Naomi Sakr is Professor of Media Policy at the University of Westminster and former Director of the Arab Media Centre (part of the University of Westminster's Communication and Media Research Institute). Her publications include *Satellite Realms: Transnational Television, Globalization and the Middle East*; *Arab Television Today*; *Transformations in Egyptian Journalism*; and, as editor, *Women and Media in the Middle East: Power through Self-Expression*; *Arab Media and Political Renewal: Community, Legitimacy and Public Life*; and *Arab Media Moguls* (all published by I.B.Tauris).

Jeanette Steemers is Professor of Culture, Media and Creative Industries at King's College London. Her publications include *Creating Preschool Television: A Story of Commerce, Creativity and Curriculum*; *Selling Television: British Television in the Global Marketplace*; and *European Television Industries* (with Petros Iosifidis and Mark Wheeler). She is co-editor of *Global Media and National Policies* and *European Media in Crisis: Values, Risks and Policies*.

'This book provides a synthesis of research and policy reports as well as professional views on producing children's media in the MENA region. As such, it sheds new light on the role of policy and ideology, as well as technology, on children's media output, covering various genres and case studies. The authors cover an impressive array of topics, including media policies, representation of gender and national identity, and the choice of linguistic code used in children's media. This is a well-written and well-argued book, which will be essential reading for students and scholars of Middle East studies.'

Noha Mellor, Professor of Media, University of Bedfordshire

Children's TV and Digital Media in the Arab World

Childhood, Screen Culture and Education

Edited by

NAOMI SAKR AND **JEANETTE STEEMERS**

I.B. TAURIS
LONDON · NEW YORK

Published in 2017 by
I.B.Tauris & Co. Ltd
London • New York
www.ibtauris.com

References to websites were correct at the time of writing.

International Media and Journalism Studies 2

ISBN: 978 1 78453 504 9 (HB)
ISBN: 978 1 78453 505 6 (PB)
eISBN: 978 1 78672 093 1
ePDF: 978 1 78673 093 0

A full CIP record for this book is available from the British Library
A full CIP record is available from the Library of Congress

Library of Congress Catalog Card Number: available

Typeset by Out of House
Printed and bound in Great Britain by T.J. International, Padstow, Cornwall

MIX
Paper from
responsible sources
FSC
www.fsc.org   FSC® C013056

Contents

Contents

Acknowledgements

This book is one of numerous published works that have resulted from research and outreach undertaken as part of a three-year project funded by the UK's Arts and Humanities Research Council (AHRC). The project as originally conceived, roughly three years before it materialized, bore the title 'Orientations in the Development of Pan-Arab Television for Children'. With the subsequent rapid development of technology, social media and changes in children's media use, the project team has come to think in terms of 'screen content' rather than television. The book's title reflects this development. As editors we wish to acknowledge the AHRC research grant (AH/J004545/1) and to thank all those who helped with both the grant and the project.

More specifically, several chapters in this volume can be traced back to presentations made at a symposium on Arab television for children, held at the University of Westminster under the auspices of the AHRC grant in May 2013. We thank everyone who took part in that event, and especially the authors whose work appears here.

Notes on Contributors

Atef Alshaer is Lecturer in the Faculty of Social Sciences and Humanities at the University of Westminster in London. He studied English Language and Literature at Birzeit University in Palestine before completing his master's in Linguistics at SOAS, University of London, where he also obtained his PhD in Sociolinguistics. His interests include linguistics, literature and the politics of the Arab world and Europe. He has published several academic and magazine articles concerned with the literary, sociolinguistic, cultural and political life of the Arab world. He is the author of *Poetry and Politics in the Modern Arab World* (2016) and *Language and National Identity in Palestine: Representations of Power and Resistance in Gaza* (forthcoming), and editor of *Love and Poetry in the Middle East* (2016).

Tarek Atia, Chief Executive Officer and founder of the Egypt Media Development Programme (EMDP), is a journalist and early online innovator in Egypt, where he founded two web portals, cairolive.com and zahma. com, in the late 1990s. Former Assistant Editor-in-Chief of *Al-Ahram Weekly*, his work has been published in international outlets including the *Washington Post* and *Neue Zürcher Zeitung*, and he has taught at Cairo University's Faculty of Mass Communications, the American University in Cairo (AUC) and the Intajour International Media Academy in Hamburg, Germany. He has worked in media development since 2006, designing and implementing capacity building programmes for over 5,000 journalists, editors and managers working across print, broadcast and online platforms. EMDP is the publisher of *Mantiqti* (My Neighbourhood), Egypt's first hyper local print newspaper, covering downtown Cairo, and the media curation site, Zahma.

Feryal Awan is a research associate at Jigsaw Consult, a social enterprise working in the international development sector, and a visiting lecturer at the Communication and Media Research Institute (CAMRI), University of

Westminster, where she was the recipient of a PhD studentship, funded by the UK's Arts and Humanities Research Council (AHRC). In June 2016, she successfully defended her PhD thesis entitled 'Occupied Childhoods: Discourses and Politics of Childhood and their Place in Palestinian and Pan-Arab Screen Content for Children' and has published and presented papers in the fields of contemporary Arab studies, childhood studies, cultural studies and political economy. She worked previously for UK and Palestinian non-governmental organizations and obtained an MSc in Political Science from SOAS, University of London.

Ehab Galal is Associate Professor in Media and Society in the Middle East at the Department of Cross-Cultural and Regional Studies, University of Copenhagen in Denmark, where he gained his PhD. His research focuses on regional and transnational Arab and Muslim media, with particular attention to religious broadcasting. His most recent project, a qualitative comparison of audience responses to Islamic television in Arabic, has involved fieldwork and research interviews in Egypt, Saudi Arabia, Denmark and the UK. He is the editor of *Arab TV Audiences: Negotiating Religion and Identity* (2014) and has published widely in academic journals and books, including *Global Mufti: The Phenomenon of Yusuf al-Qaradawi* (2009) and *Religious Broadcasting in the Middle East* (2012).

Joe F. Khalil is Associate Professor in Residence at Northwestern University in Doha, Qatar, and a visiting research fellow at the London School of Economics. He holds an MA from Ohio University and a PhD from Southern Illinois University, Carbondale, and has more than 15 years of professional television experience as a director, executive producer and consultant with major Arab satellite channels. He is co-author of *Arab Television Industries* (2009, with M. Kraidy) and has published in *Transnational Broadcasting Studies, Arab Media and Society, Television & New Media* as well as the *Encyclopedia of Social Movement Media, International Handbook of Children, Media and Culture* and *Meanings of Audiences*. He is currently working on his own book, *Youth-Generated Media*.

Daoud Kuttab is an award-winning Palestinian journalist and media freedom activist who was Ferris Professor of Journalism at Princeton University in 2007/2008. Born in Jerusalem in 1955, he started work in Arabic print media before moving to television, radio and film. He is founder or co-founder of the following: the Jerusalem Film Institute; the Arabic Media Internet Network (AMIN), Al-Quds University's Institute of Modern Media; and the Arab world's first internet radio station, AmmanNet. Kuttab is responsible for all series made so far of *Shara'a Simsim*, the Palestinian version of *Sesame Street*, which started in 1995. From 2009 the show was made by PenMedia, a Palestinian NGO formed by Kuttab as part of his Community Media Network, although work stopped in 2012 when the US government cut its financial support for the project because of Palestine's UN bid for statehood.

Nisrine Mansour is Post-Doctoral Researcher in Media, Culture and Social Policy at the University of Westminster's Arab Media Centre. She is the author of several publications on screen media, child audiences, subcultures, family relations and forced migration in the Arab region. She holds a PhD in Social Policy from the London School of Economics and an MA in Documentary Filmmaking from the University of the Arts London. Her research interests include everyday cultural practices, socio-cultural policies, audiences and qualitative research methods.

Seham Nasser is an award-winning scriptwriter and producer with over 20 years of professional experience in media, drama and documentary production, with special emphasis on educational and entertainment content for children. Based within the state-run Egyptian Radio and Television Union (ERTU), she collaborated with the European Broadcasting Union, Germany's International Central Institute for Youth and Educational Television (IZI) and worked on scripts for the USAID-funded *Alam Simsim*, Egypt's version of *Sesame Street*. Her documentary *Fatma* won a prize at the Prix Jeunesse in 2006 and her documentary *The Forgotten* won a prize from Egypt's National Council for Human Rights in 2009.

Kirsten Pike is Assistant Professor in Residence in the Communication Programme at Northwestern University in Qatar. She holds a PhD in Screen Cultures from Northwestern University and has held postdoctoral fellowships at Stockholm University and University College Dublin. Her teaching and research interests include girls' media culture, feminist media studies and critical history/theory of television and film. Her research has appeared in such publications as *Feminist Media Histories, Girlhood Studies, Mediated Girlhoods: New Explorations of Girls' Media Culture, Reality Gendervision: Sexuality and Gender on Transatlantic Reality TV* and *Princess Cultures: Mediating Girls' Imaginations and Identities.*

Tarik Sabry is Reader in Media and Communication Theory at the Communication and Media Research Institute (CAMRI), University of Westminster, where he is also Director of the Arab Media Centre. He is the author of *Cultural Encounters in the Arab World: On Media, the Modern and the Everyday* (2010), editor of *Arab Cultural Studies: Mapping the Field* (2012) and co-editor of *Arab Subcultures: Transformations in Theory and Practice* (2016, with Layal Ftouni). He is also co-founder and co-editor of the *Middle East Journal of Culture and Communication* and co-founder of the open-access online journal *Westminster Papers in Communication and Culture.* His research interests include time and modernity, migration, Arab audiences and popular cultures, and Arab contemporary philosophical thought. He has conducted a number of audience and ethnographic studies exploring global media and the dynamics of hybrid identities in the Arab world.

Naomi Sakr is Professor of Media Policy at the Communication and Media Research Institute (CAMRI), University of Westminster, and former Director of the CAMRI Arab Media Centre. She is the author of three books, *Transformations in Egyptian Journalism* (2013), *Arab Television Today* (2007) and *Satellite Realms: Transnational Television, Globalization and the Middle East* (2001), has edited two collections, *Women and Media in the Middle East: Power through Self-Expression* (2004) and *Arab Media and Political Renewal: Community, Legitimacy and Public Life* (2007), and co-edited a third, *Arab Media Moguls* (2015), all published by I.B.Tauris. Her research focuses on the political economy of Arab-owned media, with particular reference to law, regulation, human rights, journalism and cultural production.

Omar Adam Sayfo is a researcher at Utrecht University and a former visiting scholar at the Centre of Islamic Studies, University of Cambridge. He defended his PhD thesis on identity politics and Arab animated cartoons at Utrecht University in 2016. Between 2011 and 2013 he was a lecturer in media economics and intercultural communication at the University of Debrecen in Hungary. His main research field is media and political propaganda in the Arab world, with a particular focus on the Arab animation industry. He has had a number of articles published in the *New York Times*, *Huffington Post* and *Foreign Policy*, among others.

Jeanette Steemers is Professor of Culture, Media and Creative Industries at the Department of Culture, Media and Creative Industries (CMCI) at King's College, London. She gained a PhD from the University of Bath in 1990 and has worked as an industry analyst (CIT Research) and Research Manager (HIT Entertainment). She is the author of *Creating Preschool Television* (2010) and *Selling Television* (2004), co-author of *European Television Industries* (2005) and co-editor of *European Media in Crisis* (2015) and *Global Media and National Policies: The Return of the State* (2016). She has written numerous articles about the children's TV industry.

Helle Strandgaard Jensen is Assistant Professor of Contemporary Scandinavian Cultural History in the Department of History and Classical Studies at Aarhus University. She is the author of *From Superman to Social Realism: Children's Media and Scandinavian Childhood* (2017). She has written a number of articles on the history of children's media, media history in a digital age and the epistemological failures of 'moral panic' theory. Her current research project, funded by the Danish Council for Independent Research and the European Commission, is entitled 'Shaping Childhoods through Television: The Transfer and Demarcation of *Sesame Street* in 1970s' Europe'.

Note on Names and Classification of Sources

The names of individuals and organizations mentioned in this book have been transliterated from Arabic into English according to the style they themselves choose or the style most current in media coverage. This inevitably leads to inconsistencies in transliteration but tends to make the text more accessible to readers unfamiliar with Arabic. For the same reason, diacritics and apostrophes have been minimized in the rendering of Arabic words and the Arabic letter *qaf* has sometimes been represented with the English letter 'k'.

Two methods have been adopted for citing sources, depending on their type. Primary sources, such as interviews, internal reports, newspaper or magazine articles, press releases, speeches and conference presentations are cited in full in the endnotes but not in the bibliography. Secondary sources, such as books, book chapters, monographs, journal articles, academic theses and published reports are cited in both the endnotes and the bibliography. Where online sources are concerned, dates of access and URLs are not given for items that can be retrieved from a recognized archive using the source citation details provided.

1

Children's Screen Content in the Arab World

An Introduction

Jeanette Steemers and Naomi Sakr

Who pays attention to children's screen content and media use in Arab countries, and with what results? Children, defined internationally as under-18s, make up nearly 40 per cent of the total population of 18 Arab countries and nearly one third of those under-18s are below 5 years of age.[1] According to UNICEF data, shown below in Table 1, under-18s account for close to half the population in Iraq, Palestine, Sudan and Yemen, compared with a world average of just over 30 per cent. Yet local cultural production made especially for Arabic-speaking children has been slow to develop and expand. In spite of significant initiatives among Gulf-owned media companies and a regional mushrooming of animation studios, leading channels for children continue to rely heavily on imported animation. This situation may not be surprising. After years of conflict in countries across the region – Iraq, Palestine, Syria, Libya, Sudan and Yemen – and its effects in traumatizing children and denying them access to safe schooling, policy makers may regard concerns about children's access to beneficial media as secondary or even utopian. Yet, under the UN Convention on the Rights of the Child (CRC), signed by all Arab countries, children's rights to freedom of expression and information are guaranteed, as is their right to be protected from harmful content. Article 17 of the CRC affirms the 'important function' of mass media, including material of 'social and cultural benefit' from a 'diversity' of sources, in children's development.

Studies of children's media and child audiences in the region are as scarce as locally produced content that is specifically aimed at, and popular with, children. While many studies look at childhood, children's media and children's media experiences in the Global North, little has been written about these topics in the Arab world. This is despite rapid growth in the literature on wider Arab media and culture and despite the urgency of exploring influential factors in identity and worldview formation among the region's next generation of cultural and political players. The disparity in availability between research on this world region and others becomes increasingly important as globalizing forces expose tensions between different views about childhood and about the desirability of different types of media content. As communication technologies allow for ever greater diversity in what children can access and how they access it, the challenge for social science researchers becomes ever more urgent.

What we do know is that regional conflicts have disrupted children's education on a massive scale. A UNICEF report in September 2015 calculated that 13.7 million children were being denied schooling, including 3 million in Iraq, 2 million in Libya, 3.1 million in Sudan and 2.9 million in Yemen.[2] In Syria, the number of children out of school inside the country was put at 2 million with a further 0.7 million refugee children out of school in the main refugee host countries of Turkey, Lebanon, Jordan, Iraq and Egypt, despite efforts launched in 2013 to respond to this particular aspect of the refugee crisis.[3] Six-year-old Palestinian children in the Gaza Strip in 2015 had already lived through three major military confrontations with mounting impact each time; at least 551 Palestinian children were killed during the summer of 2014 and a further 3,370 injured, while nearly 0.5 million were unable to return to learning for several weeks because of damage to buildings.[4] Many who recognize the magnitude of this phenomenon are also aware of the potential for e-learning. But they rarely draw crucial links between e-learning and children's media, even though research shows not only that children in the region are adept in navigating through complex offerings on whatever platform is at hand to find what they want, but also that socio-economic background and context are factors influencing children's preferences.[5]

2

Table 1 Children as a proportion of the population

	Population ('000s)	Under-18s (%)	Under-5s (%)
Algeria	39,208	32.7	11.6
Bahrain	1,332	24.6	7.7
Egypt	82,056	36.7	11.3
Iraq	33,765	46.7	14.5
Jordan	7,274	39.9	13.1
Kuwait	3,369	28.9	9.6
Lebanon	4,822	26.4	6.3
Libya	6,202	34.6	10.3
Morocco	33,008	33.4	10.4
Oman	3,632	28.3	9.7
Palestine	4,326	47.4	14.2
Qatar	2,169	16.0	5.0
Saudi Arabia	28,829	33.6	10.1
Sudan	37,964	47.8	15.1
Syria	21,898	41.5	11.8
Tunisia	10,997	27.7	8.4
United Arab Emirates	9,346	17.8	7.1
Yemen	24,407	47.5	14.1
Total Arab	354,604	37.8	11.8
Middle East & North Africa	432,925	36.1	11.3
World	7,122,691	31.2	9.2

Source: UNICEF, *State of the World's Children 2015*

Perhaps for the same reasons that children's lives in so many countries have been so badly affected, studies of their media worlds in these politically charged environments are lacking in English and Arabic, compounding a long-standing dearth of research in this field. How much is known, for example, about who, if anyone, controls content and advertising in areas of the internet and social media that are reached by Arabic-speaking children? And how should we understand the media worlds of preschool children or the so-called tweens, between the ages of around seven to 12? With a few noteworthy exceptions,[6] the number of studies on Arab youth culture far outweighs those on young children,[7] while work on Arab countries that appears in dedicated publications, such as those issued by Nordicom's International Clearing House on Children, Youth and Media, or the *World Yearbook of Education*,[8] tend to focus more on the dimensions of child-media interactions that have to do with intentions rather than outcomes.

3

IZI, the International Central Institute for Youth and Educational Television in the German state of Bavaria, conducts regular empirical research with child audiences; its work in the Arab region is often quantitative and has concentrated mainly on Egypt.[9]

We dare to say then that this edited collection is the first in English to probe both the state of Arab media for children and how Arabic-speaking children produce and consume media. It responds to the gap in research with a holistic investigation of institutions and individuals, the practices and media experiences of children, and an examination of some iconic media texts. Three core themes of the book are as follows: regulation and policy; emerging trends in production; and representations of gender, ethnicity and language. The book is interdisciplinary and wide-ranging. It seeks to compare notions of childhood, and looks at changes in children's media through the lens of political economy, policy studies, sociology, ethnography, linguistics, management and marketing, gender studies and technology, with some short contributions alongside three of the chapters to add a further perspective. Initially focused on television, it also considers children's uses of online media platforms in the region.

The book took shape in parallel with research undertaken by the editors as part of a three-year project, entitled 'Orientations in the Development of Pan-Arab Television for Children', funded between 2013 and 2016 by the UK's Arts and Humanities Research Council (AHRC). Most of the chapters started out as presentations at the project's first outreach symposium, 'New Horizons in Pan-Arab Children's Television', which was held at the University of Westminster on 10 May 2013. There we first heard presentations on methodological approaches to research with children in the Arab diaspora, definitions of childhood, the Arab animation industry, the Egyptian series *Bakkar* and Arab children's video sharing practices. It was at this event that we discussed the 2011–2013 collapse of children's content origination in Egypt, a collapse which has since befallen Syria, another contributor to children's production before 2011. In the period between the symposium and publication of this book, we have deepened our understanding of the political economy of production and distribution of children's screen-based media, the purposes of these media as negotiated between competing elites and the cultures of reception among Arabic-speaking children.

Economic Challenges of Media for Children

Arab television for children does not exist in a vacuum. Both historically and today its operations have to be understood in relation to a particular set of economics. These inevitably mirror the economics of media industries in general. Thus population size is crucial, because children in national markets with small populations, such as many of those in the Gulf, or countries like Lebanon, Jordan or Tunisia, do not constitute a lucrative target audience for content that is funded through advertising. Where children are concerned, however, and even in societies with high levels of disposable income, the challenge of small markets is exacerbated by the fact that age brackets within the national audience are narrow. What works for pre-schoolers may not interest a child of six or above, while content that suits a 9-year-old is not interesting to someone aged 15 and so on. For viability, therefore, content needs to be designed to cross borders. But narrow age brackets also limit the economic viability of imported material that depends on subtitles, since children need to be fully literate to cope with them. The alternative, dubbing, works for cartoon characters where there is mostly no need to synchronize lip movements with speech. Cartoons are consequently much easier to trade than other genres of children's programming, leaving production of live action and factual shows at an economic disadvantage.

In the Arab world in particular, dubbing is chosen in preference to subtitles, not only for reasons of literacy but also censorship, since dubbing gives broadcasters an opportunity to remove any reference to offending material.[10] Animation specialists in the region have been known to comment on the way references to alcoholic drinks in imported content are replaced with references to 'juice' for the benefit of Arab children. As shown in Table 1 on page 3, under-5s account for 10–12 per cent of the population of many Arab countries. Yet economic pressures mean that broadcasters and advertisers want to reach under-5s across the whole region to gain a reasonably sized market. The same applies to other ages. This is where transnational players, mostly from the US, can operate almost seamlessly across borders, offering Arab broadcasters a steady diet of mostly dubbed US animation shows and sitcoms, whose costs have already been amortized over repeated showings in the US and other profitable markets. The impact of US dominance has increased with the rise in children's channels, as Alessandro d'Arma and Jeanette Steemers observed in 2013:

> Investment in children's programmes has hardly ever been profitable for domestic commercial broadcasters because of the small size of the children's advertising market. But it has become even less attractive in recent years because of the competition from transnational players.[11]

The size of child audiences in national markets is one strand in the economics of children's media; children's purchasing power and spending habits constitute another. Programmes for adults can carry advertising for everything from detergent to coffee to banking services to luxury goods. Where children are concerned the possibilities are mainly limited to toys, snacks and drinks. Various countries have seen this as a problem, especially in the case of sugary drinks and snacks that are high in fat, salt and sugar, leading to certain types of bans on advertising to children in Australia, Germany, Greece, Norway, Sweden and the UK. In the Gulf, where levels of obesity and diabetes have rocketed alarmingly and prices for soft drinks are exceptionally low, health ministers have considered imposing a 50 per cent tax on drinks. It would not be a big step from there to limiting advertising. But to limit what can be advertised is to limit the advertising revenue that can fund content creation, as UK producers discovered to their cost after a ban on 'junk food' advertising in certain slots in the television schedules took effect in 2007.[12] Why would local broadcasters, faced with depleted resources, spend on local production when they can acquire cheap animation off the shelf?[13]

Limitations on advertising, whether resulting from regulation and/or from the limited scope of children's shopping lists, mean that income from this source is frequently supplemented through sales of merchandise related to a particular film or television series – such as figurines, pencil cases, backpacks and even whole theme parks. The need to arrange for licensing and merchandizing of toys, games and other goods again favours large vertically integrated conglomerates[14] like Disney, Time Warner (owner of Cartoon Network and Boomerang) and Viacom (owner of Nickelodeon). Again it tends to diminish the range of content offered, because certain programme genres and character representations, above all animated characters, have greater retail potential than others.[15]

Policy Responses

Questions about how national authorities respond to the economic challenges of providing suitable content for their child populations are key to any analysis of regulatory and policy approaches, even though the authorities themselves may rationalize their policy choices in terms of culture and ideology rather than economics. Public subsidies are an obvious option, in return for which national broadcasters may be required to provide a specified amount of children's programming and, within this, to commission a specified quantity of first-run originations of children's programmes. Where such quotas are in place they have proved an important safeguard against shrinking output of originations.[16] Indeed, where public service broadcasters in Europe have created children's channels, these have often proved the most popular children's channels in their respective countries.[17]

Beyond instituting provisions for children through public service media, the range of regulatory options is not wide and the consequences can be unintended, as demonstrated by different approaches taken in the Global North. The impact of the intervention on junk food advertising in the UK, mentioned above, is just one example. In the US, the Children's Television Act of 1990 imposed time limits on advertising during broadcast programmes for under-12s. Yet other well-intentioned elements of the same law, notably the requirement for commercial broadcasters to provide educational content, had limited success: broadcasters simply used loose, self-serving definitions of 'educational' that were not shared by parents or children's media advocates.[18] The Philippines passed a Children's Television Act in 1997, requiring broadcasters to allocate 15 per cent of airtime to 'child-friendly' shows and creating a National Council for Children's Television, mandated to promote content aimed at developing local children's 'critical thinking and communication skills, moral values and strong sense of national identity', along with a National Endowment Fund to finance culturally relevant programmes for Filipino children. Yet it took 15 years to hammer out the implementing rules and regulations of the 1997 Act,[19] during which time only a tiny fraction of funding for new programmes was disbursed.[20]

Meanwhile struggles to compensate for market failure in relation to children's content on broadcast channels pale into insignificance compared with policy challenges vis-à-vis screen content and advertising online. On the internet, distinctions between editorial content and product placement are readily erased, as demonstrated by 'unboxing' videos on YouTube, in which people film themselves unwrapping toys or gadgets. Yet regulation has failed to keep pace with new services. Commenting on the YouTube Kids app, launched in 2015, US communications professor Dale Kunkel called it 'the most hyper-commercialized media environment for children' because it mixes promotion and content in ways that would not be allowed in broadcast television. Despite a promise from YouTube owner Google that only 'child-safe, family-friendly' content would be available, Kunkel found 'entire channels devoted to LEGO, Barbie, Play-Doh and even McDonald's' among the 100 or so channels offered by YouTube Kids.[21] In the broadcast environment many countries would regard such practices as unfair and illegal. In the online sphere, in contrast, commercial players are often able to pursue their own perceived interests with impunity, practically untrammelled by regulatory interventions.

In the Arabic-speaking world, the first breakthroughs in transnational television for children came as an afterthought to the initial growth of pan-Arab satellite channels and seemed to reflect commercial interests and regional political rivalries as much as concern for children's needs. Today children's provision is regional, international and increasingly multiplatform, with evidence that children are able to access screen content from sources and providers other than those subject to national regulation. Before pan-Arab children's channels appeared, state-owned television channels had transmitted limited hours of children's programming, much of it openly didactic and moralizing with minimal children's participation.[22] The first free-to-air pan-Arab initiative, Spacetoon Arabic, a satellite channel that started in the United Arab Emirates in 2000, grew out of a commercial dubbing operation in Syria, and its cartoons were predominantly purchased from overseas. MBC Group's creation of MBC3 for children in 2004 established a Saudi-owned channel ahead of the Qatari one that followed in 2005 in the shape of Al-Jazeera Children's Channel (JCC). The highly conservative Al-Majd network, created for Saudi and other Gulf families who considered conventional television to be forbidden by Islam,[23] arranged for satellite transmission of its dedicated children's channel in 2004.

Such was the momentum in the mid-2000s that Dubai's Arab Media Group outbid MBC in 2006 for a licence from Viacom for Nickelodeon Arabia and MTV Arabia. After the Arab Media Group venture was hit by the 2008 financial crisis, the Nickelodeon licence eventually went to MBC. For a time, initiatives in children's programming continued to multiply. The privately-owned pan-Arab Tuyur al-Jannah (Birds of Paradise) channel started life in Jordan in 2008, quickly gaining a wide audience for its charac teristic brand of children's songs and chants. Abu Dhabi promised in 2008 to nurture production of new content for children at its media free zone, twofour54, and in 2009 Qatar's JCC spawned a pre-school channel, Baraem, and educational website with video-on-demand. Turner Broadcasting launched its Cartoon Network free-to-air in Arabic from Dubai in 2010 and opened an animation academy in Abu Dhabi. Saudi Arabia introduced its own national children's channel, Ajyal (meaning 'generations'), as part of a facelift for the Saudi TV network initiated in 2010. Doha Film Institute in Qatar started the Ajyal Youth Film Festival series in 2013 and in September 2015 the long-running *Majid* magazine for children, owned by Abu Dhabi Media Group, went on air and online as Majid TV. Majid Entertainment, the company set up to create and manage the channel, drew on characters from the magazine to produce more than 150 hours of content in a period of just six months, including 70 hours of animation.[24]

However, as conflict in the region intensified and media content became increasingly polarized, the cause of local production for local chil- dren seemed to take a backseat in most other Arab countries, while debate focused on children's vulnerability to radicalization through social media content circulated by so-called 'Islamic State'. A constant refrain of contri- butions to the present volume is that, despite Arab producers' persistent pleas for more home-grown material to be made and promoted, it is not yet clear whether the regulatory and academic communities in Arab coun- tries have any consensus view on the desirable balance between local and imported programming or even effective policy responses to promote sus- tainable production that reflects a range of worldviews and not only those of various Islamist groups. That is even before the thorny issue of online digital media is broached.

Regulatory and policy issues addressed in this book are set against the backdrop of Chapter 2, in which Feryal Awan and Jeanette Steemers consider how childhood has been conceptualized in different parts of the world through the ages. They concur that there is no fixed universal concept of what it means to be a child, or even of how long childhood is supposed to last. Instead it is a social and cultural construct, always shaped by 'the social, moral and political preoccupations of a particular time and place',[25] and even the historiography of childhood is constantly being modified to address changing approaches to gender, class and ethnicity.[26] Yet conceptions of childhood matter, not least because they help us to understand why media are regulated and media texts crafted in certain ways.[27] Notions of children as vulnerable, innocent, under threat or even deviant and uncontrolled tend to lead more directly to a perceived need for negative interventions, involving bans and prohibitions, intended to mitigate harmful effects of media commercialization or propaganda. The negative effects discourse is often employed by those who fear the impact of foreign, mainly US, content on local culture. In contrast, conceptualizations that focus on child agency look more for 'positive' forms of regulation, designed to stimulate quality content for children, including content that might encourage children to see themselves as budding citizens rather than consumers. Between these two poles there are degrees of intervention that underscore the importance of context for each situation, and the fluidity of political and economic factors that determine degrees of intervention.

The spectrum of attitudes to childhood and child agency raises the question of how far values and standards relating to children's media and participation are really shared among what has been described as a 'worldwide professional network of creative leaders of children's television'.[28] These are people who work for international media companies and NGOs, and who meet at industry events such as MIP Junior and Kidscreen, but also at global conferences such as the three-yearly World Summit on Media for Children (WSMC) or festivals like the Prix Jeunesse, held in Munich every two years. Assumptions in circulation at these events are not unproblematic because they tend to be influenced by a small, usually Western-dominated, core of actors and stakeholders, whose concerns are focused on the media experiences of children in rich countries of the Global North, rather than those in developing media economies, including Arabic-speaking countries.[29] In a chapter exploring how policy ideas about children's media are transferred within and between communities,

Naomi Sakr uncovers the crucial role of some highly motivated individuals from the Global South, including Egypt and Qatar, who became actively involved in international initiatives and processes, including the Committee on the Rights of the Child, the WSMC, the Children and Broadcasting Foundation for Africa and the Giffoni Festival.

Sakr shows how these individuals engaged with the international policy community while pushing agendas specific to their own national or regional circumstances. Where the resulting policies were made centrally, however, without genuine engagement of independent companies and local non-governmental groups, their longevity was uncertain and they proved vulnerable to changes in government-appointed personnel and political priorities. A short 'Insight' piece alongside the chapter shows how policy can also be influenced through deliberations among national representatives meeting under the auspices of regional broadcasting bodies. Writing about a brief episode in the history of the European Broadcasting Union, which also encompasses Arab members, Helle Strandgaard Jensen traces the evidence documenting how the stance taken by a particular department head within the BBC affected the take-up of a model of preschool television coming from the US in other European countries.

Emerging Trends in Production

An understanding of policy-making in Arab countries thus depends, as in many contexts, on the shifting influence of key individuals within ruling national elites, who may develop a personal interest in children's welfare. The importance of these elites is a theme developed in Omar Sayfo's analysis of animation production in the region, which, according to his findings, operates within a policy environment that is 'primarily nation-bound' in terms of regulation, programming and power structures and is often shaped by the personal preferences of decision-makers within governments, state-owned broadcasters and production entities. Producers have therefore always had to pay attention to relationships within local hierarchies in order to access funding, overseas promotional possibilities, government contracts for licensing and access to the better-funded channels such as Saudi's MBC 3 and those in Qatar's Al-Jazeera network. According to Sayfo, the region's most successful animation companies have close links with state media and governments and the regimes tend to favour those productions that support their political agendas.

Sayfo's account provides an overview of animation history in the Arab world, dating back to Egypt in the 1930s. Outpriced by cheap dubbed imports, the industry has always been small, but was boosted by the arrival of pan-Arab children's channels such as JCC. Liberalizing policies for the technical side of media production in countries like Syria, Jordan and Dubai also helped, as did new animation techniques and the ability to outsource some animation processes to cheaper production locations. For example the landmark series *Freej*, produced by Lammtara Pictures in Dubai, was animated in India. With its title meaning 'neighbourhood' in local dialect, *Freej* set precedents not only as the first 3D animation to come from the Middle East but also in being so specific to the UAE, by featuring four elderly ladies in traditional costume reacting to dramatic changes taking place around them. It testified to the arrival of a new era in the Arab animation industry but also demonstrated, through its state start-up funding, how much the industry needs adequate and sustainable investment and regulatory intervention if it is not to be on the receiving end of a one-way flow of foreign products, technology and trends. Providing further evidence of dependence on moral and financial support from the government, Seham Nasser's short account recalls how established structures supporting children's media in Egypt collapsed after the 2011 uprising, not least because of their close links to the regime of deposed president Hosni Mubarak, through his wife, Suzanne.

In the next chapter, on the rebranding of JCC in 2011–2013, Naomi Sakr and Jeanette Steemers explore the complex interweaving of commercial and political considerations behind production and commissioning processes. The branding and rebranding saga shows how a children's television project can be adopted to reinforce a country's claim to regional cultural leadership, while being packaged in such a way as to depoliticize that country's institutions and composition by rooting national identity primarily in commercial interests and notions of traditional culture. JCC was established to nurture Arab and Islamic traditions and values, differentiating itself by ensuring that material would conform to what its management considered to be culturally appropriate.[30] But having been set up as a child-centred, non-commercial, fully funded enterprise that aspired to source most of its content within the Arabic-speaking region, its priorities shifted in 2011–2013 towards maximizing commercial revenues through foreign imports.

Tarek Atia also looks at content production, but his focus is on what children create for themselves. Exploring children's agency and creativity within wider commercial structures that have the potential to be exploitative, he considers how the media landscape for children has changed in the region since the January 25 revolution in Egypt in 2011. Starkly contradicting allegations that digital media generate passivity among children, Atia shows how the digital revolution has enabled children and young people to express themselves at last. Their entry point is often through gaming and virtual worlds, which lead into making and sharing video content and posting it on YouTube and other platforms such as Vine and Snapchat. Working with professional production companies and with each other, they have been able to form a community for sharing experiences and exchanging information, and a few have begun to generate revenues. But while YouTube represents an important outlet for expression, especially in the closed society of Saudi Arabia, Gulf video bloggers (vloggers) have found themselves targeted by the authorities for violating local laws that place limits on political or satirical expression.

Representation: Gender, Ethnicity, Language and Reflexivity

Children's active use of digital tools and the internet is in stark contrast to their limited representation and participation in traditional Arab media over past decades. The final four chapters of the book engage with aspects of representation and models of behaviour, including models that are presented to children through screen content and those that children infer through media use. Models here relate to gender roles, ethnicity and national belonging, and idealization of a certain form of the Arabic language as a pillar of Arab-Islamic civilization. The closing chapter, about research methods, deals with representation in the sense that it examines what two Arab ethnographers working with Arab children in London learned about themselves and their research from the way those children represented narratives and performances to them, when talking about their media use.

In their case study of the long-running Lebanese entertainment show *Mini Studio*, Kirsten Pike and Joe F. Khalil unpack the programme's constructions of girlhood and boyhood, in the process analysing connections and contradictions between advertising, representation and regulation and how this might impact children's socialization. *Mini Studio* is depicted as a show that attracts 'a specifically Lebanese, multilingual, middle class target audience' comprising mainly pre-teen girls from Lebanon's diverse communities. Its appeal is to children who are 'receptive to Western youth cultures, trends and production techniques', and this is reinforced by the economics of the show and the incorporation of clips depicting Western music stars, rather than successful Arab female vocalists whose performances have 'touched a cultural nerve' and might generate an outcry. Pike and Khalil draw attention to the 'hyper-feminine and mildly provocative' way in which girl child participants are represented, and how this is financially motivated to attract advertising and product placements that encourage consumerism and Western ideals of femininity. According to the authors, the show is a cultural hybrid which walks the line between 'grown-up sexiness' as depicted in Western videos, and a safer, but also mildly suggestive, styling of young Lebanese girls, who are represented as princesses within the show. These are programmes that are 'hybridized to cater to the proclivities of one audience after another' in pursuit of profit.[31] Instead of opening up equal possibilities for boys and girls, the show and its advertisers combine to reinforce traditional gendered roles and pursuits.

Ehab Galal's analysis of the character *Bakkar* in the Egyptian animated series of the same name explores representation from a different angle. He shows how this character is constructed for children on the one hand as a symbol of Egyptian national identity, but on the other represents the minority Nubian community, a marginalized and sometimes stigmatized group. In the series, young Bakkar is depicted as an authentic, patriotic and loyal Egyptian who has lessons for Egyptian society and embodies the values of the collective, including hard work and love for one's country. It is a portrayal that, according to Galal, represents not a politically mobilized citizen but the 'quintessential domesticated nation-centric Egyptian', embedded in a context of images and historical events that show the Egyptian state in a positive light. They represent Egypt's diversity as a foundation stone of national unity, with the nation bound by shared moral values linked to a traditional nationalist narrative. Within this narrative Nubians like Bakkar seem to be ascribed the positive characteristics of an idealized, 'salt-of-the-earth'-style authenticity, as a nostalgic counter-image to what other elements of the population have supposedly lost through modernization. From episode to episode, nationalism and moral values are conflated and Nubian signifiers are used selectively, implying that a stereotyped minority people who have their own distinct language and culture are accepted by being subsumed into the dominant culture.

In addition to visual and narrative representations of gender and ethnic origins in children's media, the Arabic language is itself portrayed in these media in ways that are complicated, culturally loaded and ideological. In Chapter 9, Atef Alshaer critiques representations of Arabic in media for children, reflecting on the culture of Arabic, not only as a language, but as an epistemological system encompassed by what he calls the 'culture of communication', which revolves around issues of authenticity and power. The use within children's screen content of formal classical and modern standard Arabic, as well as many varieties of informal, colloquial Arabic, provides a fertile ground for understanding the complexities of language acquisition and the extent to which Arabic is subject to ideological forces. Alshaer notes that classical Arabic, often chosen for dialogue in children's programmes as a way to reach children across the Arab region, tends to be regarded as the authentic and 'undeclared ambassador of Arab-Islamic civilization', while colloquial forms of the language are considered culturally inferior.

Alshaer observes, however, that even the most ardent proponents of Arab-Islamic civilization may end up using a mixture of linguistic forms to get their message across to children. Tuyur al-Jannah promotes Islamic values to children in a 'medley of linguistic forms', in contrast to the Iqra channel, which offers content for children in a form of Arabic that implies unswerving reverence for the past. But deciding what form of the language to use is not always a major preoccupation in programme-making for children, as revealed by Daoud Kuttab in his short account of where language ranked among the educational priorities selected for the Palestinian version of *Sesame Street*. Writing from his perspective as producer and practitioner, Kuttab elaborates on the factors that facilitated use of local Palestinian Arabic to communicate with children, including the funding that enabled the *Sesame Street* project to avoid having to seek financial viability through engagement with a region-wide audience.

In Chapter 10, Tarik Sabry and Nisrine Mansour reflect on the methodological issues that emerged from a pilot study in the UK, which they undertook as two ethnographers of Arab origin researching Arab diasporic children living in London. The range of issues they encountered in the field included mistrust among respondents that compounded problems of access, prompting the researchers to reflect on their own backgrounds, positionality and role in the research. The pilot was concerned with how Arabic-speaking children in London responded to Arabic language content, in order to gain insight into children's everyday media lives. The results indicated that children of Arab heritage spoke little Arabic, were eclectic in their media choices and, like other UK children, spent time online using multiple devices and platforms. But what also emerged from the results was a need to adjust the research methods in ways that could help to break down the hierarchical positions associated with being a researcher. In the adjustment process, the underlying conceptual framework also shifted, so that both the object of enquiry and data-gathering techniques moved closer to the children themselves, to take account of how they perform their identities through everyday talk, singing and dancing.

The media worlds of children in Arab families living in the UK offer glimpses into possible future media practices of hundreds of thousands of displaced children from Arab countries who sought refuge abroad in 2015. It remains unclear how media institutions – broadcasters, production companies, communications regulators – will view these children or whether they will consider their needs at all as media users. Yet the numbers of children affected by the migratory movements of recent years are the highest they have ever been. The United Nations High Commissioner for Refugees (UNHCR) reported in June 2015 that war, conflict and persecution had forced 13.9 million people to flee in 2014 alone – four times the number of the previous year and more than at any other time since records began – and that 51 per cent of all refugees in 2014 were children,[32] up from 41 per cent in 2009.[33] Of these, more than 34,300 unaccompanied or separated children, including 3,600 Syrian children, sought asylum individually, a level also unprecedented since UNHCR started collecting the data in 2006. Although unaccompanied or separated children made these asylum applications to 82 countries across the globe, one third of the total were registered with just two countries, Sweden and Germany. Large numbers were also registered with Italy, Austria, the UK, Serbia and Kosovo.[34]

With Syria, Iraq and Sudan in the top 10 countries that were the source of refugees in 2014,[35] and thousands of families also leaving Libya, there is a pressing question as to how the societies that receive displaced children will cater to their needs for media of social and cultural benefit from diverse sources, as called for by Article 17 of the CRC. A parallel question concerns the growing demand for intercultural media content that can help children born into those societies understand and relate to the circumstances of others newly arriving in their streets, schools and playgrounds. It will be incumbent on groups advocating for children's rights and children's media to raise awareness of these issues and to think innovatively about the kind of content that will promote a shared learning process across national divides.

Notes

1 UNICEF, *The State of the World's Children 2015* (New York: United Nations, 2014), pp. 66–71.

2 UNICEF, *Education under Fire* (New York: United Nations, September 2015), p. 7.

3 UNICEF, *Education under Fire*, p. 6.

4 UNICEF, *Education under Fire*, p. 4.

5 Communication and Media Research Institute, *Orientations in the Development of Screen Content for Arabic-speaking Children: Findings Report*, London: University of Westminster, September 2015, pp. 15–17.

6 For example, Chiara Diana, 'Children's citizenship: Revolution and the seeds of an alternative future in Egypt', in Linda Herrera (ed), *Wired Citizenship: Youth Learning and Activism in the Middle East* (Abingdon: Routledge, 2014), pp. 60–75; Mark Allen Peterson, 'The *jinn* and the computer: Consumption and identity in Arabic children's magazines', *Childhood* 12/2, 2005, pp. 177–200; and '*Imsukuhum kulhum!* Modernity and morality in Egyptian children's consumption', *Journal of Consumer Culture* 10/2, 2010, pp. 233–253.

7 Prominent examples include Marwan Kraidy and Joe F. Khalil, 'Youth, media and culture in the Arab world', in K. Drotner and S. Livingstone (eds), *International Handbook of Children, Media and Culture* (London: Sage, 2008), pp. 336–350, and Roel Meijer (ed), *Alienation or Integration of Arab Youth: Between Family, State and Street* (Abingdon: Routledge, 2000).

8 André Elias Mazawi and Ronald G. Sultana, *World Yearbook of Education 2010: Education and the Arab World* (Abingdon: Routledge, 2013).

9 See for example IZI's numerous studies on gender representation, or articles in its journal *TelevIZIon*. Issue No 26 in 2013, on the subject of 'How children understand stories' contains a multi-country study entitled 'Why is he running?', for which one-to-one interviews were conducted with children aged 3–6 in Egypt. No 25 in 2012, on 'TV as a learning environment', published results of a survey of 7–10 year-olds in 24 countries, including Egypt, about their ideal TV presenter.

10 Rania Nafez Mahmoud Yacoub, 'Ideological Aspects of Dubbing into Arabic for Children – With Special Reference to Language Variety', PhD thesis (University of Salford, 2009), p. 41.

11 Alessandro D'Arma and Jeanette Steemers, 'Children's television: Markets and regulation', in K. Donders, C. Pauwels and J. Loisen (eds), *Private Television in Western Europe: Content, Market, Policies* (Basingstoke: Palgrave Macmillan, 2013), pp. 132–133.

12 Naomi Sakr and Jeanette Steemers, 'Co-producing content for pan-Arab children's TV: State, business and the workplace', in M. Banks, B. Conor and V. Mayer (eds), *Production Studies: The Sequel!* (Abingdon: Routledge, 2016), p. 242.

13 Adam Sherwin, 'Advertising ban won't stop "brand bullying" says childhood expert', *Independent*, 15 September, 2011.

14 Alison Alexander and James Owers, 'The economics of children's television', in J. A. Bryant (ed), *The Children's Television Community* (Mahwah, NJ: Lawrence Erlbaum Associates, 2007), pp. 70–73.

15 Jeanette Steemers, *Creating Preschool Television: A Story of Commerce, Creativity and Curriculum* (Basingstoke: Palgrave Macmillan, 2010), pp. 169–170.

16 See for example the actions of the UK's ITV in response to changing regulations, covered in Alessandro D'Arma and Jeanette Steemers, 'Children's television: the soft underbelly of public service broadcasting'. Paper presented to the RIPE@2008 conference on Public Service Media in the 21st Century (Mainz, October 2008).

17 According to the European Audiovisual Observatory press release, 'Continued growth of children's television services in Europe', 3 June 2013, based on the Mavise Database.

18 Amy B. Jordan, 'Children's media policy', *The Future of Children* 18/1 (Spring 2008), p. 245.

19 Marinel R. Cruz, 'Children's Act given "real teeth" with IRR', *Philippines Daily Inquirer*, 2 August 2012.

20 *Manila Bulletin*, 'Wanted: More local kid's TV shows', 28 July 2012.

21 Dale Kunkel 'Digital deception: legal questions surround new "YouTube Kids" app', http://blogs.lse.ac.uk/parenting4digitalfuture/2015/11/ (accessed 30/digital-deception-legal-questions-surround-new-youtube-kids-app/ (accessed 30 November 2015).

22 Imad Karam, 'Satellite television: A breathing space for Arab youth?' in N. Sakr (ed), *Arab Media and Political Renewal: Community, Legitimacy and Public Life* (London: I.B.Tauris, 2007), pp. 83–90.

23 Abeer Al-Najjar, 'Pure Salafi broadcasting: Al-Majd Channel (Saudi Arabia)', in K. Hroub (ed), *Religious Broadcasting in the Middle East* (London: C. Hurst & Co, 2012), p. 39.

24 Emirates News Agency WAM, 'Abu Dhabi Media's Majid TV channel goes live', 28 September 2015.

25 Máire Messenger Davies, *Children, Media and Culture* (Maidenhead: Open University Press, 2010), p. 7.

26 Hugh Cunningham, *Children of the Poor: Representations of Childhood since the Seventeenth Century* (Oxford: Blackwell, 1991).

27 Alessandro D'Arma and Jeanette Steemers, 'Public service media and children: Serving the digital citizens of the future', in P. Iosifidis (ed), *Reinventing Public Service Communication* (Basingstoke: Palgrave Macmillan, 2010), p. 115.

28 David W. Kleeman, 'PRIX JEUNESSE as a force for cultural diversity', in D. G. Singer and J. L. Singer (eds), *Handbook of Children and the Media* (Thousand Oaks, CA: Sage, 2001), p. 522.

29 Jeanette Steemers, 'Production studies, transformations in children's television and the global turn', *Journal of Children and Media*, 10/1 (2016), p. 129.

30 Sakr and Steemers: 'Co-producing content', pp. 244–245.

31 Marwan Kraidy, *Hybridity, or the Cultural Logic of Globalization* (Philadelphia: Temple University Press, 2005), p. 130.

32 UNHCR, 'Worldwide displacement hits all-time high as war and persecution increase', UNHCR press release, Geneva, 18 June 2015.

33 UNHCR, *World at War: UNHCR Global Trends – Forced Displacement in 2014* (Geneva: UNHCR, 2015), p. 3.

34 UNHCR, *World at War*, p. 31.

35 UNHCR, *World at War*, p. 14.

2

Arab and Western Perspectives on Childhood and Children's Media Provision

Feryal Awan and Jeanette Steemers[1]

This chapter seeks to identify key issues affecting children's media in the Arab world, through a comparative analysis of the changing discourses of childhood in Arab and Western societies and the ways in which these discourses are articulated in policy debates and strategies for children's screen media. Assuming, as many argue, that 'childhood' is not a fixed universal concept but a social construction, then the way it is constructed will produce variations in children's media around the world because of differences in history and culture that reflect 'the social, moral and political preoccupations of a particular time and place'.[2] Society's concept of childhood as a life stage characterized by immaturity and dependency will be shaped by different rules, customs and traditions including beliefs, religious and otherwise, that affect children's lives. Society's view of childhood as a separate state will in turn affect children's relationship with society and its institutions, including the media. Yet while there are many North American and European studies relating to childhood and children's media, studies about other parts of the world, including the Middle East, are still relatively rare. This gap in research matters because globalizing forces in the media landscape, including children's media, are liable to expose tensions between different conceptualizations of childhood and types of media content that children are likely to encounter.

The chapter takes these broader economic and ideological forces into account in looking first at different constructions of childhood in Arab and Western countries. It then considers how these are reflected in debates about media provision for children. Using examples of provision and observations from media practitioners, it focuses on those issues that connect conceptualizations of childhood and children with the dual nature of regulation; namely, 'negative' regulation against harmful effects and 'positive' regulation in favour of outcomes that promote quality content.[3]

Western Constructions of Childhood

Western definitions of childhood and children as a distinct social group are complex and recent in origin,[4] but they are also specific to Western experience, rarely taking into account more 'diverse global and diverse local experiences of childhood'.[5] Among the different disciplines that have considered childhood, psychology and education usually focus on the child as a real and embodied individual, while sociology, anthropology and cultural studies have tended to concentrate more on childhood as a social institution characterized by a variety of practices, discourses and representations.[6] Applied to media consumption, psychological approaches tend to look at the media's impact on child development, while sociological approaches concentrate more on children's media use within a social and cultural context.

One way of understanding issues in Western debates about children's media use is to consider Western accounts of the history of childhood.[7] Historical perspectives have been influenced enormously by the work of Philippe Ariès,[8] who argued that childhood is a modern invention, a social construct that emerged in the 16th century and is neither biologically determined nor universal. This does not mean that children were 'neglected, forsaken or despised', but that there was no awareness of 'that particular nature which distinguishes the child from the adult'.[9] Citing the absence of contemporary children in most medieval art (apart from depictions of the Christ child and angels), Ariès maintained that the emergence of a modern Western construction of childhood, which differentiated it from adulthood, only began to develop with the expansion of education and a European middle class who began to place emotional value on their offspring and educate them.[10]

While Ariès' ideas about 'childhood' as a sociological construct are influential,[11] others have contested his view that earlier generations did not have a concept of childhood similar to modern interpretations. Ariès' evidence is largely based on the depiction of children in art. But, as Messenger Davies points out, countless mothers and nannies 'left no record' as they could not write: '[h]ence the story of childhood – which tends to be the primary responsibility of women – does not get told by those closest to it. Children, too, were not in a position to tell their own story in forms which have survived in printed or pictorial records'.[12] Nevertheless this historical definition of constructed childhood does connect with sociological approaches that emphasize children's development as a social and cultural process. It is also an approach that acknowledges that the historiography of childhood is always changing, reflecting shifting views on gender, class and ethnicity[13] as well as shifts in children's relationships with culture and media.

In the 17th and 18th centuries different philosophies of childhood came to influence Western European perceptions, and these are reflected in the ways in which children's relationship with culture and the media has been understood. The romantic notion of the innocent, pure, spontaneous child draws on the ideas of French philosopher Jean-Jacques Rousseau (1712–1778),[14] suggesting that a child needs protection from a hostile environment fashioned by adults.[15] This notion of natural childhood innocence liberated from adult rules[16] persists as a strong ideal in Western culture, echoed in initiatives to protect children from negative media influences associated with commercialization, sexualization and violence. English philosopher and physician John Locke (1632–1704)[17] fostered the idea of the child as a blank slate (*tabula rasa*) who could be trained, educated and guided to become rational. These ideas were repeated in initiatives to establish compulsory schooling in the 19th century,[18] opening up a separate space for the study of children and childhood.[19] Compulsory education reinforced the separation of childhood from adulthood and marked a change in the way that children, especially working-class children, were perceived, as they became valued less for their economic value and ability to work, and more for their emotional value to their parents.[20] According to Lynn Whitaker, the *tabula rasa* construction accords with the principles of public service broadcasting and the education of taste, and also appears in contemporary discourses about media literacy.[21]

Christian doctrine has also shaped constructions of childhood, with religious discourses identifying the child as inherently wicked and in need of redemption,[22] necessitating the inculcation of Christian values and punishment for transgressions.[23] In its early 19th-century guises this doctrine was evident in moralizing children's literature based on Christian precepts that warned against the dire consequences of wrongdoing.[24] One example is *Struwwelpeter* (1845), a German children's book comprising 10 tales depicting disastrous and sometimes fatal outcomes for children who misbehave. According to Whitaker,[25] this construction of a child naturally predisposed toward excess and self-gratification is manifested in contemporary debates about 'junk' food and 'junk' television.[26]

In contrast to historical approaches, developmental psychology, the major 20th-century Western framework for analysing childhood, concentrates on distinguishing and recording the physical and cognitive stages of childhood. Jean Piaget's stage theory,[27] emphasizing distinctive stages in a child's cognitive development, has been important for its influence not just on educators but also on those involved in producing educational and entertainment media[28] as well as toys and games that are marketed as 'age appropriate'. Yet some have disputed the universalism of psychological approaches, arguing that they concentrate on developmental norms without paying enough attention to the social world and cultures that children inhabit[29] where age is not always a reliable predictor of development.

Sociological approaches, which became more prominent in the latter half of the 20th century, concentrate instead on children's socialization into society, a process marked less by biology and age and more by children's relationships with their environment and the demands that societies make of them.[30] Sociological approaches are significant for understanding children's relationship with the media, positioning children either as victims of corrupting and trivializing media products[31] or as active participants who use media in sophisticated and empowering ways.[32] Rather than the universal understanding of child development promoted by developmental psychology, the 'new sociology of childhood'[33] emphasizes different types of socially constructed childhood, which are culturally determined; are likely to differ across time and place; are shaped by local practices and beliefs relating to class, gender and ethnicity; and involve children as active social agents and meaning-makers.[34] Sociological approaches build on Ariès' idea of childhood as a social construction, recognizing that 'children are not formed by natural and social forces but rather that they inhabit a world of meaning created by themselves and through their interaction with adults'.[35] From this perspective, the distinction between childhood and adulthood, the transition between 'being and becoming'[36] becomes less distinct. This has implications for the international study of childhood, which 'has been differently understood, institutionalized and regulated in different societies at different points of history – and experienced differently by children'.[37]

Childhood can also be viewed from a policy perspective where adults identify children's needs or problems, necessitating a policy response. For Stainton Rogers[38] the needs discourse reflects the distinctive status assigned to children by Western values that prioritize individual autonomy. This approach fits awkwardly with other societies, including those with stronger orientations to family, community or religious doctrine, where a different type of adulthood may be aspired to. Some alternative policy discourses focus on promoting children's rights, taking account of their views. These resonate with the legally binding principles of the UN Convention on the Rights of the Child (CRC), adopted in 1989, which placed child welfare as an issue of legal concern for the first time, and which asserts, in Article 12, that children have the right to express their views on matters affecting them and for these views to be taken seriously. However, the rights discourse can also be problematic because of different constructions of childhood in different parts of the world. For example, it is argued that the CRC's emphasis on chronological age (the age of adulthood is set at 18) and allegedly Western ideals of childhood do not always suit social, political, cultural, religious and ethnic conditions in all countries.[39]

Clearly there are different constructions of childhood in Western countries, which have changed over time. They are important for our understanding of policy issues relating to children and their use of the media in the West, while it is also clear that the values underpinning Western constructions may not suit other parts of the world.

Arab Constructions of Childhood

One distinguishing aspect between Arab and Western conceptions of childhood is the fundamental role of Islam as a belief system that spans a diverse and increasingly geographically dispersed set of Arabic-speaking communities. In general terms, Islam is 'ingrained in the everyday structures of Arab societies' and 'permeates many spheres of Arab social and cultural life'.[40] While Christianity has certainly had a significant role historically in defining Western perceptions of childhood, religious mores have come to have less dominant impact in large parts of contemporary Western societies. This is not the case in many Arab countries, where interpretations of Islam touch every aspect of life, including adult obligations to children, and offer alternative legal touchstones to those perceived to underpin the CRC. The Quran contains little that deals with children directly, but efforts to reconstruct the way it was taken as a declaration of social and economic values[41] do 'shed light on the long-term impact of the Quranic message in the domain of family ethics and the ways that this message has been accommodated to changing circumstances'.[42]

Children, as defined by the CRC, make up a large and growing proportion of the Arab population. UNICEF data published in 2015 show that the total number of under-18s in 18 Arab countries[43] stood at more than 134 million.[44] Yet children's media experiences in the Arab world have rarely been the focus of research by scholars based in the region or outside it. Instead, as Martin Woodhead notes, Western discourses about the origins of childhood 'have been exported and become globalized standards for judging other people's childhoods',[45] with limited sensitivity regarding the nature of childhood elsewhere. Woodhead goes on to point out that, whereas age and developmental norms have come to be seen as important childhood milestones in the West, there may be less attention to age in those places where the course of life is based on different expectations about work, gender and the age of maturity. Across the world, childhood varies in terms of how long it lasts and the length and degree of dependency on adults. In Arab countries with high youth unemployment, the category of 'waithood' has been applied[46] to a phase between childhood and adulthood during which young people with no job and mixed feelings about parental dependence are 'waiting' to negotiate their identities.[47] At the other end of the age spectrum, 'preschool' can cover varying age brackets within Gulf countries, where research sponsored by the Arab Bureau for Education in Gulf States (ABEGS) has shown rates of kindergarten enrolment to be markedly different between nationals and expatriate groups.[48] Meanwhile, different rules for young people before and after they reach puberty add another layer of complexity, since there may be several years of difference between the onset of puberty for boys and girls. Ethnographic studies have discussed the consequences of differential treatment of adolescents in various parts of the Arab world.[49]

As with Western constructions of childhood, history affords us some ideas of how childhood has been conceptualized in Arab countries. For example, Avner Giladi argues that the concept of childhood existed in medieval Muslim society dating back to the 10th century. Using David Herlihy's criteria of emotional and economic 'investment',[50] and drawing on paediatric, religious, educational and legal writings of the time, Giladi makes a case for childhood having been accorded a distinct status in pre-modern Arab society and separated from adulthood. According to Giladi, medieval Arab society invested in children on three levels, 'the intellectual, the emotional and the economic'.[51] He cites the existence of the *kuttab*, an elementary educational institution dating from the eighth century, as well as limited references to the care and protection of children in the Quran and *hadith* (narrative stories about the Prophet's life).[52] As with Ariès, whose approach has been criticized for over-reliance on representations of children in art, Giladi's approach is reliant on written sources, in this case theological and legal texts.[53] Also as with Ariès, the analysis lacks contemporary accounts by parents and by women in particular.[54]

While contemporary Western approaches to childhood tend to focus on the individual child, in Arab and Muslim societies the family continues to play a more central role, as it did previously in Western countries. In those times and places where the bearing of children is linked almost exclusively to marriage and family, it is the changing complexities of the relationship between family, religion and gender that can shed light on transforming conceptualizations of childhood. In Arab societies, colonial and post-colonial legacies are also at play. Ethnographic literature paints the Arab family as a 'society in miniature',[55] reflecting patriarchal structures, that became the 'last relatively independent refuge' from European colonial influence.[56] Under colonial rule and after independence, formal education provided the basis for modelling and remodelling childhood[57] and shaping future citizens.[58] At times, post-independence remodelling challenged gender roles and provided a new site for the creation, maintenance and negotiation of childhood, thereby usurping some of the family's traditional responsibility for the cultural socialization of children.[59]

Ethnographic studies by Elizabeth Fernea in Iraq, Egypt and Morocco in the 1950s, 1960s and 1970s reveal how societal norms were taught at an early age with gender and religious socialization taking place at home, in the mosque, and for boys in Quranic schools.[60] In societies where children were viewed as incomplete and irrational,[61] Fernea describes a socialization process that was both hierarchal and patriarchal, where children were required to conform according to the expectations of parents (primarily the father) and the extended family, as well as to religious and social ideas about gender and 'the values of honour, morality, religiosity, generosity, hospitality, respect for parents (especially the father) and responsibility for their care in old age'.[62] More recent biographical accounts of childhood have concentrated on a yearning to escape these patriarchal family strictures.[63] Yet, in countries where there is no alternative institutional system of welfare or security, belonging to a family or kin group remains an important driver of personal identity[64] and inevitably influences constructions of childhood.

Others, however, dispute the narrative of male power over children, pointing out that patriarchal structures within the Arab family are being disturbed. Several commentators suggest that the media, including television, have introduced women and children to alternative ideas about the family, gender and society.[65] Suad Joseph maintains that the Arab family is not homogenous, fixed and static, but that relationships within it are fluid, complex and cannot simply be reduced to a matter of class and gender.[66] Family endures as an important social institution, reinforced by religious belief and the lack of other strong social institutions, but growing youth rebelliousness reveals a different story characterized by unemployment, violence and growing estrangement from the family[67] seen at its most extreme in suicide bombings. The Arab uprisings of 2011 sparked new studies of Arab youth and increasing awareness of the traumatic impact on children of brutal conflicts in the region.

27

Arab constructions of childhood, like their Western counterparts, are varied and shifting, in response to changing economic and political circumstances and conjunctures. Nevertheless, the above overview of these constructions can provide some understanding of policy issues, as discussed below.

Constructions of Childhood and Debates about Children's Media Provision

We argue that the way childhood is perceived by different societies also affects the way children's relationships with the media are understood by scholars and society at large. The core issue is not just about children's everyday use of the media, but how broader forces within society shape children's consumption.[68] Children may be active meaning-makers of media content, but they are active within boundaries that might not be of their own choosing. Children's active agency[69] is only one part of the story about their relationship with the media, which is also shaped by a variety of social, political, cultural, religious, corporate and economic constraints.

Children's relationship with the media becomes a policy issue arising from concerns about cultural standards, about the opportunities afforded by the media, as well as recurring panics about media impact. Responses reflect particular and different constructions of childhood, which are 'simultaneously present'.[70] These often build on discourses about a more general crisis in childhood, which is seen to necessitate protection for children from media's perceived harmful effects. Or they may build on developmental approaches, whereby children are seen to have needs that require certain types of content to enhance their development. Internationally some of these concerns were reflected in the Children's Television Charter drafted at the first World Summit on Children and Television in Melbourne in 1995. Key issues then included the importance of high quality 'indigenous' production, the accessibility of wide-ranging material to all children, content that allows children to 'affirm their sense of self, community and place', awareness and appreciation of other cultures, and the promotion of high standards facilitated through funding and government support. Since then the three-yearly world summits have encompassed media more generally, but the objectives of the Charter remain in place.

In the UK, the issues highlighted by the Charter have been the subject of industry and public debate for many years, being echoed in the remit of public service broadcasters as well as in frequent public reviews and reports. In 2008 and 2013 the BBC Trust reviewed the BBC's Children's Services, evaluating the BBC's performance against its public purposes.[71] In 2007, responding to a perceived crisis in the funding of original programmes for children, the UK regulator Ofcom published a review of children's television programming; it also publishes annual surveys on children's media use. Concerns are raised by the advocacy organization, the Children's Media Foundation, which advises parents on what types of media might be 'bad' for children, whether video games make children aggressive, whether too much time spent on media will affect children's social skills or education, the risks associated with going online, and questions about quality.[72]

In Arab countries, in contrast, opportunities for informed public debate about children's media have been much more limited, partly because little content was produced specifically for Arab children until recently and partly because government control over media output denied space to independent voices speaking on issues of broadcast regulation for the benefit of children. Malika Alouane, former director of programmes at Al-Jazeera Children's Channel (JCC), told a conference on pan-Arab children's television at the University of Westminster in 2010,[73] that JCC had been launched in 2005 to help to stimulate production of children's content by creating a market. Yet, she said, the lack of regulation for children's broadcasting was problematic. 'We're not asking for censorship', she said, 'but regulation would help broadcasters to position themselves better'. Speaking at the same event, Nadine Hassan, then head of MBC3, part of the private Saudi-owned MBC Group, agreed. Pointing out the effect of climate on regional viewing patterns, with daytime temperatures of 40–50 degrees in the Gulf creating a physical environment conducive to long hours spent indoors in front of the television, Hassan said broadcasters could not act individually and independently to respond to children's needs without appropriate wider regulation of children's broadcasting in the region.

Another reason for a lack of informed public debate about Arab policy and regulation lies in the political obstacles to conducting credible surveys or monitoring. Surveys are needed to provide an evidence base for policies, but these risk raising questions about the effectiveness of existing political leaderships. Although there are a number of Arabic language channels besides Spacetoon, MBC3 and JCC, including Saudi-owned Majd Children's Channel and JCC's preschool offshoot, Baraem, much recent expansion in the region has been by non-Arab children's channels based in the US, notably Nickelodeon Arabia (now part of MBC3) and Arabic versions of Turner Broadcasting's Cartoon Network with its preschool channel Boomerang. The rise of animation studios in the Gulf[74] has been accompanied by some government-backed initiatives to promote children's media. Examples include the Doha Film Institute's Ajyal Youth Film Festival, started in 2013, the radio station attached to Dubai's Jalila Childhood Centre, which opened in 2013, and the preschool Gulf television series *Iftah ya Simsim*, relaunched in 2015 by Abu Dhabi–based Bidaya Media in collaboration with the US Sesame Workshop, Abu Dhabi's Mubadala investment company and the Arab Bureau for Education in Gulf States (ABEGS). Yet imported content continues to dominate the broadcasting schedules and, despite producers' persistent pleas for more home-grown material to be made and promoted, it is not yet clear whether the regulatory and academic communities in Arab countries take a consensus view on the balance between local and imported programming or effective policy responses.[75]

While Arab public debate rarely focuses on children's media, there are elements of wider debates about the media that have implications for children's content, especially those relating to preservation of Arab and Islamic culture. Kraidy and Khalil[76] echo others[77] in their claim that a direct clash between globalized youth culture and local norms in the Arab world is indisputable, as young people are put in touch with cultures other than their own. As well as raising questions about identity, the penetration of global media such as satellite television and the internet into Arab homes coincides with changing dynamics of the family and the position of the child within it, blurring boundaries between the public and the private sphere and between home and the external world, as children and young people start to form alternative peer networks alongside the more hierarchical relationships that exist within the family.[78]

Thus constructions of childhood inform policy debates on children's media in both Arab and Western countries. The following sections highlight concerns related to protection and regulation as well as ideas about the promotion of quality content and its relationship to local culture.

Protection and Negative Regulation

One of the dominant and recurring themes in academic and journalistic debates about the relationship between children and the media has always been the potentially corrupting force of electronic media, ranging from the perceived dangers of American cartoons and commercial exploitation to the perils of technological overload and surveillance. The perennial 'toxic childhood' discourse in the West highlights the dangers of the media for children's emotional, social and cognitive development.[79] This contrasts with a discourse, more common among media professionals, which views children as empowered and media savvy,[80] although empowerment is also recognized as a marketing tactic used by commercial companies.[81] The concern to protect involves shielding children from knowledge and content, which they are deemed too immature to deal with.

Although evidence of harmful effects from media consumption is often complex and difficult to disentangle from other influences, these concerns do reflect wider debates about a perceived crisis in childhood, where children's lives are apparently 'tainted' by overexposure to electronic media, a lack of places to play and an overemphasis on academic testing. Although not new,[82] these concerns appear to have taken on a new intensity since the mid-20th century with children's greater exposure to visual culture, commercialism and new technologies. Yet there is still only limited understanding of how children use and understand media and new technologies, how the media are embedded in their lives and how their media use is also affected by the economic, social and political environment of the societies they inhabit.[83] The protectionist discourse is ever present, but the solutions are not straightforward in a multiplatform world, which operates alongside changes to family life and media consumption – changes that are not always easy to subject to regulatory control or prohibition.

The negative media effects discourse is also prevalent in Arab studies of children's media, as demonstrated by titles in the annotated bibliography compiled by Cairo University professor Sami Tayie, which contain phrases such as 'negative influences', 'psychological dangers', 'impact of advertising' and 'televised violence'[84]. In public debates the negative discourse frequently has a religious angle. As Barbara Ibrahim and Hind Wassef point out, older generations in the Arab world mostly regard younger age groups as being in need of 'saving from deviation'.[85] Traditionalists worry that too much foreign content is jeopardizing what many refer to as 'Arab-Islamic culture', a term mostly treated as uncontentious and self-explanatory.[86]

Concerns like these inevitably result in calls for policy interventions in order to protect what is perceived as a vulnerable audience.[87] Negative regulation, such as bans and prohibitions, arise out of societal pressures to deal with the perceived negative effects of exposure to media violence, pornography or over-commercialized content. They are evident, for example, in measures taken by countries like Sweden, which banned advertising on all programming for under-12s in 1991, or Greece, which banned television advertising for toys, and, most recently, the UK, which saw a ban in 2006 on advertising for foods high in sugar, fat and salt around children's programming. At the same time there is some recognition that banning or censoring content is not always adequate for shielding children from potential harm, leading to initiatives by regulators such as Ofcom which focus more on education and on enhancing media literacy.[88]

In the Arab world, although government interventions in the media are ubiquitous, there are few explicit regulations or laws about children and the media. Lebanon, for example, does require locally licensed television channels to provide a minimum amount of children's programming under its Audiovisual Law of 1994,[89] but enforcement is another matter. Without explicit external regulation of the broadcasting sector, control becomes an internal matter for broadcasters themselves. In JCC's case, for example, the channel's own Compliance Department considers all content in respect of dress codes; gender segregation; references to non-Muslim celebrations such as Christmas, Easter and Valentine's Day; and values and beliefs about matters such as relationships with parents, relationships between the sexes and so on.[90] One area of difference with Western content is the perceived need to have authority figures present in children's content, reflecting attitudes of the family in Arab society. An interviewee involved in compliance intimated that he personally had noticed the 'lack of mother and father' in the narrative of much children's content imported from the West. 'Either the mother and father are abusive or they're not there or [the child is] being raised by someone else', he said. He went on to note that 'if we were to try to do something about it (which we haven't) and we decided that this isn't appropriate, I think we'd lose most of our content, because ... that's the starting point [of every story]'.[91]

This view highlights a tension between the inclination of someone involved in internal regulation in an Arab broadcaster and mainstream Western children's narratives, such as Disney's *Hannah Montana*, in which the child is empowered and takes 'centre stage' without much intervention by authority figures. At JCC, the emphasis is on 'building the family' and depicting relationships in culturally acceptable ways:

> there are things we can't control. We can't control how it's going to be interpreted. But I do think generally you can see trends in values ... put into children's programmes and I think when you notice them, and recognize them, it's important to block them out. Some would be very innocent in the West but we would have more difficulty with them in the East here, especially in terms of love, and marriage and things like that.[92]

Some religious broadcasters seek to counter Western influence by explicitly offering children alternative identity positions. Ehab Galal's analysis of programmes broadcast by the Iqra and Majd Children's Channel, two religious channels owned by private Saudi financiers, shows that both position the child as Muslim, wholly defined by religious behaviour, which governs all aspects of life.[93] The narrow remit of such channels does not provide a holistic view of the world, but credible statistical evidence is lacking as to how many children view them or what impact they may have. It is because of a disconnect between protective intentions and actual viewership that some perspectives on children's media place the emphasis instead on positive regulatory influences to promote local production, as discussed in the following section.

'Quality' Content and Local Culture

People involved in children's media call for validation of local culture for children everywhere, as expressed in the following three quotations:

> We want local children, either Emirati or others living in the Emirates, to learn through best practice. We want to equip them with all the tools to take pride in their own culture and thus take their place in the world.[94]

> Children need and deserve programmes which reflect their own rich and diverse heritage of language, literature, values and environment, as well as those of other countries and cultures.[95]

> Young Arab audiences, like all young viewers, deserve the best content from their own culture as well as from around the world.[96]

In contrast to the negative regulation associated with regulating against harmful effects, regulation for positive outcomes recognizes that children's media can be a potentially positive social influence.[97] This is seen most clearly in the institution of public service broadcasting (PSB), found in Europe, some African countries and Japan, which is often designed to provide children with a diverse range of content that not only entertains, but also educates and contributes to children's development as citizens.[98] The concept of the child here is of an individual who can be educated (the *tabula rasa*) to become a discerning and appreciative connoisseur of quality. It is a view that can be seen as both child-centred and paternalistic. It assumes that public service broadcasters can produce high quality home-grown children's content that will enhance citizenship, and that this material is superior to imported material, usually US cartoons.

However, 'quality' is a highly contested term in academic discourse[99] and the equation of quality with domestically produced content is problematic because it is often assumed that imported programming (particularly US content) is culturally inferior, again without much evidence.[100] Although little tangible evidence has been collected to support assumptions about the benefits of home-grown content, politically it has been tied to arguments around childhood and identity[101] and, as noted above, is frequently highlighted in pronouncements by both advocacy groups and media practitioners. The extent to which PSBs offer popular quality content is variable, with well-resourced PSBs like the BBC in a better position to achieve this goal than less well-resourced players.[102] Quotas, production subsidies and tax breaks are also used to promote domestic content, but these tend to support industry objectives[103] rather than the needs of children.

In the Arab world, meanwhile, there is no public service broadcasting and few initiatives that are wide-ranging enough to promote local production at all stages of the supply chain. Samer Hamarneh of Rubicon Holding Group, a Jordanian-owned company with offices around the world, believes this lack of investment has far-reaching cultural consequences. He told a panel on animation at the Big Entertainment Show in Dubai on 19 November 2013:

> Our culture is really rich. We have lots to talk about. But our kids are growing up with no connection to society because they watch programmes that don't relate to them.[104]

Zaidoun Karadsheh, partner in the Amman-based Sketch in Motion animation studio, echoed the point to the same panel. 'We have an identity crisis in this region', he said. 'My kids watch *Spongebob Squarepants*, but this represents different ethics, different clothes. We need to create a local hero.'[105] Asked about solutions to the problems of content creation in light of these identity issues, Hamarneh's arguments were similar to those of former executives of JCC and MBC3 quoted earlier in this chapter, to the effect that a transparent system of standard-setting is needed for the industry as a whole. Governments could make a joint code or charter to 'set standards for pan-Arab content to make it good', he said.[106]

> Nothing that gets shown here gets checked for standards except inside companies and I need that to be transparent ... It is a child's right to have access to their own culture and not to be fooled, as for example when the dubbing says 'juice' but the character is obviously drinking alcohol.[107]

Previous and existing Arab-inspired initiatives for specially designed children's content demonstrate a strong concern to foreground Arab and Muslim culture and values. When academics at Baghdad University evaluated *Iftah ya simsim*, a Kuwaiti version of *Sesame Street* first launched in 1979, they found that it promoted 'Islamic principles, positive social behaviour, personal manners, and the importance of traits such as honesty, respect for parents, loyalty, and social interaction' as well as the Arabic language.[108] Mahmoud Bouneb, JCC's first general manager when it launched in 2005, said he wanted to build a 'new concept' in Arab television for children – one that would avoid 'letting Western values be [seen as] the only ones'.[109] When JCC's preschool offshoot, Baraem, came on the scene, Malika Alouane was quoted as saying that it was designed 'not only [to] educate and entertain children, but to make Arabic culture a part of their everyday lives'.[110]

However, in both Arab and Western countries, many factors intervene to complicate the equation between home grown content and quality. Independent producers of Arabic-language content frequently contrast state backing for children's programming that is available in non-Arab countries with an absence of such support in the Arab context. Nathalie Habib, General Manager and Executive Producer of Blink Studios in Dubai, told the 2013 Big Entertainment Show in Dubai that the production of children's content in countries like Japan, Canada, France benefits from government subsidies, tax credits and so on. 'In the Arab world', Habib said,

> there are more than 300 million people using the same language but no government thinks 'how do we fund content for our children?'. If they thought about children the process of creation would come from the right end but, instead, animation studios are trying to shape the process from the wrong end. Governments have to realise this is an industry to put money into.[111]

The same point is made by Fayez Al-Sabbagh, founder and chief executive of the Dubai-based Spacetoon Group. He insists that it is the job of governments to support the ample talent that exists in the Arab region:

> In the Middle East they want animation but they don't build the industry, they build small things here and there and then these small companies, unfortunately later on they close … If you have a nice professional camera it doesn't mean you can make a movie; if you have a computer and software it doesn't mean you can do animation … It is the job of the government to build the industry and spend money for the pre-production pipeline of writers, scripts as well as the animator themselves.[112]

At the same time production talent is sometimes blocked by a fear of innovation. Ian Prince, a British producer who was involved in creating a young people's discussion programme in Morocco, found that local producers wanted to make it 'just like all the other political discussion programmes', which are 'deathly boring and cheap to make' but which 'no-one watches'. 'There was', he said, 'a reticence to do something new and also a reticence to take responsibility for breaking the mould'.[113] As this reticence suggests, the quest for exciting Arabic content for children is complicated by the underlying politics of government-broadcaster relations. Paradoxically, in the case of the JCCTV channel for children aged 7–12 years, relaunched as Jeem TV in 2013, pressure to increase viewership after management changes at the station in 2011 led to renewed reliance on highly rated imports. Domestically produced series that were commissioned by the old management team were axed in 2012 in favour of US and UK imports, including a large purchase of Disney material in March 2013. Perceived as having high quality and proven popularity, these imports were intended to secure better audiences at a time when Jeem TV was looking to achieve improved financial sustainability through the introduction of advertising. According to Saad Al Hudaifi, JCC's executive manager and director of programmes:

> If we don't have quality our viewership satisfaction won't increase. As you know, we have done deals with Disney and BBC and both of them represent very high quality. ... we select the best programmes according to who matches the culture and the area.[114]

Conclusion

Constructions of childhood do leave a mark on children's media in different parts of the world, and are evident in broadcast regulation and commitment to children's content. In both Western and Arab countries, unease about rapid developments in the media is linked to concerns about the changing nature of childhood. While it is clear that ideas about childhood are socially constructed, these varying social constructions affect the purposes assigned to children's media. Ideologies of childhood differ between the regions, with Western broadcasters and researchers placing greater emphasis than their Arab counterparts on the child as an individual with agency, while Arab media institutions focus more on the child's status within the framework of the family and family traditions, and on religion. In both regions, however, commercial priorities increasingly shape the construction of childhood, not least because many representations are produced by US-based conglomerates for a transnational audience. This raises questions about the specificity of children's media for representing, and thus serving, distinctive audiences. The increasing commodification of childhood in both Arab and Western media reveals how the ability to compete in the marketplace, and stay profitable, often clashes with the construction and reflection of dominant national, religious and cultural sensibilities.

Notes

1 Research for this chapter was conducted as part of a project funded by the UK's Arts and Humanities Research Council (see the Acknowledgements of this volume). The chapter includes references to interview data collected by Naomi Sakr as part of the same research project.

2 Máire Messenger Davies, *Children, Media and Culture* (Maidenhead: Open University Press, 2010), p. 7.

3 Alessandro D'Arma and Jeanette Steemers, 'Public service media and children: Serving the digital citizens of the future', in P. Iosifidis (ed), *Reinventing Public Service Communication* (Basingstoke: Palgrave Macmillan, 2010), p. 115.

4 David Buckingham, 'The commercialisation of childhood? The place of the market in children's media culture', *Changing English: Studies in Culture and Education*, 2/2 (1995), p. 17.

5 Martin Woodhead, 'Childhood studies: Past, present and future', in M. J. Kehily (ed), *An Introduction to Childhood Studies,* 2nd ed. (Maidenhead: Open University Press, 2008), p. 17.

6 Mary Jane Kehily 'Understanding childhood: An introduction to some key themes and issues', in Kehily (ed), *An Introduction to Childhood Studies*, p. 1.

7 Hugh Cunningham, *Children and Childhood in Western Society Since 1500* (Harlow: Pearson Education, 1995); Diana Gittins, 'The historical construction of childhood' in Kehily (ed), *An Introduction to Childhood Studies*, pp. 35–49; Harry Hendrick, 'Origin and evolution of childhood in Western Europe, c.1400–1750', in J. Qvortrup, W. Corsaro and M. Honig (eds), *Palgrave Handbook of Child Studies* (Basingstoke: Palgrave Macmillan, 2009),

pp. 99–113; Nicholas Orme, *Medieval Children* (New Haven: Yale University Press, 2001); Steven Ozment, *Ancestors: The Loving Family in Old Europe* (Cambridge, MA: Harvard University Press, 2001).

8 Philippe Ariès, *Centuries of Childhood: A Social History of Family Life* (trans. Robert Baldick) (New York: Vintage Books, 1962).

9 Ariès, *Centuries of Childhood*, p. 125.

10 Ariès, *Centuries of Childhood*, p. 125; Cunningham, *Children and Childhood*, p. 11.

11 See Allison James and Alan Prout (eds), *Constructing and Reconstructing Childhood: Contemporary Issues in the Social Study of Childhood*, 2nd ed. (Abingdon: Routledge, 1997).

12 Messenger Davis, *Children, Media and Culture*, p. 23.

13 Hugh Cunningham, *Children of the Poor: Representations of Childhood since the Seventeenth Century* (Oxford: Blackwell, 1991).

14 Jean-Jacques Rousseau, *The Social Contract* (trans. Maurice Cranston) (Harmondsworth: Penguin, 1968).

15 Kehily: 'Understanding childhood', p. 5.

16 Bruno Bettelheim, 'Do children need television??' In P. Löhr and M. Meyer (eds), *Children, Television and New Media* (Luton: University of Luton Press, 1999), pp. 3–31.

17 John Locke, *Some Thoughts Concerning Education*. (Internet Modern History Sourcebook, 1692), Available at http://www.fordham.edu/halsall/mod/modsbook.html (accessed 1 June 2013).

18 Cunningham, *Children and Childhood*; Hendrick, 'Origin and evolution of childhood'; Colin Heywood, *A History of Childhood: Children and Childhood in the West from Medieval to Modern Times* (Cambridge: Polity Press, 2001).

19 Alan Prout and Allison James, 'A new paradigm for the sociology of childhood: Provenance, promise and problems', in A. James and A. Prout (eds), *Constructing and Reconstructing Childhood*, p. 9.

20 Viviana Zelizer, *Pricing the Priceless Child: The Changing Social Value of Children* (New York: Basic Books, 1985); Cunningham, *Children and Childhood*, p. 177.

21 Lynn Whitaker, 'Producing UK Children's Public Service Broadcasting in the 21st Century: A Case Study of BBC Scotland', PhD Thesis (University of Glasgow, 2011), pp. 45–46.

22 Chris Jenks, *Childhood*, 2nd ed. (Abingdon: Routledge, 2005).

23 Gittins, 'The historical construction of childhood', pp. 41–42.

24 Peter Hunt, 'Children's literature and childhood', in Kehily (ed), *An Introduction to Childhood Studies*, pp. 50–69.

25 Whitaker, *Producing UK Children's Public Service Broadcasting*, p. 44.

26 See also David Buckingham, Hannah Davies et al, *Children's Television in Britain* (London: BFI Publishing, 1999).

27 Jean Piaget, *The Language and Thought of the Child* (London: Routledge, 1977).

28 Gerald Lesser, *Children and Television: Lessons from Sesame Street* (New York: Random House, 1974); Messenger Davies, *Children, Media and Culture*, p. 44; Jeanette Steemers, *Creating Preschool Television* (Basingstoke: Palgrave Macmillan, 2010).

29 Chris Jenks, 'Constructing childhood sociologically', in Kehily (ed), *An Introduction to Childhood Studies*, pp. 93–111; James and Prout (eds), *Constructing and Reconstructing Childhood*; Allison James, Chris Jenks and Alan Prout, *Theorizing Childhood* (Cambridge: Polity Press, 1998).

30 Jenks: 'Constructing Childhood Sociologically', p. 102.

31 Stephen Kline, *Out of the Garden: Toys, TV and Children's Culture in the Age of Marketing* (London: Verso, 1993); Neil Postman, *The Disappearance of Childhood* (New York: Delacorte Press, 1982); Marie Winn, *The Plug-in Drug* (New York: Bantam, 1977).

32 Marsha Kinder, *Playing with Power in Movies, Television, and Video Games: From Muppet Babies to Teenage Mutant Ninja Turtles* (Berkeley: University of California Press, 1991); Ellen Seiter, *Sold Separately: Parents and Children in Consumer Culture* (New Brunswick: Rutgers University Press, 1993).

33 James and Prout (eds), *Constructing and Reconstructing Childhood*.

34 James and Prout (eds), *Constructing and Reconstructing Childhood*, pp. 8–9.

35 Jenks, 'Constructing childhood sociologically', p. 106.

36 Whitaker, *Producing UK Children's Public Service Broadcasting*, p. 118.

37 Woodhead, 'Childhood studies: Past, present and future', p. 20.

38 Wendy Stainton Rogers, 'Promoting better childhoods' in Kehily (ed), *An Introduction to Childhood Studies*, p. 148.

39 Jo Boyden, 'What place the politics of compassion in education surrounding non-citizen children?', *Educational Review*, 61/3 (2009), pp. 265–276.

40 Tarik Sabry, *Cultural Encounters in the Arab World: On Media, the Modern and the Everyday* (London: I.B.Tauris, 2010), p. 245.

41 Maryam Elahi, 'The rights of the child under Islamic law: Prohibition of the child soldier', in E. Fernea (ed), *Children in the Muslim Middle East* (Austin, TX: University of Texas Press, 1995), p. 368.

42 Avner Giladi, 'Some notes on the Quranic concepts of family and childhood', in F. Georgeon and K. Kreiser (eds), *Childhood and Youth in the Muslim World* (Paris: Maisonneuve & Larose, 2007), pp. 15–26.

43 Algeria, Bahrain, Egypt, Iraq, Jordan, Kuwait, Lebanon, Libya, Morocco, Oman, Palestine, Qatar, Saudi Arabia, Sudan, Syria, Tunisia, United Arab Emirates, Yemen.

44 UNICEF, *The State of the World's Children 2015* (New York: United Nations, 2014).

45 Woodhead, 'Childhood studies: Past, present and future', p. 21.

46 Diane Singerman, 'The economic imperatives of marriage: Emerging practices and identities among youth in the Middle East', Middle East Youth Initiative

Working Paper (Washington and Dubai: Wolfensohn Center for Development and Dubai School of Government, 2007).

47 Singerman, 'The economic imperatives of marriage', p. 38.

48 Bidaya Media Managing Director, Cairo Arafat, interviewed by Naomi Sakr, by telephone, 20 December 2013.

49 Elizabeth Fernea, 'Children in the Muslim Middle East', in Fernea, *Childhood in the Muslim Middle East*, pp. 3–16; Susan Dorsky and Thomas Stevenson, 'Childhood and education in highland North Yemen' in Fernea (ed), *Children in the Muslim Middle East*, p. 93–108; Susan Schaefer Davis and Douglas Davis, 'Love conquers all? Changing images of gender and relationship in Morocco' in Fernea (ed), *Children in the Muslim Middle East*, pp. 93–108.

50 Avner Giladi, 'Herlihy's thesis revisited: Some notes on investment in children in medieval Muslim society', *Journal of Family History*, 36/3 (2011), pp. 235, 242.

51 Giladi, 'Herlihy's thesis revisited', p. 243.

52 Giladi, 'Herlihy's thesis revisted'; Avner Giladi, 'Concepts of childhood and attitudes towards children in medieval Islam: A preliminary study with special reference to reaction to infant and child mortality', *Journal of the Economic and Social History of the Orient*, 32/2 (1989), pp. 121–152.

53 Jonathan Berkey, 'Review of Avner Giladi "Children of Islam: Concepts of childhood in medieval Muslim society"', *Speculum*, 69/3 (1994), pp. 780–781.

54 Oliver Boyd-Barrett, 'Pan-Arab satellite television: The dialectics of identity' in H. Tumber (ed), *Media Power, Policies and Professionals* (London and New York: Routledge, 2000), pp. 314–331.

55 Halim Barakat, *The Arab World: Society, Culture and State* (Berkeley and Los Angeles, University of California Press, 1993), p. 46.

56 Fernea, 'Childhood in the Muslim Middle East', p. 12.

57 Aicha Belarbi (trans. Moncef and Wafaa Lahlou), 'The Child as economic investment: Preliminary reflections' in Fernea (ed), *Children in the Muslim Middle East*, p. 231; Timothy Mitchell, *Colonising Egypt* (Cambridge: Cambridge University Press, 1988), p. 71.

58 William Armbrust, 'What would Sayyid Qutb say? Some reflections on video clips', *Transnational Broadcasting Studies* 1 (2005), pp. 18–29.

59 Fernea, 'Childhood in the Muslim Middle East', p. 4; Mitchell, *Colonising Egypt*, p. 85.

60 Fernea, 'Childhood in the Muslim Middle East', p. 9.

61 Hamed Ammar, *Growing Up in an Egyptian Village* (London: Routledge, 1954); Belarbi, 'The child as economic investment', pp. 230–234.

62 Fernea, 'Childhood in the Muslim Middle East', p. 11.

63 Tetz Rooke, 'Escape from the family: A theme in Arab autobiography' in Meijer (ed), *Alienation or Integration of Arab Youth*, p. 222.

64 Fernea, 'Childhood in the Muslim Middle East', p. 228.

65 Dorsky and Stevenson, 'Childhood and education in highland North Yemen'; Robert Fernea, 'Gender, sexuality and patriarchy in modern Egypt', *Critique: Critical Middle East Studies*, 12/2 (2003), pp. 141–153.

66 Suad Joseph, 'Connectivity and patriarchy among urban working-class Arab families in Lebanon', *Ethos*, 21/4 (1993), pp. 452–484; Suad Joseph, *Intimate Selving in Arab Families: Gender, Self, and Identity in Arab Families* (New York: Syracuse University Press, 1999).

67 Luis Martinez, 'Youth, the street and violence in Algeria' in Meijer (ed), *Alienation or Integration of Arab Youth*, pp. 83–113.

68 See David Buckingham, New media, new childhoods? Children's changing cultural environment in the age of digital technology' in Kehily (ed), *An Introduction to Childhood Studies*, pp. 124–139.

69 James Lull, 'The social uses of television', *Human Communication Research*, 6 (1980), pp. 197–209; David Morley, *Family Television: Cultural Power and Domestic Leisure* (London: Comedia, 1986).

70 Buckingham et al, *Children's Television in Britain*, p. 149.

71 BBC Trust, *Review of the BBC's Children's Services* (London: BBC Trust, 2013). Available at: http://downloads.bbc.co.uk/bbctrust/assets/files/pdf/our_work/childrens_services/childrens_services.pdf (accessed 17 September 2015).

72 http://www.thechildrensmediafoundation.org/parent-portal.

73 The conference, entitled 'Children's Television in the Arab World', was organized by the University of Westminster's Arab Media Centre and took place on 4 June 2010.

74 See Chapter 4 in this volume.

75 See Chapter 3 in this volume.

76 Marwan Kraidy and Joe F. Khalil, 'Youth, media and culture in the Arab world', in K. Drotner and S. Livingstone (eds), *The International Handbook of Children, Media and Culture* (London: Sage, 2009), pp. 336–350.

77 For example, Barbara Ibrahim and Hind Wassef, 'Caught between two worlds: Youth in the Egyptian hinterland', in Meijer (ed), *Alienation or Integration of Arab Youth*, p. 161.

78 Pamela Karimi and Christiane Gruber, 'Introduction: The politics and poetics of the child image in Muslim contexts', P. Karimi and C. Gruber (eds), *Images of the Child and Childhood in Modern Muslim Contexts*, special volume of *Comparative Studies of South Asia, Africa and the Middle East*, 32/2 (2012), p. 291.

79 Kline, *Out of the Garden*; Sue Palmer, *Toxic Childhood* (London: Orion, 2006); Postman, *The Disappearance of Childhood*.

80 See Buckingham et al, *Children's Television in Britain*.

81 Juliet Schor, *Born to Buy: The Commercialized Child and the New Consumer Culture* (New York: Scribner, 2004), p. 55.

82 Martin Barker and Julian Petley (eds), *Ill Effects: The Media Violence Debate* (London: Routledge, 1997).
83 Buckingham, 'New media, new childhoods?', p. 134.
84 Sami Tayie, 'Children and mass media in the Arab world: a second level analysis', in U. Carlsson, S. Tayie et al (eds), *Empowerment through Media education: An Intercultural Dialogue* (Göteborg: Nordiskt Informationscenter, 2008), pp. 67–87.
85 Ibrahim and Wassef, 'Caught between two worlds'.
86 Naomi Sakr, *Arab Television Today* (London: I.B.Tauris, 2007), p. 151.
87 D'Arma and Steemers, 'Public service media and children', p. 115.
88 Buckingham, 'New media, new childhoods?' p. 134.
89 Dima Dabbous-Sensenig, 'Ending the War? The Lebanese Broadcasting Act of 1994', PhD thesis (Sheffield Hallam University, 2003).
90 Staff at JCC Compliance Department, interviewed by Naomi Sakr, Doha, 25 November 2013.
91 Sakr interview at JCC Compliance Department.
92 Sakr interview at JCC Compliance Department.
93 Ehab Galal, 'Reimagining religious identities in children's programs on Arabic Satellite-TV: intentions and values' in J. Feldt and P. Seeberg (eds), *New Media in the Middle East*, Working Paper Series No. 7 (Odense: University of Southern Denmark, 2006).
94 Dina Abu Hamdan, Jalila Childhood Centre, interviewed by Naomi Sakr, Dubai, 19 November 2013.
95 House of Lords, Select Committee on Communications, 1st Report of Session 2009–10, *The British Film and Television Industries – Decline or Opportunity?* Volume II Evidence (London: The Stationery Office, 2010), p. 340.
96 Estelle Hughes, 'Partnering in the Arab world', *C21Media*, 28 June 2011.
97 Máire Messenger Davies, 'Academic literature review: the future of children's television programming' (London: Ofcom, 2007). Available at http://www.ofcom.org.uk/consult/condocs/kidstv/litreview.pdf (accessed 18 February 2014).
98 Messenger Davies, *Children, Media and Culture*, p. 4; D'Arma and Steemers, 'Public service media and children', p. 115; Buckingham et al, *Children's Television in Britain*, p. 157.
99 Charlotte Brunsdon, 'Problems with quality', *Screen*, 31/1 (1997), pp. 67–90; Mark Jancovich and James Lyons, *Quality Popular Television: Cult TV, the Industry and Fans* (London: BFI Publishing, 2003).
100 See David Buckingham et al., *The Impact of the Commercial World on Children's Wellbeing: Report of an Independent Assessment* (London: Department for Children, Schools and Families and Department of Culture, Media and Sport, 2009); Jeanette Steemers and Alessandro D'Arma, 'Evaluating and regulating

the role of public broadcasters in the children's media ecology: The case of home-grown television content', *International Journal of Media and Cultural Politics*, 8/1 (2012), pp. 67–85.

101 Messenger Davies, *Children, Media and Culture*, p. 63.

102 Alessandro D'Arma, Gunn Enli, and Jeanette Steemers, 'Serving children in public service media' in G. Ferrell Lowe (ed), *The Public in Public Service Media*, (Göteborg: Nordicom, 2010), pp. 227–42.

103 D'Arma and Steemers, 'Public service media and children'.

104 Remarks transcribed by Naomi Sakr.

105 Remarks transcribed by Naomi Sakr.

106 Hamarneh, Remarks.

107 Hamarneh, Remarks.

108 Misbah al-Khayr and Hashim al-Samira'i (trans. Ahmed Sweity), 'Iftah Ya SimSim (Open Sesame) and Children in Baghdad' in Fernea (ed), *Children in the Muslim Middle East*, p. 464.

109 Mahmoud Bouneb, interviewed by Naomi Sakr, Doha, 20 April 2009.

110 Quoted by Martin Buxton in '*Meet the buyers: Al Jazeera*', *C21Media*, 3 November 2009.

111 Remarks transcribed by Naomi Sakr.

112 Fayez Al-Sabbagh, interviewed by Naomi Sakr, Dubai, 20 November 2013.

113 Ian Prince, interviewed by Jeanette Steemers, London, 26 April 2013.

114 Saad Al Hudaifi, interviewed by Naomi Sakr, Dubai, 18 November 2013.

3

Forces for Change in Official Arab Policies on Media and Children

Naomi Sakr

Prizes, summits, charters and festivals around the world testify to a widespread recognition that special stimuli are needed to underpin standards in children's media. Those stimuli are special in being neither commercial nor legislative, because, as discussed in Chapter 1 of this book, experience has shown the pitfalls of relying on markets or the law to guarantee space or safety nets in this field. If markets and the law fail to stimulate local investment or innovation in a sufficiently diverse range of children's media genres, characterizations or narratives, it falls to public policy to find alternative ways to promote these things.

Initiatives aimed at shaping public policy and content in children's media have had an international reach for several decades, whether in relation to children's audiovisual content, promoting media literacy among children or raising media awareness of children's rights. The US-originated preschool educational television programme *Sesame Street*, launched in 1969, has been making international co-productions since 1972. Germany's Prix Jeunesse, founded in 1964 to promote excellence in children's television, has worked with willing partners in Asia, Africa and Latin America since the 1990s. UNESCO's ongoing efforts to enhance critical understanding and competent use of electronic and print media through media literacy at all levels – preschool to university to lifelong learning – date back to an international congress that produced the Grünwald Declaration on Media Education in 1982. As for the challenge of protecting children's rights vis-à-vis the media, that was one plank of the Child Rights Information Network, which came together in Geneva in the early 1990s through mainly Swedish, Swiss and UNICEF collaboration and expanded to include organizations from the Global South in 1995.[1] Its trigger was the UN Convention on the Rights of the Child (CRC), which came into effect in 1991 having been ratified by 191 countries. Recognition of the central role played by the child-media relationship in every aspect of child rights was articulated in the 'Oslo Challenge', sent out in 1999 from a meeting organized by UNICEF and the Norwegian government.[2]

As the collaborations behind these gatherings and initiatives suggest, part of the ethos of promoting children's interests in terms of media content, media awareness and media responses to children's needs, rests on a sense of shared values and intentions among communities of specialist children's media professionals that potentially span continents and even the globe. Assuming that the sharing of values, standards and intentions is an active two-way process, this chapter aims to explore interactions that have taken place between international bodies that are the mainstays of those cross-border communities and Arab individuals and institutions that may or may not be part of them. To that end the chapter draws on theories about the transfer of policy ideas within and between communities and applies them to a discussion of two initiatives relating to children's media in the Arab world. The first initiative selected for analysis is a series made for and by children on Egyptian state TV in 2008, which is considered in relation to Egyptian involvement in two out of the seven World Summits on Media for Children held between 1995 and 2014; namely, those in Greece in 2001 and South Africa in 2007. The second is a film festival for children launched by Qatar's Doha Film Institute (DFI) in Qatar in 2013, which grew out of several years of partnership between DFI and the international Giffoni Film Festival for children, based in Italy.

Norms, Processes and the Transfer of Practices and Ideas

A desire to share best practice in policy approaches to children and media across national borders sounds uncontroversial. Yet, when the processes involved and the assumptions underlying those processes are unpacked in light of the scholarly literatures on policy transfer and children's rights, thorny issues start to emerge. These have to do with power relationships, the origins and content of particular policies and the narratives used to rationalize them, as well as the identities and motives of policy actors.

For example, many players may refer to children's rights, but schools of thought about interpreting and implementing these rights range along a spectrum that attributes varying levels of competence to children and thus accords them varying degrees of rights and equality with adults. So-called paternalists focus exclusively on a right to protection, while 'welfarists' prioritize protection over rights to provision and participation, 'emancipationists' prioritize participation over provision and protection and 'liberationists' focus exclusively on participation rights.[3] These schools of thought respond differently to issues such as child labour, votes for children, compulsory schooling and so on.[4] Several articles of the CRC are directly relevant to media, in the sense of children's rights to the following: have their views heard and be given weight [Art. 12]: seek, receive and impart information and ideas of all kinds [Art. 13]: freedom of thought, conscience and religion [Art. 14]; and access to socially and culturally beneficial information and material from diverse national and international sources [Art. 17]. Yet different norms and traditions emphasize different sub-clauses of these articles. Thus Article 17 can be read as supporting Articles 13 and 14 in the way it encourages 'mass media' to co-produce and disseminate content of benefit to children. Or it can be seen primarily as supporting the child's right to protection from material 'injurious' to 'well-being'. Article 12 implies a right to participate in public policy-making on issues that affect children's lives, through children's councils and parliaments. Yet some say it is the least implemented provision of the CRC, perhaps because it is perceived as a threat to adult authority.[5]

One way to track the spread or transfer of particular approaches underlying policies adopted is to treat an implemented policy as an 'assemblage of texts, actors, agencies, institutions and networks' that has been made and held together by 'political and technical work'.[6] That is to say, it is an outcome of links and causal mechanisms in which certain ideas are transmitted in preference to others. Yet whereas the implemented policy or related initiative is observable, the links and causal processes behind it – being much less visible – need to be uncovered through research. Two key exponents of the qualitative method of process tracing note that causal mechanisms are 'ultimately unobservable physical, social, or psychological processes through which agents with causal capacities' operate to transfer information to other entities.[7] Process tracing calls for careful description of steps along a trajectory of change,[8] using histories, documents, interviews and other sources to 'see whether the causal process a theory hypothesizes or implies in a case is in fact evident in the sequence and values of the intervening variables in that case'.[9]

Setting out to track any influence of international bodies and movements on Arab policies regarding children and media, the present research hypothesized that influence would occur through 'complex processes of policy assembly' in which 'divergent political motivations' are likely to have been aligned and 'translations' effected[10] to contribute to certain practices being adopted in Arab locales. 'Translations' in this context refers to the texts and discourses through which objects of policy are made 'thinkable' in a new place.[11] What this chapter contemplates is not the 'hard' transfer of policy instruments, institutions and programmes but the 'soft' transfer of ideas, ideologies and concepts that may occur within transnational advocacy networks.[12] According to Diane Stone, networks represent a 'soft, informal and gradual mode for the international diffusion and dissemination of ideas and policy paradigms' and these networks have the potential to influence policy if decision-makers are actively involved.[13]

Stone considers advocacy networks to be somewhat distinct from 'epistemic communities' in that the latter share knowledge that is professionally constituted and codified, whereas the emphasis in advocacy is more on building norms.[14] Both networks and communities are relevant to policy on children and media, because of questions about norms for children's participation and because the concept of an epistemic community resonates with J. Alison Bryant's notion of the 'children's television community', in which she includes content creators, programmers, 'toy tie-in companies, advertisers, governmental bodies, advocacy groups and philanthropic organizations'.[15] It also chimes with the policy 'community' as seen by John Kingdon, consisting of a more or less tightly knit network of officials, academics, consultants, analysts and advocates.[16]

Kingdon's classic notion of the 'policy entrepreneur' is also potentially insightful for the present analysis of networks, texts and actors. This recognizes that certain people 'in or out of government, in elected or appointed positions, in interest groups or research organizations' are willing to invest their 'time, energy, reputation, and sometimes money' in the hope of achieving policies they favour, but also possibly in the hope of attaining 'personal aggrandizement' or 'satisfaction from participation' in a policy community.[17] In the Arab region, prominent policy entrepreneurs in the field of children's media are often female relatives of heads of state. Stephen Heydemann believes that regimes in the Middle East have learned from each other how to contain civil society by sponsoring it and depriving it of autonomy: to exemplify this form of policy transfer he cites the activities of the first ladies of Egypt, Syria and Jordan as sponsors of semi-official 'non-governmental' organizations (NGOs).[18] These activities have been focused on children to a significant extent. Suzanne Mubarak, wife of Egypt's former dictator, led Egypt's delegation to the UN World Summit for Children in 1990, chaired the policy-making arm of Egypt's National Council for Childhood and Motherhood (NCCM), and was a patron of the Egyptian co-production of *Sesame Street*. Children's rights and schooling form an important strand in the charitable work of Jordan's Queen Rania.[19] Sheikha Moza, a wife of the former ruler of Qatar, was the leading figure behind the launch of Al-Jazeera Children's Channel in 2005. Princess Haya, wife of the ruler of Dubai, heads the board of trustees of the Al Jalila Child Culture Centre,[20] named after their daughter, Shaikha Jalila. In neighbouring Sharjah, the ruler's second wife, Shaikha Jawaher Al Qasimi, was behind Sharjah's first children's film festival, while her daughter, Sheikha Bodour, has won awards for her work in promoting children's literature and literacy.

Given the range of possible motivations of policy entrepreneurs, the study also pays regard to texts and discourses legitimating policies introduced. In research on policy transfer affecting higher education in Egypt and Morocco it was revealed that policy advisors' incorporation into international circles led them to frame the issues in general terms, reflecting international norms that were then imposed in a top-down fashion, rather than in relation to the specifics of each country's domestic situation.[21] On the other hand, Dafna Lemish's research on children's television producers' views about gender, culture and intercultural exchange shows that, for media practitioners at least, the relationship between international norms and domestic specificities is actually the reverse: the 'kind of cosmopolitan dialogue' these individuals engaged in at international events did not translate into any expression of a desire for intercultural dialogue on screen when they were interviewed by Lemish, beyond the acquisition of broadcasting rights to good quality programmes from each other.[22]

Each of the following sections begins by describing an observed policy outcome, in the form of a media initiative, with some contextualization in terms of its significance, the actors and agencies implementing it and the discourses adopted to present it to the local population. For each initiative the study then traces sequences of events and factors that led to it, looking at processes inside the country and external influences. The conclusion discusses how the internal and external interact.

Egypt, *Esma3oona* and the World Summit Movement

A weekly show called *Esma3oona* (officially translated as 'Hear us Out') started on Egypt TV's Channel 2 in January 2008 and continued in one form or another for the next several years. It began as one component of a larger Child Media Project aimed at advocacy and training to promote public awareness of children's rights, and resulted from collaboration among several organizations based inside and outside Egypt. Finance, to the tune of some US$900,000, came from the Finnish mobile phone company Nokia and the Swedish International Development Agency (SIDA).[23] This initial sum paid for a first season of 48 episodes in which children from around the country would talk about issues affecting them, such as violence in schools, early marriage, street children, talking to parents, disability and so on. The aim was for children themselves to make the 20-minute episodes, helped by graduate students from the American University in Cairo and Al-Karma Edutainment, a Cairo-based production house that had been making *Alam Simsim*, the US-financed Egyptian co-production of *Sesame Street*, since 2000. On the pre-production side were Plan-Egypt, the local branch of Plan International, which works with communities to improve the lives of marginalized children, and Egypt's own NCCM, a government agency created in 1988 to coordinate protection and development activities relating to mothers and children and liaise with international bodies. Broadcasting the series was the responsibility of the government-run Egyptian Radio and Television Union (ERTU). The first season went out at 11 a.m. on Fridays, just before midday prayer time on Egypt's main weekly rest day. It was followed in 2009 and 2011 by two more seasons of 16 and 12 episodes respectively, also funded by Nokia and SIDA. The 2009 series aired at 2.30 p.m. on Fridays. It was succeeded in 2014 by another Plan-Egypt/Al-Karma co-production called *Efhamouna* ('Understand Us'), with a different format and older age group, ranging up to 29.

The years of planning and launching *Esma3oona*, 2007–08, were important in the chronology of child-related legislation in Egypt, which is why one description of the programme said it aimed to 'provide accurate information on the needs of young people that will assist in enlightened decision-making and action'.[24] June 2008 saw the passage through the People's Assembly of several amendments to the Child Law No 12 of 1996, which were cautiously welcomed by children's rights campaigners.[25] The age of criminal liability was raised from seven to 12 years and punitive measures against children at risk[26] were abolished, while local child protection committees were to be formed with representation from relevant ministries and civil society. The legal minimum age for marriage was raised from 16 to 18. Against a backlash from Muslim Brotherhood MPs, who said the amendments ran counter to the 'norms, customs, and nature of the Egyptian people',[27] Egyptian government machinery reinforced the message of *Esma3oona* by ensuring its nomination for a prize at the Cairo International Film Festival for Children (CIFFC) in March 2009. It won the festival's Silver Award for Best TV Programme and was entered for a European Broadcasting Union award. Described in the CIFFC catalogue as going 'beyond entertainment' because it aims at 'developing the society itself',[28] the show's sponsors pitched it in terms of protecting children by empowering them to participate. Plan-Egypt's media coordinator, Mohamed Kamel, said: 'One of *Esma3oona*'s top priorities is to protect children against all types of abuse and violence within the social justice system, health care and [enable them to] participate fully in decisions that regard themselves and their community'.[29]

The heads of both Al-Karma and the NCCM emphasized the series' role in giving children a voice. Al-Karma's Amr Qoura said: 'Kids don't have a chance to talk about their rights and opinions. This programme will give them that chance.'[30] Moshira Khattab, NCCM Secretary-General, also highlighted the issue of rights, especially in relation to street children. She indicated that getting children to express themselves would help government and NGOs to manage the issues more effectively.[31] Khattab, holder of a doctorate in children's rights with a thesis written on implementation of the CRC, began a diplomatic career in the 1990s, becoming Egypt's first ambassador to South Africa after its first post-apartheid elections in 1994. She took responsibility for the NCCM on leaving her South Africa posting in 1999 and, as head of NCCM, was given ministerial status in 2009. When Khattab's ministerial appointment ended in February 2011, with the revolution, cabinet portfolios changed; the NCCM lost its privileged position of reporting directly to the prime minister and was put under the Ministry of Health.

Khattab insists that activities promoting children's rights in Egypt during the 2000s were a result of good networking among 'thousands' of people within Egypt who shared the 'right vision' and 'right attitude' – the right attitude, in her view, being one that recognizes children as 'rights holders' who have the 'right to be heard, the right to free expression, the right to receive information, the right to exercise – to be part and parcel of the cultural life of their country'.[32] She names children's writer Fatma Al-Maadoul and filmmaker Layaly Badr as key partners in local media campaigns. But she explains her own motivation by reference to her experience abroad, as an ambassador living in South Africa for five years, where she attended 'every single meeting'[33] of the Nelson Mandela Children Fund, whose mission is to give 'voice and dignity to the African child by building a rights-based movement'.[34] Khattab says that living abroad opened her mind to 'so many things' because she could compare 'how people are living' with the situation in Egypt, where she saw people 'denying problems, pretending everything is perfect'.[35] Having found experts in Egypt, including media professionals committed to shedding light on children's lives but 'needing some entity that has the mandate', Khattab says, 'All I did was I decided to open all the files', which led her, for example, to commission a national survey on child labour despite facing resistance on the grounds that such a survey would 'embarrass Egypt'.

Sitting on the CRC Treaty Body, the Committee on the Rights of the Child in Geneva, was another motivating factor for Khattab. Describing the way the UN treaty bodies give feedback to states that have signed up to human rights conventions, Khattab highlights the contradiction she would have faced in telling other countries 'you have to do the right thing' if she had been 'sitting at home, closing my eyes to many wrongdoings'. We 'had to be consistent', she says.

> So we started opening all these files and we have to give Suzanne Mubarak the credit that she did not say 'no'. She could have stuck to the niceties, you know, just have nice girls, celebrate children's day. Instead of that we had the Child Action Plan, protecting children from trafficking and drugs and for children with disabilities.[36]

Layaly Badr, one of the media professionals who collaborated with Khattab to help bring realities of children's lives to Egyptian state TV, is not originally Egyptian. A Palestinian who worked in Kuwait in the 1980s, at the Gulf Cooperation Council's Joint Programme Production Institute (JPPI), Badr was assistant producer on *Salamtak* ('Your Health'), a JPPI health programme for children and adults. Being a children's writer at the time, Badr recounts that she was so fascinated with JPPI's success with *Iftah ya Simsim* ('Open Sesame'), the Arab co-production of *Sesame Street* first broadcast in 1979, that she read the entire archive of documents relating to how each episode was developed; she read them 'one by one' and 'learned a lot from them'.[37] After studying filmmaking in Germany, Badr joined ART, a Saudi-owned pay-TV satellite network that started in 1994 and included a children's channel in its bouquet, showing mostly foreign cartoons.

Badr is proud that, with backing from her US-educated Saudi boss, she managed to overcome outright opposition from Egyptian censors within ART to initiate interactive shows in which children were encouraged to voice their opinions on current issues, such as one for 11- to 14-year-olds called *Taala faker maana* ('Come Think with Us'). She extended the interactivity by launching ART Teenz Channel and persuading ART owner Saleh Kamel to make it free to air. It was on this channel that, as Badr tells it, 'we started to make for the first time, programmes made by children, for and by children'. In a series called *Esmaouna*,[38] created in 2000 and supervised by young presenters and researchers who later became famous in the industry, children aged 14 to 18 had an opportunity to choose the topic of each episode, ranging from pocket money and music to religion and death, and discuss it with an adult expert in the studio live on air. When a 14-year-old girl in one episode questioned why being a Muslim should not be a matter of choice rather than birth, this was so contrary to local norms of religious conduct and deference to adults that Badr recalls: 'I thought they'll fire me tomorrow'.[39]

Badr is not at all concerned that the name she adopted for the ART Teenz show in 2000 resurfaced in 2008 for a series on Egypt TV.[40] In the intervening years, having met Badr at the CIFFC, Khattab had asked her to help with shaking up attitudes to children among practitioners at the ERTU. Khattab was acutely conscious that ERTU children's programmes were 'very monotonous', with children as mere spectators and adult personalities 'with full make-up' speaking 'all the time'.[41] She was also sure that any change in national attitudes towards children required media involvement and told Badr of her wish to conduct research about ERTU content for children, which she could use as evidence to change it. Badr duly wrote a report in 2006–2007 and presented it to ERTU channel heads, who were furious at its critical nature and rejected it. Khattab, present at the meeting, complimented Badr on the report but asked her publicly to add in 'what is good in each programme'. Badr says that, with difficulty, she found nice things to add and, through Khattab's mediation, the report was accepted.[42]

It was at this point, in 2006–2007, that Khattab, besides hosting regional consultations to produce recommendations for the UN Study on Violence against Children, also contributed to preparations for the 5th World Summit on Media for Children (5WSMC), held in Johannesburg in March 2007. Khattab recounts that, at the time, 'you could feel the positive energy' in the Arab League's Advisory Committee on Children, where, for example, early denials that any violence against children took place in their territories had given way to a willingness to 'be realistic; it started to come out, they started to talk'.[43] According to Firdoze Bulbulia, chair of the Johannesburg summit's host, the Children and Broadcasting Foundation for Africa (CBFA), who had met Khattab during her time as ambassador to South Africa, 'Moshira was a good supporter ... [she] really really supported our work'.[44] Bulbulia recalls that Khattab had also organized regional Arab and African preparatory meetings in Cairo to reach unified positions for the UN Special Session on Children that was held in May 2002. When it came to preparing for the 5WSMC, Khattab arranged an Arab pre-summit meeting of 100 delegates at Egyptian and Arab League expense.

The Cairo pre-summit served a purpose that Bulbulia felt had not been achieved by previous World Summits. The CBFA, which was formed as a lobby group after the first World Summit on Media for Children in Australia in 1995, wanted the 5WSMC to bring in 'voices from groups that were not historically linked to the Summit movement' and, 'unlike previous Summits', to ensure full-scale participation of hundreds of children in the summit's plenary sessions and their own daily summit workshops.[45] Bulbulia, noting South African schoolchildren's crucial role in fighting apartheid, as in the Soweto uprising of 1976, is scathing about events (like the Australia summit) where children are absent, saying they are 'for children, about children, without children'.[46] An email circulating ahead of the 5WSMC suggested that Patricia Edgar, founder of the World Summit movement and president of the Australia-based World Summit on Media for Children Foundation, saw Bulbulia's relentless drive to enlist worldwide support for the 5WSMC as a bid to start a separate movement.[47] Whatever misunderstandings took place in the run-up to March 2007, the World Summit Foundation website excludes Johannesburg from its list of past 'world' summits, relegating it to a list of 'regional summits and forums' that 'form part of the World Summit movement'.[48] A contrast between Bulbulia's participatory approach and Edgar's more paternalist orientation and rich-world concerns was evident in Edgar's speech at the 5WSMC. Blaming the global television industry for 'systematically destroying children's bodies along with their minds', through obesity and promoting a 'dysfunctional mismatch' between social and biological maturation, Edgar argued for media that would produce 'educated, engaged children', leading to 'fewer teenage pregnancies, higher school achievement, fewer dropouts and a better employment record'.[49]

Indeed, from an African perspective, the Australia summit in Melbourne was a 'First World' affair of rich countries talking to each other about television, whereas what Bulbulia calls the 'majority world' still needed to talk about radio. She questions how many of those present in Melbourne understood the 'experiences of people living in poverty ... all the challenges of the developing world'. She recounts how different groups in Africa were mobilized to develop the African Charter on Children's Broadcasting, which built on the Children's Television Charter that came out of Melbourne and was adopted at the 1995 Prix Jeunesse in Munich. The World Summit Charter put forward a vision of content that would affirm children's sense of self, community and place and an appreciation of their own and other cultures, alongside a vision of a policy that would ensure adequate funding to promote the highest programming standards. Reviewing the role of the Charter, subsequent additions to it in different regions, and the 'varying ideologies' of the World Summit series since Melbourne, children's media specialist Máire Messenger Davies describes the 5WSMC in Johannesburg as 'exceptional in its emphasis on children's agency', noting that a thousand children and a thousand adults took part.[50]

A feeling of division between the children's broadcasting communities of the 'first' and 'majority' worlds continued through the second and third summits, held in the UK and Greece respectively, as it was not until the Brazil summit in 2004 that the supposedly global event was hosted in a country of the Global South. Against this background, it is notable that the organic two-way link between influential individuals campaigning for children's right to expression and participation in South Africa and Egypt, which had grown over years of personal contacts, was quite different from the relationship with Egypt that the organizers of the 2001 WSMC in Greece sought to establish from scratch. The Egyptian delegation to the WSMC in March 2001, being 13 strong (and including Al-Karma,[51] makers of *Alam Simsim* and *Esma3oona*), was certainly large. It was second only to South Africa's 45-member representation among Global South countries attending the event.[52] Brazil also sent 13 and India 10, while the Arab countries present – Algeria, Jordan, Kuwait, Lebanon, Palestine and UAE – had no more than one or two delegates each. Yet despite Egypt's commitment to the summit as reflected in the size of its delegation, Khattab was dubious about the vision of the Greek hosts. She is clear that, if Athina Rikaki, organizer of the Greek summit, had not gone out of her way to invite Egyptian participation, she would not have attended. Khattab quotes Rikaki as telling her 'this will not be a conference, but a market'. Khattab comments: 'I have to say, for me this was new … We were invited but then we took matters in our own hands'.[53] Taking matters into Egyptian hands led over the early 2000s to the series of steps outlined above: opening sensitive 'files' on child labour, trafficking, female genital cutting and other issues; Arab and African regional meetings taking place in Cairo to prepare for the UN Special Session on Children, the UN Report on Violence against Children and the 5WSMC; domestic networking and campaigning; legal amendments to Egypt's Child Law; and the *Esma3oona* television bid to get children's voices heard. The activity of that period stands in marked contrast to public neglect of children's rights in Egypt after 2011.

Qatar's Ajyal Film Festival and the Giffoni Experience

Qatar's Doha Film Institute (DFI), founded in 2010, took an innovatory step in November 2013 when it held its first international film festival for children under the name Ajyal Youth Film Festival. The word Ajyal, meaning 'generations', was chosen because the festival, besides following what the DFI called its 'history of community-based programming', was an invitation to 'generations to come together to discuss cinema ... opening up a fun, collaborative environment where young people can express themselves'.[54] In its first year the event hosted more than 400 young jurors of 45 nationalities, aged between 8 years and 21, who awarded cash prizes of US$5,000 to US$15,000 to winning films.[55] The majority of jurors were from abroad, with around 30 per cent being Qatari,[56] while the 65 films shown came from 30 countries[57] and were divided into four categories, named Bariq, Mohaq, Hilal and Bader, for ages 4–7 years, 8–12 years, 13–17 years and 18–21 years respectively.[58] Alongside the film screenings the DFI also hosted a two-day Industry Forum, under the slogan 'Our children first!', bringing together around 70 content producers, festival organizers and other practitioners from 28 countries to 'raise awareness and find solutions for quality media for all our children'.[59] The festival was repeated just over a year later, in December 2014, with 90 films from 43 countries shown over seven days, including some 20 films directed by Qataris or residents of Qatar.[60] Once again 450 children were jurors, although this time only 25 were from outside Qatar, representing 12 different countries, including four Gulf states (Kuwait, Oman, Saudi Arabia and the UAE) and two other Arab states, Tunisia and Lebanon.

Meanwhile, other Gulf states were taking what looked like similar initiatives, except that Ajyal was distinctive in inviting children to give formal verdicts on the films shown. Just a month before the first Ajyal in 2013, the UAE emirate of Sharjah held the Sharjah International Children's Film Festival (SICFF) for children aged from 7 to 18 years, describing it as 'the first of its kind in the region', with 78 films from 32 countries.[61] SCIFF, repeated in October 2014 with more films for a wider range of ages starting from 4 years up,[62] was publicized as intended to teach media literacy to children and promote filmmaking for, by and about young people.[63] Its winning films were chosen by adults.[64] A few months after the first Ajyal, in April 2014, Dubai likewise started its own Children's International Film Festival (CIFF), showing high-profile films as well as 30 student films for children (out of 80 student films submitted), together with workshops covering all aspects of filmmaking, from scriptwriting to editing.[65] As Qatar's DFI planned a third edition of its Ajyal festival for December 2015, Dubai held its second CIFF, building on the reported 15,000 attendance at the 2014 event and showing 53 films made by children and students in the UAE along with 67 international films.[66] The CIFF, like the SICFF, chose adult jurors. Thus, barely two years after Ajyal's launch, the Arab Gulf states had gone from having not a single children's film festival to having hosted seven. Even so, only Ajyal had invited children to judge the winning films.

Introducing the inaugural Doha event, the festival director spoke of the benefits of encouraging children to talk about film. Fatma Al Remaihi said Ajyal had 'addressed a clear need in this part of the world' in 'creating a platform for young audiences to discover new facets of cinema, engage in new types of conversations and expand their imagination'.[67] That is to say, DFI's focus on child film audiences as family members (the 'generations' theme) and a concern to make them culturally aware went hand-in-hand with promoting children's creativity and conversation. DFI publicity for the second edition of the festival said it would 'bring generations of film-goers together for an enlightening and entertaining experience', offering 'films for kids as young as three' as well as all genres of film, including 'fascinating, informative documentaries that bring the world's stories home to Qatar'.[68] In addition, the DFI promised a 'special focus on films made right here in Qatar'.[69] Its promise chimed with Qatar's *National Vision 2030* to transform itself from a hydrocarbon economy to a knowledge economy in a matter of decades. But it also provides an insight into some of the policy struggles – over the right balance between domestic interests and foreign input – that beset the DFI in its early years. These were the struggles from which the decision to initiate Ajyal emerged.

The DFI, founded in 2010, grew out of an interest in film on the part of its founder and chair, Shaikha Mayassa, daughter of Shaikha Moza and Shaikh Hamad bin Khalifa Al Thani, who ruled Qatar from 1995 to 2013 before handing his position over to his son and Mayassa's brother, Shaikh Tamim. Born in 1983, Mayassa graduated from Duke University in North Carolina in 2005 with a double major in literature and political science, moving from there to Columbia University in New York to pursue postgraduate studies in public administration. In 2006, aged 23, she was appointed to head the Qatar Museums Authority, a new body which replaced the country's National Council for Culture, Art and Heritage. By the time she resettled in Doha, Mayassa had completed two internships with institutions in New York. One, in the summer of 2006, was with the company behind the Tribeca Film Festival (TFF), the other with the UN. TFF, an outgrowth of the Tribeca Film Centre, run by actor Robert De Niro and director Jane Rosenthal, was created in 2003 as a regeneration effort for the Tribeca and Lower Manhattan districts, which had been home to the twin towers of the World Trade Centre, destroyed by the 9/11 suicide attacks of 2001. The Tribeca model was thus geared to community and outreach, as well as helping, according to TFF publicity, to widen public access to independent film. Mayassa reportedly wanted to gain film production experience with Tribeca. She told the press that her father 'loved films' and she and her siblings had consequently watched 'lots growing up'; she apparently also wanted to experiment with turning a novel into a film.[70] She regarded the UN internship as consistent with this interest, seeing film as complementary to diplomacy and international affairs.[71]

The Doha-Tribeca Film Festival (DTFF), first held in 2009, preceded formal inauguration of the DFI and credit for launching it seems to be shared among several people. It has been described as the 'brainchild' of Shaikha Mayassa,[72] who clearly had direct contacts with TFF at a time when its co-founders were looking for ventures abroad[73] and found themselves in sympathy with Qatar's educational investments and aspirations.[74] But another protagonist was Australian-born Amanda Palmer, aged 33 in 2009 and employed as head of entertainment at the Doha-based Qatari-owned channel Al-Jazeera English, where she hosted a programme on international cinema called *The Fabulous Picture Show*. Palmer states that Mayassa asked her advice on possible film festival partnerships.[75] Noting Tribeca's 'fantastic educational all-year-round community-outreach programmes', Palmer considered it an obvious choice. She also believed that, with two thirds of Qatar's population aged under 30, Tribeca-style workshops run in Doha in August and September 2009 would keep young people engaged and excited.[76]

When Shaikha Mayassa formally launched the DFI at the Cannes Film Festival in May 2010, Palmer was its Executive Director. The Institute was, according to its early press releases, dedicated to film appreciation and education with the ultimate goal of making Qatar a cultural centre with a 'sustainable film industry'.[77] Besides its partnership with Tribeca Enterprises, DFI also announced cultural partnerships with Martin Scorsese's World Cinema Foundation and Mira Nair's Maisha Film Lab, which offers courses for aspiring filmmakers. By the time Palmer left the DFI, in July 2012, a partnership with Giffoni Film Experience in Italy had been added, through an incremental process that began in November 2010, when the DTFF arranged for 60 'local Doha children' to join with six international guests to act as jurors for a selected set of films.[78] The Giffoni film festival, started in 1971 in a village near Salerno in southwest Italy, stands out among children's film festivals worldwide because its format revolves around juries composed entirely of children. Claudio Gubitosi, who founded Giffoni when he himself was 18 years old and changed its name from 'Festival' to 'Experience' in 2009, told the second 'Doha-Giffoni Experience' in 2011 that he felt 'at home' at DTFF because it had a dedicated section that is 'sensitive and attentive' to young people, which is 'impressive', he said, 'for a festival that is only three years old'.[79]

Fatma Al Remaihi, described on the DFI website in 2015 as 'the driving force behind the establishment of a strategic partnership with the Giffoni Film Festival', drew on her own experience as a mother of small children in promoting children's active participation. Having graduated from

Qatar University with a degree in English Literature, Al Remaihi joined DFI from its inception as Cultural Adviser to the first DTFF in 2009.[80] In September 2009 she told *Time Out Doha* that she possessed 'hundreds and hundreds of movies' and felt she 'had to be involved' the minute she heard that Tribeca was coming to Doha; Palmer told the same media outlet that she relied on Al Remaihi to make sure that 'everything feels like it comes out of Qatar' because everything 'has to be as authentic as possible'.[81] In fact Al Remaihi took part along with five other Qataris in the inaugural Doha-Tribeca workshop in August 2009, two months before the first DTFF. She made a one-minute film, entitled *Like Father, Like Son*, featuring her eldest son in a humorous treatment of a father's advice.[82]

Charged with maintaining cultural authenticity, Al Remaihi seems to have been instrumental in linking the Doha-Giffoni Experience not only to the Giffoni festival in Italy but also to film education events for children in Qatar, which in turn required outreach to local schools. Three teenagers, two boys and a girl aged 13–15, were chosen to represent Qatar at Giffoni in Italy in July 2011, based on the reviews they had written of films screened at DTFF in 2010; the children attended a three-day workshop in Doha beforehand to develop the necessary skills. It was at this point that Palmer spoke of plans to 'build a youth film hub here, through our own Festival'.[83] The number of local and international child jurors at the DTFF in Doha increased from 60 in 2010 to 100 in 2011 and 220 in 2012, each child taking lessons in film criticism and engaging in question-and-answer sessions with directors. Jurors aged 8–12 were asked to vote for five short films while those aged 13–18 voted for one of two feature films and one of five shorts.[84] Given the challenges of gaining local Qatari children's participation, the numbers involved in these events are noteworthy. A facilitator who worked with child jurors at DFI says it can be hard to persuade Qatari parents to permit their children to travel, or to ensure that they turn up regularly or on time.[85]

The DTFF held in 2012 turned out to be the last. However, far from signaling the end of the Doha-Giffoni Experience, the demise of DTFF led to formalization of the DFI-Giffoni relationship and to the Ajyal festival, based on the Giffoni model. Indeed, the attention paid to children's participation and children's film by Fatma Al Remaihi represented an element of continuity during a period of uncertainty at DFI and a hiatus in other local media education work with schoolchildren. The latter work was carried out by the Doha Centre for Media Freedom (DC4MF) with 80 Qatari schools[86] until the removal of its director, Jan Keulen, just days after Ajyal finished in 2013, left the DC4MF without direction for more than a year.[87] At the DFI, Palmer was replaced in October 2012 by a Qatari banker, Abdel-Aziz Al Khater, with no background in the film industry, who initiated a first round of about 30 redundancies at the Institute soon into his tenure and another 40 redundancies in January 2014.[88] After splitting with Tribeca in 2013, Khater promised two new DFI festivals: Ajyal to launch in November 2013, under Al Remaihi's directorship; and Qumra, due to start in March 2014 as an event for first- and second-time filmmakers and deliberately timed to facilitate and improve coordination with film festivals in the UAE.[89] Qumra was eventually postponed to 2015. But Ajyal went ahead, with one of Al Remaihi's own children among the hundreds of young jury members. 'He's having the time of his life', Al Remaihi told a reporter, and 'the best bit is he doesn't know he is learning a lot at the same time'.[90]

Cemented in July 2013, ahead of the first Ajyal festival, the DFI's cultural partnership with Giffoni was a two-way affair in which Giffoni, in the person of Gubitosi, also actively sought to team up with the DFI, as another new counterpart outside Italy. Since 2001, when Gubitosi created the Giffoni World Alliance, he had exported the Giffoni model to other parts of Europe as well as the US and Australia. Giffoni managed to link with the Dubai International Film Festival (DIFF) in 2007 through Giffoni Hollywood, which invited 1,000 child jurors from 30 countries, of whom three, aged 13–14, were from the UAE.[91] Announcing the partnership with DFI, Al Remaihi melded the Giffoni focus on giving children 'a place where they can express themselves freely' and a 'sense of engagement'[92] with Qatar's emphasis on its *National Vision* for the future. She explained that 'with Giffoni's help', the DFI would 'give young people the space to express themselves creatively and honestly ... so that they can become the artists of tomorrow'.[93]

Conclusion

The case studies presented here deal exclusively with processes that led to certain public media initiatives being adopted, not with any impact those initiatives may have had. Unpicking the causal processes behind adoption reveals how much the latter depended on certain motivated individuals – 'agents with causal capacities'[94] – who were effectively policy entrepreneurs,[95] other than the First Ladies referred to earlier in the chapter. It also reveals how multifaceted, incremental and transnational the processes were.

In the Egyptian case the World Summit movement and its associated Children's Television Charter barely feature as links in the chain of policy-making, despite the size of the official Egyptian delegation to the Third World Summit in Greece in 2001. Where they do feature it is mainly because Moshira Khattab, in a position of relative power in the NCCM, personally supported the work of Firdoze Bulbulia of the CBFA, who saw the World Summit movement as a lever in mobilizing for change across the continent of Africa. Both women were instrumental in pushing the 5WSCM in Johannesburg forward according to agendas they perceived to be different from those of 'First World' forces dominant in the movement's early years. Instead of any single moment of encounter, the links leading to policy changes in Egypt were culturally subtle and geographically diverse. For Khattab, they included her experiences in South Africa at a time of high post-apartheid aspirations and at the UN Committee on Children's Rights in Geneva. They also included her interactions with a series of entrepreneurial figures in children's media, including Layaly Badr, a Palestinian who spent formative years in Kuwait and Germany and was able to push for innovation at the Cairo studios of a Saudi-owned TV network and at the ERTU. At the same time, public and private funding from Scandinavia and Plan International's community-oriented approach were crucial elements in the assemblage of actors, agencies, networks and texts behind the *Esma3oona* series. The policy narrative stressed the urgency of hearing children speak for themselves, to describe their own circumstances for the first time with the specific purpose of informing adult officialdom.

In the Qatari case, the Giffoni International Experience was an important player for four years leading up to the first Ajyal festival because it provided inspiration for an event that emphasized children's agency. But the forces for change that ultimately led to Ajyal's launch can be traced back much further, to the career paths of two Qatari individuals. Shaikha

Mayassa, a ruling family member and policy entrepreneur behind the DFI, was embedded in global networks through her educational background and cultural management responsibilities. Fatma Al Remaihi seems to have been motivated by an interest in the cultural education of children like her own and by her personal interest in film. The work of assembling the Ajyal policy and holding it together involved visions of a future Qatari film industry as part of a knowledge economy and a narrative that stressed the family as the appropriate environment within which to develop children's creativity and self-expression.

A corollary of the key role of individuals in both countries is the potential fragility of initiatives that depend on the support of a senior state agency official. Opening Egyptian state television up to discussing children's hardships took the head of the NCCM to push for it and the wife of the head of state to approve it. Local grassroots civil society groups could not reach the state media in the same way, as evidenced by the decline in attention paid to children's rights in post-2011 Egypt. In Qatar the DFI's origins and trajectory can be explained in part through Shaikh Mayassa's chance internships. Its subsequent focus on children was a top-down policy driven by an awareness of Qatar's demographics and a concern to appear relevant to local families. Possibilities for complementing the Ajyal film education initiative with media education in schools were cut short by sudden personnel changes at the DC4MF during same period. Centralized policy-making, from which local non-governmental actors are missing, raises questions about the sincerity of promises of participation and self-expression for children.

Tracing the process of policy formulation revealed here that individuals may draw norms and ideas from their personal transnational networks, but personal networks are different from epistemic communities insofar as the latter share professional values and practices.[96] Khattab's personal contacts outside Egypt were in the spheres of diplomacy and children's rights, while Shaikha Mayassa's contacts outside Qatar were in film and the art market. Various professional communities, both national and transnational, that could loosely be classed as 'epistemic', can be glimpsed at stages in the processes leading to *Esma3oona* and Ajyal. Examples include the CBFA, Tribeca Enterprises, the Giffoni Experience, as well as the *Sesame Street* world that encompassed Badr and Al-Karma, or the shortlived ART Teenz nurturing of young Egyptian TV presenters. Compared with examples of communities that share values and practices it becomes clear that the World Summit movement is far from a transnational epistemic community and the DFI in 2010–2014 was far from a national one. Given the range of possible approaches to children's agency and participation in media development, any attempt to establish shared values and practices within and across borders faces a big challenge.

INSIGHT 1

The EBU as a Transfer Hub for Media Policy

In considering the role of international bodies and individuals in policy transfer and diffusion, it is interesting to note how a particular policy relating to children's television appears to have spread from one source to others through the European Broadcasting Union (EBU) in the 1970s. The EBU, so named because it was open to members from the European Broadcasting Area, which includes parts of the Mediterranean, was founded in 1950 by a group of 22 European and Mediterranean countries that included Egypt, Lebanon, Morocco, Syria and Tunisia.[97] The broadcasters of Egypt and Syria resigned from the EBU in 1958 in protest at the entry of Israel's state broadcaster.[98] By the early 1970s, however, the EBU counted the state broadcasters of Algeria, Jordan, Morocco and Tunisia in its membership, with Algeria and Jordan having just joined in 1970.[99] The Arab States Broadcasting Union (ASBU), the EBU's Arab counterpart, was new at that stage. It came into existence in 1969 and collaborated closely with the EBU, including over the subject of educational broadcasting.[100] Here historian **Helle Strandgaard Jensen** *explores how the EBU served as a hub for diffusion of policy ideas related to preschool television.*

Soon after *Sesame Street* was first broadcast in the US in October 1969, the New York–based programme maker Children's Television Workshop (CTW) offered the programme to European broadcasters, including the UK's public service broadcaster, the BBC.

The BBC only wanted to buy some Muppet sequences, but CTW wanted to sell the entire programme: all or nothing. When the BBC's commercial competitor, ITV, stepped in to buy the programme instead, the success of the series in the UK put the BBC under pressure from the British public to justify turning it down.[101] In the summer of 1971 the head of the Children's Department, Monica Sims, found herself defending BBC decisions everywhere: within the institution, in the press and in letters to individuals.[102] This prompted her to draft a range of texts explaining her views. She took one of the more elaborate papers, running to nine pages, to a European Broadcasting Union (EBU) meeting in Oslo in October 1971, where *Sesame Street* was screened.[103]

Sims' paper contained a detailed criticism of *Sesame Street*. Drawing upon scholarly research, she characterized its aims and production methods as 'indoctrination', arguing: 'Brain washing for a good purpose may seem attractive, but once the technique is admitted there is danger of its proliferation for less desirable motives and one must hope that, however good "*Sesame Street*'s" intentions, its brain-washing methods will not become generally accepted'.[104] She quoted Mary Waddington, a University of London professor of early childhood education, who accused the programme of being unsuitable for pre-school children because it was 'based on the theory that commercials make people concentrate'. Sims' third overarching point was *Sesame Street*'s inability to speak properly to children because it did not 'start from the child's own particular environment'. Her paper dismissed the vast majority of positive effects CTW had ever claimed the programme had on pre-school children.

A heated dispute between CTW and the BBC ensued over whether the document had been distributed on purpose as part of a BBC press kit, or had been shown in confidence by Sims to a small number of delegates and later Xeroxed without her knowledge for a wider distribution. Whatever the precise circumstances of its circulation, the paper ended up in the offices of 27 broadcasters represented at the meeting.[105] CTW was furious. Because of the BBC's prominence in the EBU (as the member that had convened the organization's founding conference and supplied its first president[106]), CTW's Michael Dunn claimed in a telephone call to the BBC's David Attenborough that the paper was 'part of a stupid campaign by the BBC to destroy *Sesame Street*'.[107] Dunn accused Sims of 'waging a personal vendetta, that her document was officially circulated in official brochures to all members of the Oslo meeting, that it was full of gross inaccuracies, and that he [Michael Dunn] was marshalling all the most influential people in the United States, from the Government downwards, to bring pressure to bear on the British Government and the BBC'.[108] This reaction clearly demonstrated not only that CTW believed that BBC opinions were very important within the EBU but also that it saw the EBU as an important hub for the transfer of media policy. After meetings in New York and London between high-ranking BBC and CTW officials, CTW managed to pressure Sims to write an official letter correcting her paper and retracting most of her claims.[109] After CTW had approved its content, this letter was sent to all the EBU members.

Nevertheless, Sims' – and by extension the BBC's – stance did have an effect on European broadcasting decisions. Her opinions and those of the BBC were referenced directly and indirectly in internal and external discussions in Norway, Denmark, Italy and West Germany about whether to buy or co-produce *Sesame Street* with the CTW.[110] Broadcasting traditions in these countries were quite different, especially as regards the pre-school audience: in Scandinavia, television was supposed to be a 'children's spokesman', whereas producers in Italy and West Germany took a more traditional, educational approach.[111] Despite this, discussions in all five countries echoed the core points of criticism in Sims' paper. In the end, producers at the West German Norddeutscher Rundfunk (NDR) decided to broadcast the programme in 1972 and later co-produce with CTW (*Sesamestrasse*). In Denmark and Norway the public service broadcasters, DR and NRK, never bought the programme, as the alleged 'authoritarian' approach to learning and its commercial undertones were seen as inappropriate for children's television.[112] In Italy, *Sesame Street* was eventually launched as *Sesamo Apriti* by the public service broadcaster, RAI, in

1977, but only after a major restructuring of the entire corporation had replaced the former head of the children's department with CTW-friendly Paula De Benedetti.[113]

In the Arab world, *Sesame Street* made its first appearance in 1979, in the form of a Kuwait-based co-production shared with other Gulf states. There was no co-production with an Arab member of the EBU until the Egyptian version, *Alam Simsim*, started more than 20 years later.

Notes

1   http://crinarchive.org/about/crin-history.asp.

2   http://www.unicef.org/magic/briefing/oslo.html.

3   Karl Hanson, 'Schools of thought in children's rights', in Manfred Liebel (ed), *Children's Rights from Below: Cross-Cultural Perspectives* (Basingstoke: Palgrave Macmillan), p. 73.

4   Hanson, 'Schools of thought', pp. 72–78.

5   Aisling Parkes, *Children and International Human Rights Law: The Right of the Child to be Heard* (Abingdon: Routledge, 2013), p. 260.

6   Russell Prince, 'Policy transfer as policy assemblage: making policy for the creative industries in New Zealand', *Environment and Planning A*, Vol 42 (2010), pp. 172–173.

7   Alexander George and Andrew Bennett, *Case Studies and Theory Development in the Social Sciences* (Cambridge, MA: MIT Press, 2005), p. 137.

8   David Collier, 'Understanding process tracing', *Political Science and Politics: PS* 44/4 (October 2011), p. 823.

9   George and Bennett, *Case Studies and Theory Development*, p. 6.

10 Prince, 'Policy transfer as policy assemblage', p. 170.

11 Prince, 'Policy transfer as policy assemblage', p. 169.

12 David Benson and Andrew Jordan, 'What have we learned from policy transfer research? Dolowitz and Marsh revisited', *Political Studies Review*, 9 (2011), pp. 369–370.

13 Diane Stone, 'Learning lessons, policy transfer and the international diffusion of ideas', University of Warwick Centre for the Study of Globalisation and Regionalisation Working Paper No 69/01 (April 2001), p. 15.

14 Stone: 'Learning lessons', p. 16; Peter M. Haas, 'Introduction: Epistemic communities and international policy coordination', *International Organisation*, 46/1 (Winter 1992), pp. 1–35.

15 J. Alison Bryant, 'Understanding the children's television community from an organizational network perspective', in J. A. Bryant (ed), *The Children's Television Community* (Mahwah, NJ: Lawrence Erlbaum Associates), p. 40.

16 John W. Kingdon, *Agendas, Alternatives and Public Policies*, 2nd ed. (Glenview, IL: Longman, 2011), pp. 116–117.

17 Kingdon, *Agendas, Alternatives and Public Policies*, p. 123.

18 Stephen Heydemann, *Upgrading Authoritarianism in the Arab World*, Brookings Institution Saban Center for Middle East Policy, Analysis Paper No 13 (October 2007), pp. 4 and 8.

19 Felia Boerwinkel, *The First Lady Phenomenon in Jordan: Assessing the Effect of Queen Rania's NGOs on Jordanian Civil Society* (Amsterdam: University of Amsterdam and Hivos, Knowledge Programme Civil Society in West Asia, March 2011), p. 16.

20 *The National*, 'Praise from Sheikh Mohammed as the Al Jalila Child Culture Centre opens', 3 December, 2014.

21 Florian Kohstall, 'Free transfer, limited mobility: A decade of higher education reform in Egypt and Morocco', *Revue des mondes musulmans et de la Méditerranée*, 131 (June 2012), pp. 91–109.

22 Dafna Lemish, *Screening Gender on Children's Television: The Views of Producers around the World* (Abingdon: Routledge 2010), p. 70.

23 Jered Stuffco, 'Kids on TV: New program aims to give kids a voice', *Daily News Egypt*, 29 December 2006.

24 'Esma3oona channels Egypt's children's voices', *Community Times*, March 2008, p. 18.

25 Adel Azer, Sohair Mehanna, Mulki al-Sharmani and Essam Ali, *Child Protection Policies in Egypt: A Rights Based Approach*, Monograph in the *Cairo Papers in Social Science* series, 30/1 (2010), pp. 94–95.

26 For more on what was called 'risk of delinquency' see Human Rights Watch, *Charged with Being Children: Egyptian Police Abuse of Children in Need of Protection* (Washington: Human Rights Watch, February 2003), p. 39.

27 According to Saad Katatny, leader of the Muslim Brotherhood bloc in the People's Assembly, quoted by Liam Stack in 'Egypt's child protection law sparks controversy', *Christian Science Monitor*, 24 July 2008.

28 *What Do Children Want? 19th Cairo International Film Festival for Children 5–13 March 2009* (Cairo: Ministry of Culture, 2009), p. 107.

29 Quoted by Reem Gamil in ' "Esma3oona" children speak up', http://whatwomenwant-mag.com/2012/12/esma3oona-children-speak-up/ August 2009.

30 Quoted in Stuffco, 'Kids on TV'.

31 Stuffco, 'Kids on TV'.

32 Author's interview, Cairo, 3 June 2015.

33 Author's interview, Cairo, 3 June 2015.

34 Mission statement at http://www.nelsonmandelachildrensfund.com/who-we-are/about-the-fund/.
35 Author's interview, Cairo, 3 June 2015.
36 Author's interview, Cairo, 3 June 2015.
37 Author's interview, Cairo, 3 June 2015.
38 This is the transliteration of the standard Arabic word. The Arabic spelling, and associated transliteration of the later programme, *Esma3oona*, reflect a pleading emphasis in pronunciation.
39 Author's interview, Cairo, 3 June 2015.
40 Author's interview, Cairo, 3 June 2015.
41 Author's interview, Cairo, 3 June 2015.
42 Author's interview, Cairo, 3 June 2015.
43 Author's interview, Cairo, 3 June 2015
44 Author's interview, Doha, 22 November 2013.
45 CBFA, 'World Summit arrives in Africa', conference brochure, no date.
46 Author's interview, Doha, 22 November 2013.
47 According to a source who saw the correspondence, one of the emails could have been interpreted as an attempt by the Australia-based Foundation to disown the South Africa summit.
48 See http://www.wsmcf.com/past_summits/past.htm (accessed 29 July 2015).
49 Patricia Edgar, Address to the 5th World Summit on Media for Children, Johannesburg, South Africa, March 2007, http://27.253.36.134:8080/Patricia EdgarAndDonEdgar/Content/Speech/addresstothe5WS (accessed 6 February 2015). The numbering accorded to the summit on this site is not repeated on the timeline of the WSCM site referred to in Note 48.
50 Máire Messenger Davies, *Children, Media and Culture* (Maidenhead: Open University Press, 2010), pp. 55–58.
51 According to Moshira Khattab, interviewed by the author, Cairo, 3 June 2015.
52 3rd World Summit on Media for Children: Final Activity Report. www.wsmcf. com/past_summits/pdf/finrep3.pdf (accessed 1 March 2015).
53 Author's interview, Cairo, 3 June 2015.
54 DFI introduction to the Ajyal webpages in 2013 at http://www.dohafilminstitute. com/filmtalk/ajyal-youth-film-festival/ajyal-youth-film-festival-2013.
55 Wendy Mitchell, 'Doha's Ajyal fest wraps with youth jury awards', *Screen Daily*, 1 December 2013.
56 Alex Ritman, 'Whatever happened to the Qatari film industry?', *Guardian*, 6 March 2014.
57 Mitchell, 'Doha's Ajyal fest'.
58 DFI press release, 28 October 2013 at http://www.dohafilminstitute.com/ press/doha-film-experience-to-empower-young-film-enthusiasts-at-ajyal-youth-film-festival.

59 According to the Industry Forum brochure.

60 DFI press release, 7 December 2014 at http://www.dohafilminstitute.com/press/2nd-ajyal-youth-film-festival-concludes-with-young-jurors-selecting-winners-at-doha-film-experience.

61 Roberta Pennington, 'Film festival to children [sic] opens in Sharjah', *The National*, 21 October 2013.

62 Malavika Vettath, 'Second edition of Sharjah's International Children's Film Festival to screen 112 films over six days', *The National*, 29 September 2014.

63 Pennington, 'Film festival'.

64 Vettath, 'Second edition'.

65 Chris Newbould, 'Children's film festival opens today in the UAE', *The National*, 23 April 2014.

66 Chris Newbould, 'Children's film festival returns for second edition', *The National*, 21 April 2015.

67 Quoted by Mitchell, 'Doha's Ajyal fest'.

68 DFI publicity at http://www.dohafilminstitute.com/filmfestival/festival.

69 DFI publicity at http://www.dohafilminstitute.com/filmfestival/festival.

70 Amy Yee, 'Qatar sets scene for film industry', *Financial Times*, 11 February 2009.

71 Yee, 'Qatar sets scene'.

72 Yee, 'Qatar sets scene'.

73 Larry Rohter, 'Mixing oil and Hollywood: Tribeca festival expands to the Persian Gulf', *New York Times*, 23 October, 2009.

74 See the remarks of Jane Rosenthal, quoted in *The National*, 25 October 2009, http://www.thenational.ae/arts-culture/the-organisers-have-insisted-that-doha-tribeca-wont-just-be-the-new-york-festival-transplanted-to-a-new-venue-its-programme-seems-to-confirm-this.

75 *The National*, 'The organisers have insisted'.

76 *The National*, 'The organisers have insisted'.

77 For example, DFI press release on 16 May 2010 at http://www.dohafilminstitute.com/press/qatar-s-h-e-sheikha-al-mayassa-launches-the-doha-film-institute.

78 DFI press release, 9 November 2010 at http://www.dohafilminstitute.com/filmtalk/doha-tribeca-film-festival/giffoni-experience.

79 DFI press release, 26 October 2011 at http://www.dohafilminstitute.com/press/young-locals-participate-as-jurors-for-dfi-s-doha-giffoni-experience.

80 According to the biodata posted when Al Remaihi was promoted to DFI executive director, at http://www.dohafilminstitute.com/institute/leadership.

81 *Time Out Doha* Staff, 27 September, 2009, 'The Doha Tribeca film festival', http://www.timeoutdoha.com/print/features/10774-doha-tribeca-film-festival.

82 *I love Qatar*, 'Debutant filmmakers showcase humor, horror and tradition', 18 August 2009, http://ilq.isuf.co.uk/iloveqatar/news/content/debutant-filmmakers-showcase-humour-horror-and-tradition.

83 DFI, press release, 12 July 2011.
84 DFI, press release, 26 October 2011.
85 Author's telephone interview, 27 July 2015.
86 Author's conversation with DC4MF staff, Doha, 24 November 2013.
87 Peter Kovessy, 'Leaderless for a year, Doha Centre for Media Freedom appoints new head', *Doha News*, 16 February 2015.
88 Ritman, 'Whatever happened to the Qatari film industry?'.
89 Kaleem Aftab, 'For Ajyal and Qumra, the new Doha film festivals, cooperation is the aim', *The National*, 19 May 2013.
90 Alex Ritman, 'A film festival for kids', *The National*, 1 December 2013.
91 DIFF press release, 13 May 2007
92 *People*, 'A coffee with... Claudio Gubitosi', 26 June 2015 at http://www.wherenaples.com/discover-naples/people/item/1812-a-coffee-with-claudio-gubitosi/1812-a-coffee-with-claudio-gubitosi.html.
93 DFI press release, 22 July 2013.
94 George and Bennett, *Case Studies and Theory Development*, p. 137.
95 Kingdon, *Agendas, Alternatives and Public Policies*, p. 123.
96 Haas, 'Introduction', p. 3.
97 Maria Michalis, *Governing European Communications* (Plymouth: Lexington Books, 2007), p. 61, note 27.
98 Hans Brack, *The Evolution of the EBU through its Statutes from 1950 to 1976* (Geneva: European Broadcasting Union, 1976), p. 30.
99 For the year of admission for member states see https://www3.ebu.ch/.../EBU-Active-Members.pdf.
100 Yahya Abu Bakr, Saad Labib, Hamdy Kandil, *Development of Communication in the Arab States: Needs and Priorities*, UNESCO Reports and Papers on Mass Communication No 95 (Paris: UNESCO, 1983–English translation from Arabic published 1985), p. 30.
101 BBC written archives T47/113/1.
102 BBC written archives T47/113/1.
103 In the letters from CTW and the BBC there is some confusion as to whether the meeting was actually held in Oslo or Stockholm. CTW's copy of the official list for invitations distributed by the EBU gives the location as Oslo (CTW archive, Hornbake Library, Maryland, US, Box 361, Folder 16).
104 Copy of Monica Sims paper held in CTW's archive, Box 361, Folder 2.
105 This number is referred to in an internal memo from the BBC, held in the BBC written archives T47/113/1. In an official list of recipients of the paper in CTWs own archives 24 broadcasters are mentioned (CTW archive, Box 361, Folder 13).
106 Brack, *The Evolution of the EBU*, pp. 8–9.
107 Phone call from Michael Dunn (CTW) to David Attenborough (BBC), as referenced in internal briefing for 'the Chairman' before a meeting with Lord Harlech. BBC written archives T47/113/1.

108 Internal briefing, BBC written archives T47/113/1.

109 CTW archive Box 361, Folder 13.

110 Denmark: DR's archives at the National Archives: B&U, Småbørnssektionen, 1, Diverse 1973–1979. Germany: Klaus Schleicher, *Sesame Street für Deutchland? Die Notwentigheit einer Vergleichender Mediendidaktik* (Düsseldorf: Schwann, 1972). Italy: CTW archive, Italy papers, Box 369, Folder 1. Norway: NRK's archives at the National Archives: Nordvision reports, the Children and Youth Committee 1971–1972.

111 Helle Strandgaard Jensen, 'TV as children's spokesman: Conflicting notions of children and childhood in Danish children's television around 1968', *Journal for the History of Childhood and Youth*, 6/1 (2013), pp. 105–128.

112 DR's archives at the Danish National Archives: B&U, Småbørnssektionen, 1, Diverse 1973–1979.

113 CTW archive, Italy papers, Box 369, Folders 3 and 4.

4

Arab Animation between Business and Politics

Omar Adam Sayfo

For many decades, spots on Arab television channels dedicated to children were dominated by imported animated cartoons. Starting from the 1970s, generations of Arab children grew up watching dubbed Asian and Western animations. During the past few years, however, this situation has changed dramatically and in less than a decade the number of home-grown productions has significantly increased. The growth of Arab animated cartoon production can be seen most clearly in the proliferation of television series and web cartoons, while the production of feature-length productions still remains low. Television channels from Tunisia, Egypt, Saudi Arabia, Jordan and the Gulf are proudly presenting animated serials revolving around national themes, as was demonstrated by the Dubai sitcom animation *Freej*, which gained visibility not only on screen but also via brand extension, thereby inspiring similar productions in other Arab countries. Pan-Arab channels such as MBC3 and Al-Jazeera Children's Channel (JCC) have presented geo-linguistically relevant series such as *Saladin: The Animated Series* as well as educational material. Some culturally relevant productions – such as the Egyptian-made series *Stories in the Qur'an* – are even moving beyond the national and regional level and finding their way to the screens of non-Arab Muslim countries.

The aim of this chapter is to provide a brief introduction to the history of animated cartoon production in the Arab world and to explore factors that can explain why this production suddenly grew in the early 2000s, including the changing nature and levels of production and distribution. Animated cartoon production in the Arab world is culturally, economically and politically far too diverse to be described by a single or even a handful of production strategies. Attempting to draw a complete map of networks and collaborative projects would be extremely challenging owing to fuzzy boundaries and diverse practices. The aim here, therefore, is to analyse examples that can illustrate some of the main trends in production development and give insights into the way a combination of government policies and changing technologies led to the rise of national, regional and global production and distribution networks.

From Celluloid to CGI

Modern Arabic adopted the English term 'cartoon' (*cartoun*) and animation films are referred to as *film cartoun/aflam cartoun* (pl). They are sometimes also called *al-rusum al-mutaharrika*, a literal translation of 'moving drawings'. In Arab popular discourse, this term is generally associated with animations aimed at children and is often considered a non-serious medium. On the other hand, the most significant and popular homemade animated series are capable of gaining special prestige when they make their debut on primetime television in the month of Ramadan, when whole families gather around the television sets.

The history of animation production in the Arab world shows how much it has been inspired and affected by global flows of content and technology. It goes back to the 1930s, when cinemas in Alexandria and Cairo began to screen American productions. The widespread success of *Mickey Mouse* and *Felix the Cat* inspired young local artists to produce their own works. The first short celluloid films were produced in the workshop of the Frenkel Brothers, the three sons of Russian-Jewish immigrants. Their first animation, *Marco Monkey*, debuted in 1935. When it received harsh critiques for merely copying American productions, the concept of *Mish Mish Effendi*, a largely localized black-and-white production, was born.[1] Between

1937 and their departure to France in 1950, the Frenkels produced nine episodes of *Mish Mish Effendi* and a number of cinema commercials. Since then, Arab animation production has largely been driven by the desire to create culturally relevant productions for Arab audiences and hence to provide an alternative to global giants like Walt Disney.

Starting from the late 1930s, a number of native Egyptian artists produced short, culturally relevant animations. Egypt was the first Arab country to introduce higher education in art. The School of Fine Arts (*Madrasa al-Funun al-Jamilah*), established in 1908, was later reorganized and followed by a number of other state-sponsored institutions. An animation unit was founded at Egyptian Television in 1961. Due to the high costs of technical equipment for celluloid production, the vast majority of practising Egyptian animators, such as Antoine Selim (b. 1910), Mustafa Hussein (b. 1935), Muhammad Hakem (b. 1929), Ali Moheb (b. 1935) and Noshi Iskander (b. 1938), could only work if they were well integrated into local academic and/ or media hierarchies – a situation that persisted until the late 1990s. Although the vast majority of animations were commercials made to order for cinema or television, some animators also managed to produce their own short stories. After the presidency of Gamal Abdel-Nasser ended in 1970, animation production declined. The free market (*infitah*) policies of Nasser's successor, Anwar al-Sadat (1970–1981), led to a flood of foreign goods onto the Egyptian markets.[2] Businessmen turned from expensive time-consuming animated advertisements to cheap and quickly accessible live-action ones. Producing and presenting culturally relevant cinema and television content was no longer a political priority.

From the 1960s, several Algerian (Mohamed Aram, Mohamed Mazari, Menouar Merabtene, et al) and Tunisian (Amor Ben Mahmoud, Mongi Sancho, Zouhair Mahjoub, et al) animators working in national television industries produced short animations. But the number remained low because institutional support was lacking, and circulation was limited to local screens and film festivals. From the introduction of terrestrial television broadcasting in Arab countries in the mid-1950s,[3] to the arrival of satellite television in the 1990s, Arab television was almost exclusively run by government institutions and penetration of television content was largely confined within national borders, meaning that local media authorities and censors could act as gatekeepers. As the local animation was extremely rare, television slots dedicated to children were dominated by cheap, locally produced live content, and dubbed foreign animations. Choosing the sources of imports during the Cold War era was often a political decision. Socialist Arab countries such as Syria, Libya and Iraq preferred products from France and the Eastern bloc, while Gulf countries tended to import from the US. However, certain anima tions, such as *Tom and Jerry*, circulated regardless of political orientation, and there was also admiration for Japanese anime across the entire Arab world. While a number of Arab state-run channels established their own dubbing departments, traditional and new regional centres of cultural production such as Egypt and Syria began to distribute foreign animated content dubbed into literary Arabic to other markets, and hence became gatekeepers not only on the national, but, to a certain extent, also on the regional level.

Due to the high costs of the necessary equipment for celluloid anima tion production, Arab animators generally operated within local television production institutions supervised by governmental institutions until the late 1980s. Early Arab animation shared many similarities with European artisan-style animation, such as a focus on artistic quality, but was characterized by high costs, high risks and lower budgets resulting in lower quality.[4] One major difference in the case of Arab producers was their exclusive association with national academic hierarchies and cultural industries, which often reduced the producers' personal risks to zero. Even so, early animators in Egypt, Algeria and Tunisia could only survive with great deal of persistence and a willingness to take jobs in local media industries and institutions by producing advertisements and animated parts for television programmes.

Although computer-generated imagery (CGI) was introduced in the US and Europe in the 1960s, it did not reach the Arab world until the late 1980s.[5] CGI productions use computers to draw and colour the frames instead of the human hand, but overall the technology remained expensive and labour-intensive. Wells notes that dominant visual styles of animated cartoons generally recall figurative illustration traditions of the country of origin.[6] That Arab artists showed limited interest in producing animated cartoons can most probably be ascribed to the fact that the decorative and illustrative arts in the Arab world were largely dominated by non-figurative decoration (mosaic, calligraphy), avoiding figurative illustration. No CGI studios were established in the Arab world until the late 1980s. In the case of early CGI technology, it was difficult to separate the creative tasks from the technical and mechanical ones.[7] Because communication was slow and production costly, constant personal supervision was needed from authors to make the animation process efficient. In response, some Arab animation producers moved the entire production process to technically more advanced countries, and often also travelled there themselves to keep control over the texts. This was the case with *Al-Amirah wal-Nahr* ('The Princess and the River'), a propagandistic Iraqi feature-length production in 1982. While scriptwriting and dubbing was performed in Iraq, the entire production process was moved to East Germany and the scenario was written by an Australian expert.[8] Another example is represented by the pioneer works of the so-called 'Islamic Animation' (*Cartoun Islamiyy*), a special genre produced mainly by religious foundations from Saudi Arabia and the Gulf.[9] The pioneer producer of the genre, a Saudi company called Ella, moved the production of its early feature-length films to Turkey.[10]

The first Arab production company to set up a local CGI studio was Cairo Cartoon, established in Egypt in 1988 by Mona Abul-Nasr. Given Abul-Nasr's close ties to local political, media and academic hierarchies, Cairo Cartoon received both financial support and commissions from the Egyptian state-run channel. Cairo Cartoon's first significant productions were animated spots for a local children's programme, *Kani wa Mani* ('Kani and Mani'), in 1989, followed by a number of animated series and productions, among them *Bakkar*, recounting the adventures of a Nubian boy, in 1998.[11] Cairo Cartoon became an incubator for a number of young Egyptian animators, who later established their own CGI and 3D studios and signed their own productions. A couple of years later, television workers from Syria with experience in dubbing foreign animations decided to establish their own dubbing studios, followed by their own animation department.[12] However, because of the slight increase in quantity and the slow improvement in quality, Arab cartoons of the 1990s were still largely outnumbered by imported animation productions even on their own turf.

Step Changes in Productivity and the Rise of 3D

The late 1990s heralded a new dawn for Arab animation production, with local output increasing in both quality and quantity. This dramatic growth was principally driven by three factors: the proliferation of Arab satellite channels, the liberalizing policies of a number of Arab governments regarding media ownership, and the introduction of modern animation technologies.

The expansion of satellite technology and Arab satellite transmission in the 1990s eroded government monopolies over television programming, introducing channels owned by private entrepreneurs, political and religious institutions, and other actors. With the proliferation of Arab satellite channels, the demand for local television productions grew. Eventually a number of Arab children's channels were established, run by profit-oriented companies as well as governmental and religious institutions, with the goal of presenting culturally relevant productions to children. These channels broadcast many old cartoons, but at the same time catered to the enormous demand for new productions, both imported and home-grown. Local animation studios and production houses quickly responded to the demand created by the proliferation of broadcasters, but the gap between demand and supply remained a problem.

Due to its head start in media production and relatively liberal environment for certain types of business, Egypt quickly rose to become the centre for producing animated cartoons. From the early 1990s onward, other Arab governments also introduced economic reforms that paved the way for the creation of new production houses and animation studios. In Syria, Investment Law No 10 of 1991 encouraged private sector entrepreneurs to develop television programmes for commercial entertainment. Private individuals and entities started to invest in television production, a domain that was originally reserved to the public sector.[13] In Jordan, a four-year national economic and social plan was launched in 1993. The declared goal of the Jordanian government's initiative was to build a knowledge-oriented society, with special emphasis on information and communications technology, including research, development and scientific and technological services. In the early 2000s, a number of start-up animation studios were established in Egypt and advanced production companies decided to produce animated content either by founding their own studios or by sub-contracting with new animation companies. Meanwhile, Dubai established Dubai Media City in January 2001 as part of its development strategy aimed at turning the emirate into a regional media hub.

The third factor that led to the improvement of Arab animation production can be found in global technological and media trends. The huge critical acclaim and financial success of Disney's *Toy Story* in 1995 opened the gates for a new worldwide interest in animation. In less than a decade, new 3D technologies replaced old CGI animations, and large companies such as Disney and Fox closed down their old studios to focus on 3D animation. In the new millennium, the vast majority of Western animations were already computer-made. Compared to traditional CGI animation, 3D requires less labour and less talent. Technological development led to a boom in 2D productions as well, as specialized computer programmes increased artists' productivity six-fold or more.[14]

A fall in computer hardware prices in the early 2000s, combined with easy access to 3D animating software, provided an opportunity for a number of Arab individuals and companies to start to catch up with Western and Asian companies that already had a long tradition in the animation business. In a short time, a large number of animation studios sprang up, with actors who had gained some measure of experience in the media business. A few animators gained advantageous experience working abroad, but many were self-taught, using freeware and in some cases – due to the absence or weak enforcement of intellectual property laws – unregistered copies of animation software to train themselves before starting their business. The production process of 3D animated cartoons enabled production phases to disperse geographically: producers lacking their own capacity for animation production could outsource technology-intensive phases to experts beyond the geographical borders, as discussed below.

Particularities of Arab Production Networks

Producing 3D animated cartoons consists of four main stages: conceptualization, pre-production, production and post-production.[15] Distribution can also be counted as an integral fifth stage of the production process.[16] Conceptualization covers the definition of basic ideas and preparing the script that details the general concept and the main elements such as scenes and characters. Pre-production generally covers the production of models according to the concept, the script fleshed out in models and storyboards and, finally, story reels. The production stage includes developing the specifications, visual effects, background paint, ink and paint, and modelling and animating characters including all colours, textures and styles. Post-production consists of sound effects, the final music score, sound mixing and colour correction.[17]

In the chain of Arab animation production, the stages of conceptualization and pre-production are relatively strong, as the numbers of potential authors and original ideas is large and most directors have already earned a reputation through directing movies and television dramas. In contrast, the production stage still suffers from various weaknesses compared to Western and Asian animation. As there are relatively few academies or courses teaching 3D animation, a number of studios are forced to hire talented self-taught young animators and then train them.[18] The cultural factors of Arab media also pose challenges for producers. The majority of producers schedule their series to start broadcasting in the month of Ramadan, when watching television becomes an important family event. Therefore, while the stages of conceptualization and pre-production continue throughout the year, the high season for production starts three to four months before Ramadan, when producers hand over the scripts to the animators. Very few animation studios employ all their animators all year round; instead, to save money, they hire freelancers in what might be called the animation season. At that point competition for talented animators becomes fierce, whereas these same people are hard put to find jobs outside the season.[19] Cash-strong producers have the ability to overcome these problems by signing with animation studios beyond the Arab world. *Freej*, for example, despite becoming a national icon in Dubai, was animated in India.

In the production process of 3D computer animation, a distinction is generally drawn between mechanical and creative work. Creative work such as character ideas, script and direction could be geographically separate from labour-intensive drawing, colouring and animating. The mechanism of production enables creative control to be maintained even if the working process takes part in distant locations.[20] Geographic dispersal of labour-intensive tasks gives rise to both national and transnational production networks.[21] With the formation of new structural boundaries, regional and local producers receive new resources to work with, both material (finance and technology) and symbolic (ideas and models).[22]

The three main institutional actors in the Arab animation production chain are TV channels, production houses and animation studios. The governance of animation production is generally dictated by the institutions which control whether content is produced and how it is distributed.[23] In this respect, the role of television channels as funders, customers and ultimate censors is particularly important. On the other hand, television channels also depend on the other two actors as they rarely have the necessary expertise or infrastructural background to supply their own animated cartoons. Hence channels are forced to sign deals with production houses, either commissioning exclusive new content or purchasing material that has already been produced. Many of these production companies are new to the animation business; having started out by making films and drama serials, they now often sign contracts and partnership deals with professional animation studios as a means to outsource labour-intensive work phases. According to Wells, in animation production it is the directors and producers who should be regarded as authors.[24] Viewed from this perspective, animated cartoons can be considered Arab even if part of the labour that goes into them is performed by non-Arabs, as long as the project leader is Arab. For example, *Freej*, which was produced by Mohammed Saeed Harib's Lammtara Pictures, should be viewed as a Dubai animation despite the fact that it was animated in India. The role of directors and producers as authors is extremely important, as they hold the responsibility for balancing between the demands and sensibilities of their clients (TV channels) and the artistic ambitions of the animators and other workers.

Following the global trend observed in Hollywood filmmaking since the 1950s, Arab animation industries consist of vertically disintegrated production systems, whereby television channels, production houses and animation studios collaborate on an ad hoc basis around particular projects.[25] While closely knit production networks do exist, Arab animation industries largely consist of shifting networks of large, middle-sized and small firms, many with a short life-span, spread across borders and characterized by heterogeneous practices. My interviews with Arab animators and producers revealed that informal and personal relationships play an important role in the way production chains for Arab animated cartoons are formed.[26] This is not surprising, since vertical disintegration largely rests on the increased use of social mechanisms and relationships that serve the sharing of information and building of trust between potential partners.[27] Transnational production requires a great deal of reflexivity, face-to-face meetings and intensive communication. Recent growth in the numbers of Arab animated cartoons is partly a consequence of institutional frameworks and modern means of communication that have made it possible to span national borders and physical distance.

As is the case with European animation industries, those in the Arab world have created a spatially extended 'project ecology' that shares many qualities with those tightly agglomerated clusters that form the focus of much scholarship in the discipline of geography.[28] Producers with governmental and institutional support are able to build durable production networks. Overall, however, Arab animation industries consist of shifting networks of firms of various sizes and life-spans spread across an indistinct and expanding geography. Companies recruit from both the local and the regional labour pools, as it is also common for young Arab animators to move from one country to another in pursuit of jobs. Production centres in Egypt and the Gulf generally employ not only citizens or residents of these countries but also others from elsewhere in the Arab world. At a more modest level, smaller studios from Jordan and Tunisia hire talents from neighbouring countries.

Even though globalization theorists tend to highlight the importance of global actors in media production, the nation state remains the dominant structure on both the political and the institutional level. States generally enjoy the prerogative of structuring most ground rules for the media, starting with market structures, ownership rules, production incentives and subsidies, financial rules, assignment of communication frequencies, technical standards and content regulation. These institutional structures provide rules, boundaries and resources to those who work within them. The primary structural elements for television are economic frameworks, technological bases and institutional forms of organization and operation. Straubhaar argues that these structural elements are boundaries within which cultural agents such as producers operate, since they frame or limit possibilities.[29] Arab television is also primarily bound to the nation state in terms of regulation, programming and 'power structures'.[30] Arab states and state-related institutions largely dominate broadcasting on both the political and the institutional level, so that animation producers, who rely on television channels for commissioning and exhibition, become subject to the state framework.

As mentioned before, the boom in Arab animation production is partly a result of the liberalizing policies of different governments that enabled the creation of private production and animation companies across the Arab world. However, as Sakr notes, it is hard in the context of Arab broadcast media to separate between private and public.[31] Economic liberalization in Arab countries is a highly centralized and top-down process, aimed at maintaining the regime's control over the population,[32] and loyalist entrepreneurs are therefore usually the first to benefit from it. In the case of Arab television, patronage relations define production at a high level. In other words, even though many actors and owners in the Arab animation industry are private companies and individuals, market power is rarely wielded by independent actors. According to veteran political commentator Rami Khouri, cultural productions are 'appendages of the ruling political and economic order in the Arab world, not challenges to it'.[33]

While it is fair to say that Arab governments generally have no direct policies regarding animated cartoon production, it is the case that this production is influenced by the same policies that define cultural productions in general and television production in particular. These in turn can depend on many predictable and unpredictable factors. Unpredictable factors are the personal preferences and priorities of decision-makers, as well as the personal networks of producers who can influence them. Predictable factors are mainly political or religious agendas, market size and wealth. Thus, for example, in Egypt under the presidency of Hosni Mubarak (1981–2011), where government institutions controlled a fairly large domestic market and declared an aim to preserve and improve Egypt's cultural dominance in the Arab world, the state provided generous support for local producers. Similarly, governments with long-term visions or policies of nation-building such as Baathist Iraq (1968–2003) and Baathist Syria (1963–2011) were willing to invest in animation productions produced by loyalists serving the agendas of ruling elites. The same can be said of Jordan, Dubai and Saudi Arabia.

It is striking that the companies producing the animated cartoons with the biggest budgets, supported by effective marketing, usually maintain close ties with particular governments. Mona Abul-Nasr, producer of *Bakkar*, one of the first Arab CGI animation series, had strong connections to the Mubarak regime. Syria's Tiger Production, the producer of quality feature-length productions such as *Khayt al-Hayat* ('Yarn of Life', 2007) and *Tuyur al-Yasmin* ('Jasmine Birds', 2009), was established by individuals with extensive professional experience in the Syrian state TV's dubbing department and good contacts, through personal networks, with local hierarchies. Jordan's highest budget animated series, *Ben wa Essam* ('Ben and Izzy', 2008), was produced by Rubicon, a multimedia production company funded by the King Abdullah II Fund for Development.[34] The Jordanian state also supported the production through promotion, as the English version was launched at an extravagant gala in New York's Metropolitan Museum of Art in 2006 with the participation of Queen Rania.[35] Lammtara Pictures, the Dubai producer of *Freej*, was funded by Sheikh Mohammed Bin Rashid's Establishment for Young Business Leaders in 2005.[36] Partly as a result of governmental tailwind, *Freej* soon became a national icon and a part of local popular and even commercial culture, through contracts with state companies such as FlyDubai and the opening of a theme park. Well-funded children's channels with close ties to particular states, such as MBC3, part of the Saudi-owned MBC Group, and Qatar's JCC, tend to offer better quality animations than those produced by smaller channels. *Saladin: The Animated Series*, an exclusive production of Al-Jazeera Children's Channel, met high technical standards.[37]

Where foreign animated cartoons represent significantly higher visual quality than lower budget local productions, they have a greater potential for success among audiences. Higson contends that the key to local popularity for national cinema lies in attaining an international (Hollywood) standard.[38] This argument is even more valid in the case of animated cartoons. As Arab audiences became used to the visual quality of Walt Disney and other Western animations, they demanded local productions of similar calibre. However, in animation production, the quality of production is directly proportional to the invested capital because increasingly specialized technical positions are needed for high-end 3D animation.[39] Affluent producers can sign large budget contracts with renowned studios capable of quality work; therefore, as a general rule, animation productions with larger budgets have more potential to gain audience acclaim.

Dynamics of Liberalization and Transnational Operation

While governmental and institutional support provide definite advantages to a select group of companies, liberalizing policies also open opportunities to start-up animation companies outside the preferred circle. These companies can follow numerous strategies to succeed: they can focus on creative content, enter niche markets, subcontract to well-to-do companies or join or set up transnational production networks.

Even though visual quality is a key factor in the success of animated cartoons, the example of American-made *South Park* shows that productions of lesser visual quality can still gain popularity if there is a sufficient creative spark. Creativity and original ideas are equally keys to success for Arab animations. One example is *Wesh Cylinder* ('Cylinder Face'), an Egyptian adaptation of Pixar's *Cars*, produced by Evolution Post-Production, a start-up company from Cairo. Even though the series' visual layout does not match up to that of Arab productions with a larger budget, *Wesh Cylinder* became highly popular on Nile Comedy channel and gained the highest viewing figures on YouTube, most probably due to its funny dialogues and children's general fascination with cars.

Smaller companies can also build skills and portfolio by subcontracting to larger production firms or larger animation companies, or by producing advertisements. Both are precarious ventures with little added value, providing only a slight chance to build reputation that is essential for creative industries.[40] Although newcomers usually lack the resources to produce feature-length productions or even their own series, they can still enter niche markets such as preschool and educational animations that require significantly less capital than series. A large number of education and edutainment animations shown on Arab children's channels are produced by small Arab firms.

As Arab children's channels generate demand for a significant volume of culturally relevant productions, those channels are generally willing to meet demand by purchasing content from studios and production houses based in other parts of the Arab world. The transnational networks fostered by this dynamic provide opportunities for animation and production companies to be independent of local hierarchies. Here success relies heavily not only on talent and quality but also on management and networking skills. One example is Kuwaiti Magic Selection, which sells its output not on the national, but on the pan-Arab market.[41] Likewise, Egyptian companies such as Al-Sahar and Matrix, with weaker links to local media decision-makers, principally focus on the geo-linguistic regional market rather than local ones. They do this by subcontracting to production companies from the Gulf and also by selling complete productions to Arab television channels.

Audience demand for foreign-based channels meanwhile gives animation producers a chance not only to win contracts, but also to consolidate production. This is what happened with a small Jordanian company, Sketch in Motion Animation Studio. After signing a number of contracts with Jordanian, Iraqi and Palestinian partners, the company developed the idea of an animated sitcom series about the life of a fictional Bedouin tribe, called *Al-Masageel*. After making a demo, they signed with Saudi-owned MBC1, which became a sponsor of the forthcoming series. Benefiting from the skills and profit gained while producing *Al-Masageel*, Sketch in Motion Animation Studio acquired the wherewithal to produce its own projects.

With the globalizing tendencies of television industries, production is anyway no longer tied only to nation state structures. Jan Nederveen Pieterse argues that globalization in structural terms means an 'increase in the available modes of organization: transnational, international, macroregional, national, micro-regional, municipal, local'.[42] These levels do not necessarily conflict. Arab media production in general and animated cartoon production in particular have three main levels: national, regional and global. But the national mode is nowadays restricted mainly to Egypt. Perhaps because of their long tradition in film and media production, Egyptian television channels, as well as production houses and animation studios, are relatively unusual in the Arab world in relying mainly on national production networks. In contrast, companies from other Arab countries with less established media industries are often forced to seek partners beyond national borders. Arab producers who do not have local capacity for animation processes that are intensive in their need for both labour and talent may decide to outsource certain production phases abroad. It is noteworthy, however, that even when they do this they generally prefer companies located in other Arab or Muslim countries. It seems they assume that cultural proximity makes Arab and Muslim animators easier to work with than Western or even Asian companies.[43] One production network that thrives on this demand centres on Tarek Rashed Studio in Egypt, which has a majority of Gulf producers among its customers, all intent on making nationally relevant productions.[44] There are also production networks specializing in religious material, such as Ella, a Saudi Arabian producer of Islamic feature-length productions since the 1990s. Ella's owner, Osama Khalifa, chose Turkish animation studios over Western ones due to their assumed cultural understanding of Islamic topics. Similarly, *Saladin: The Animated Series* was a co-production between Qatar's JCC and Malaysia's Multimedia Development Corporation.

As noted above, budget is generally crucial to visual quality. Cash-strong producers can sign contracts with studios capable of quality work. For example, *Freej*, produced by Lammtara in Dubai, and *Tesh Eyal*, produced by Saudi-owned MBC, were both outsourced to India and represent a noticeably higher quality of animation than the majority of Gulf animations outsourced to Egypt. But relatively few production networks today operate beyond the Muslim world. Among the few examples, we find the Tunisian Computer Graphic Studio, creator of the renowned sitcom animation *Tunis 2050*, which signed with a number of French production houses and studios.[45] Another is Jordan's Rubicon Holding, which signed for the animation production of *Postman Pat* and *The Pink Panther*.[46] It is extremely rare for Western producers to prefer Arab animation companies over Asian ones when subcontracting.

As with production, the distribution of animated cartoons also has three main levels: national, regional (geo-linguistic) and global. The very basic level of distribution is the national market, where local producers – usually with personal connections to decision-makers – sell culturally relevant productions to local state-owned or private television channels. While locally produced animated cartoons often enjoy a favoured position on national channels, being launched in Ramadan, the majority of productions shown on Arab television channels are still US and other Western animations dubbed into Arabic. The second and more significant level of distribution is regional, with the Arab world constituting a geo-linguistic market. The trend of the late 20th century was the regionalization of television into multi-country markets linked by geography, language and culture. These markets can be defined as 'geo-cultural' or 'cultural linguistic' markets rather than 'regional markets', since not all of the linked populations, markets and cultures are geographically contiguous.[47] Geo-cultural or geo-linguistic markets are usually centred in particular countries or geographical regions, and are primarily unified by language, even if dialects differ from one sub-region or country to another. Apart from language, people are also bound by history, religion, ethnicity, common cultural values, family structure, living patterns and identity. Therefore, audiences may appreciate productions made in countries that share cultural elements such as language.[48] Straubhaar contends that the formation of such markets is primarily led by local audiences' demand for 'cultural proximity' and material that 'culturally resonates with their experiences'.[49]

Arab national industries produce a substantial amount of television content and hold a leading position in national and geo-linguistic markets, as demonstrated by long-standing Egyptian and Lebanese exports of cultural products to other Arab countries. Sakr defined Arab television as 'an interconnected set of cultural industries, where production and exchange takes place across a market circumscribed not by tariffs or jurisdiction but by language'.[50] Regionalization of Arab television has boosted the animation business in the sense that, in order to reach pan-Arab audiences, children's channels such as MBC3 and JCC are willing to purchase productions from countries where those audiences live.

Global Distribution of Animation with an Islamic Theme

Straubhaar's observations on demand for culturally relevant productions and Sakr's point about interconnected cultural industries apply not only to geo-linguistic markets but also to cultural and Islamic ones – a phenomenon already demonstrated earlier by the surge in popularity of Turkish soap operas in the Arab world.[51] Arab animated cartoons with Islamic content find their way easily to non-Arab Muslim markets. However, the distribution channels of individual religious animations are widely different. Educational material with a Shi'a or Salafi orientation has a relatively limited circulation, being mainly restricted to television channels with a compatible agenda. On the other hand, Islamic content that is relatively free of political or other sectarian parameters travels readily to other Muslim markets. The centre for the latter type of production is Egypt, where the authority of Al-Azhar regarding Islamic affairs means that, once an animated cartoon gains the approval of the religious scholars, it can easily be sold on other Muslim markets. No wonder, then, that many Egyptian animation studios and production houses produce their own animated Islamic series. One example is *Hikayat al-Hayawan fil-Qur'an* ('Animal Stories in the Qur'an'), an animation series produced by Associates for Media Production in Egypt in 2011. After premiering on Egypt's Al-Hayat channel, the series was sold to Iraq, Kuwait, Qatar and Saudi Arabia as well as to non-Arab Muslim countries such as Turkey and Indonesia.[52]

However, despite their tremendous growth since the mid-1990s, Arab animated cartoon productions still suffer from a lack of competitiveness on international markets. Buying foreign animated content remains significantly cheaper than originating exclusive productions. Arab channels that do not prioritise the scheduling of culturally relevant productions usually choose to purchase foreign animations. Meanwhile, home-grown productions are fuelled by a desire to present culturally relevant content to local and regional audiences, but this very relevance limits the global circulation potential of Arab animations. Very few Arab animation studios and production houses have been able to reach beyond the borders of the Arab and Muslim worlds and one of the few that has did so by reaching Arab and Muslim expatriate communities. This is *The 99*, an animated adaptation of comic books featuring Muslim superheroes, produced in 2011 by Naif Mutawa, a Kuwaiti-American entrepreneur. As Santo concluded, whereas the series became popular among Muslim children living in the US, it faced resistance from Western audiences and critics.[53]

This means that, as a general trend, the showing of Arab animated cartoons outside the Arab world is largely restricted to international film and animation festivals. Arab animators, like Arab animation producers, tend to stay within geo-linguistic borders, making full use of their cultural advantages to cultivate networks nationally and regionally. Those who take a chance to go beyond these borders, by contacting and sending demos to non-Arab producers and studios, are in a small minority. For this reason, Arab animation can hardly be described as global. In animated cartoon production and distribution, the contact between global and local Arab markets can be described as a one-way flow of foreign products, technology and trends to the Arab world.

Conclusion

Although the early phase of Arab animated cartoon production dates back to the 1930s, it was not able to gain a foothold in local and regional television markets until the 2000s. The proliferation of satellite channels, the apparent liberalization of business ownership and the global technological trends of the 1990s provided an opportunity for a large number of animation companies to start up across the Arab world. Sakr notes that Arab media are mostly nation-bound in terms of regulation, programming and power structures.[54] Unlike the majority of US productions, Arab animation production is not always based on market signals. Despite the large number of start-ups, the most successful companies have remained those with close ties to particular regimes – ties that enable them to pre-empt market risks. At the same time, however, some companies lacking governmental or institutional support have managed to succeed by focusing on creative content, entering niche markets, subcontracting to affluent companies or either joining or establishing transnational production networks.

The main actors of recent Arab animation production networks are television channels, production houses and animation studios that form vertically disintegrated, geographically indistinct networks engaging in ad hoc collaborations on particular projects. Despite the significant growth of the last decade, Arab animation production is still uncompetitive on global markets. Given that the funding of Arab animation production is largely led by the desire to create culturally significant content for national or pan-Arab audiences, the potential of this production to enchant global audiences is limited. Only a few Arab animators and studios have taken the bold step of subcontracting to non-Arab producers or animation studios. As Arab studios generally lack both the financial resources and experience to produce animated cartoons on a scale, and with sufficient quality, that would enable them to compete with Western and Asian productions, they rely primarily on national, linguistic and cultural markets. Because the Arab world forms a geo-linguistic market, cultural proximity plays a highly important role in the functioning of production and distribution networks. As Straubhaar argues, when 'local champions' emerge and consolidate their position this process acts as a catalyst for the formation of multilayered media flows.[55] Thus, even though their presence on global markets is limited, Arab animations, as 'local champions', occupy an important position on national and geo-linguistic markets, thereby demonstrating the strength of countervailing forces to global media giants.

INSIGHT 2

Prominent Personalities and the Fortunes of Children's Media in Egypt

The role of centralized political support structures in the development of children's media was particularly pronounced in the case of Egypt under former president Hosni Mubarak because the First Lady, Mubarak's wife, Suzanne, associated herself with initiatives to promote children's learning. Here, filmmaker and television producer **Seham Nasser** *compares approaches to media for children in Egypt before and after the uprising of January 2011.*

Two ministries in Egypt have been responsible for controlling film and broadcasting, both public and private, for most of the past several decades: the Ministry of Information and the Ministry of Culture. Under Egypt's 2014 Constitution, responsibility for radio and television was supposed to be moved from the Ministry of Information to separate regulatory bodies. Before the new structures were set up, however, the separation remained unclear. The Ministry of Culture initiated the Cairo International Film Festival for Children (CIFFC) in

1990 and continued it in an unbroken series until 2011, at which point the aftermath of the uprising prevented arrangements for the festival from going ahead. For at least the next three years, children's media in the country, being so closely linked to government institutions, was subject to the fluctuations and uncertainties affecting control of the ministries.

I have held positions at both ministries, including 10 years at the Ministry of Information, during which I was a Member of the Committee of Children's Programmers, and one year as a member of the Supreme Committee on Children at the Ministry of Culture. This gave me a close view of what happened before and after the uprising. Between 2005 and 2010 the Egyptian Radio and Television Union (ERTU) had exchanges with the European Broadcasting Union (EBU), which created opportunities for us in the ERTU to produce various genres of programme for children, including short fiction and documentary films, with the EBU encouraging us to give children the chance to speak for themselves. This was in contrast to the customary practice in most Egyptian shows for children, which were studio based, with adult presenters doing all the talking, and talking down to children. As part of the ERTU-EBU exchanges, the ERTU gained rights to broadcast high quality productions from other countries, but unfortunately the relevant ERTU department heads saw no benefit in this. That is to say, more than 45 documentaries, 300 short films and 30 feature films were stored in the library and not shown because the channel heads chose not to.

That lack of interest reflected the absence of any clear vision or plan for children's media among officials working at the information and culture ministries. Instead of a plan, initiatives took place based on personal contacts of powerful people. Suzanne Mubarak's involvement in the Egyptian co-production of *Sesame Street* demonstrates this. She was prominent as patron of the Egyptian series, *Alam Simsim*, which premiered in August 2000 and ran for 10 years with funding from the US agency for international development, USAID. *Alam Simsim* was developed with the Egyptian Ministry of Education and supported by the Ministry of Information, under the patronage of Suzanne Mubarak, who herself appeared on the show. In 2005, during a visit to Egypt by the US First Lady, Laura Bush, both women featured on the programme. The late Mona Abul-Nasr also had a good relationship with the First Lady of Egypt and thus with the ERTU, which broadcast her animated series *Bakkar* for seven years.[56] Together with the Egyptian-made puppet series *Bougy wa Tamtam*, which ran for 17 years on state television, these three shows were the most famous locally made offerings for children on Egyptian TV. As with *Bakkar*, however, which stopped for eight years when its original director died, *Bougy wa Tamtam* also ceased when director and puppet designer Mahmoud Rahmy died in 2001. This was despite efforts by Mona Abul-Nasr's son, Sharif Gamal, and Mahmoud Rahmy's son, Bassem, to continue production. It was not until 2015 that a new series of *Bakkar*, directed by Sharif Gamal, and a new series of *Bougy wa Tamtam*, directed by Bassem Remy, appeared on a private channel. But the comebacks were not part of any long-term plan, since systematic budgets are not set aside for such programmes.

After the January 25 revolution in Egypt, when presidential-level support for specific children's media initiatives disappeared with the demise of Mubarak, children's programming ground to a complete standstill. The Nile thematic channel previously known as the Family and Children's Channel effectively became just the Family Channel, and the children's programmes were cancelled. The CIFFC was held in 2012, but senior people who had run it since the start considered it a flop and in 2013, under the shortlived Muslim Brotherhood regime of Mohammed Morsi, the festival failed to take place, without even any explanation from the Ministry of Culture. Managers and owners of private Egyptian-owned satellite channels showed no interest in children's material, either as regular programme slots or as a dedicated channel. The idea of creating an online channel has limited appeal because of the large number of Egyptian children who cannot access the internet and there is no financial support from the government or any private organization.

Notes

1 *Al-Ahram*, 31 July 1936.
2 Lila Abu-Lughod, *Dramas of Nationhood: The Politics of Television in Egypt* (Chicago: University of Chicago Press, 2005), p. 135.
3 Terrestrial television broadcasting was introduced in Algeria in 1956, Egypt 1960, Iraq 1956, Syria 1960 and Tunisia 1966.
4 Michael Storper and Robert Salais, *Worlds of Production* (Cambridge, MA: Harvard University Press, 1997).
5 CGI technology refers to designing and animating cartoon characters with computer-aided 2D technologies.
6 Paul Wells, *Animation Genre and Authorship* (London: Wallflower Press, 2002), p. 3.
7 Ted Tschang, 'Production and political economy in the animation industry: Why insourcing and outsourcing occur', a paper presented at the DRUID Summer Conference 2004 on Industrial Dynamics, Innovation and Development, Elsinore, Denmark, 14–16 June, 2004.
8 *Al-Amirah wal-Nahr* was produced by Babylon, a semi-private production company (est. 1980); the director was Faissal al-Yasseri, while scripts were written by an Australian scenario writer John Palmer.
9 Such 'Islamic animations' are defined by educative content, historical topics and the absence of soundtracks.
10 Muassasat Alla lil-Intag al Fanniyy wal-Tawzi' (Alla Institution for Art Production and Distribution) was established in 1992 by Osama Khalifa. The company made a number of feature-length animation productions on historical and Islamic topics, amongst them *Muhammad al-Fatih* (1995), *Rihlat al-Khuloud* (1996), *Asad Ayn Jalout* (1998) and *Tareq ibn-Ziyad* (1999).
11 See Chapter 8 in this volume.
12 Muna' Hejazi, who worked in the dubbing department of Syrian TV, established Venus for Art Production (al-Zahra) in 1992.
13 Lisa Wedeen, *Ambiguities of Domination: Politics, Rhetoric, and Symbols in Contemporary Syria* (Chicago: University of Chicago Press, 1999), pp. 90–91.
14 Tschang, 'Production and political economy'.
15 Catherine Winder and Zahra Dowlatabadi, *Producing Animation* (Boston: Focal Press, 2001).
16 Stefan Krätke, 'Network analysis of production clusters: the Potsdam/Babelsberg film industry as an example', *European Planning Studies*, 10 (2002), pp. 27–54.
17 Winder and Dowlatabadi, *Producing Animation*.
18 The lack of training opportunities remains a problem in Algeria, Egypt, Kuwait, Saudi Arabia and Tunisia, while it is improving in Jordan and the UAE.

19 The competition for professional animators in high seasons was verified by a number of producers from Egypt, Jordan and Tunisia whom I interviewed, including Sameh Mustafa (Cairo, 7 September 2012) Riadh Ghariani (Tunis, 23 March 2013) and Tarek Rashed (Cairo, 5 September 2012). Meanwhile, the number of animators available poses no serious problems for producers from Dubai.

20 Alexander Cole, 'Distant neighbours: the new geography of animated film production in Europe,' *Regional Studies*, 42 (2008), pp. 891–904.

21 Hyejin Yoon and Edward J. Malecki, 'Cartoon planet: Worlds of production and global production networks in the animation industry', *Industrial and Corporate Change*, 19/1 (2009), p. 240.

22 Joseph Straubhaar, '(Re)Asserting national television and national identity against the global, regional, and local levels of world television', in J. Chan and B. McIntyre (eds), *In Search of Boundaries: Communication, Nation States and Cultural Identities* (Westport, CT: Praeger, 2002), pp. 181–206.

23 Tschang, 'Production and political economy'.

24 Wells, *Animation Genre*, pp. 74–76.

25 Several works by Susan Christopherson and Michael Storper in the late 1980s describe how the vertically integrated studio system of Hollywood's classic period prior to the 1950s was gradually replaced by a vertically disintegrated production system.

26 A fact verified by a number of my interviewees regardless of their country of origin. Among them were Mohamed Elmazen (Cairo, 2 September 2012), Tarek Rashed (Cairo, 5 September 2012), Omar al-Moghazy, Matrix (Cairo 8 September 2012) and Sulafa Hejazi (by telephone, Beirut 12 December 2012).

27 Charles F. Sabel and Jonathan Zeitlin, 'Neither modularity nor relational contracting: Inter-firm collaboration in the new economy. A critique of Langlois and Lamoreaux, Raff, and Temin', *Enterprise and Society*, 5/3 (2004), pp. 388–403.

28 Cole, 'Distant neighbours'.

29 Straubhaar, '(Re)Asserting national television'.

30 Naomi Sakr, *Satellite Realms: Transnational Television, Globalization and the Middle East* (London: I.B.Tauris, 2001), p. 66.

31 Naomi Sakr, *Arab Television Today* (London: I.B.Tauris, 2007), p. 166.

32 Toby Dodge, 'Bringing the bourgeoisie back in: globalization and the birth of liberal authoritarianism in the Middle East', in T. Dodge and R. Higgott (eds), *Globalization and the Middle East: Islam, Economy, Society and Politics* (London: Royal Institute of International Affairs, 2002), pp. 169–187.

33 Quoted by Sakr in *Arab Television Today*, p. 2.

34 *Ben and Izzy* was first released in English, then dubbed into Arabic. The plot revolves around the friendship between two 11-year-old boys, one American, the other of Jordanian background, travelling back in time. The series

promotes a message of tolerance between Islamic and Western cultures that largely accords with official Jordanian politics.

35 Jacques Steinberg, 'A children's cartoon from the Middle East has a new Mideast peace plan', *New York Times*, 30 April, 2006.

36 Lammtara was established in September 2005, with around 3 million UAE dirhams provided by the Mohamed bin Rashid Establishment for Young Business Leaders. *Freej* centres around the story of four elderly Emirati ladies, dealing with the dynamic world around them.

37 *Saladin: The Animated Series* (2009) is a Malaysian-Qatari co-production about the fictitious adventures of Salahuddin Ayubi and his companions.

38 Andrew Higson, 'The concept of national cinema', *Screen*, 30/4 (1989), p. 42.

39 Tschang: 'Production and political economy'.

40 Richard Caves, *Creative Industries: Contracts between Art and Commerce* (Cambridge MA: Harvard University Press, 2000).

41 Magic Selection is a Kuwaiti-based animation production studio, founded in 2002, producer of a large number of educational and edutainment animation series, purchased by channels such as Syrian-owned Spacetoon, Saudi-owned MBC2 and MBC3 and Qatari-owned JCC.

42 Jan Nederveen Pieterse, 'Globalization as hybridization', in M. Featherstone, S. M. Lash and R. Robertson (eds), *Global Modernities* (London: Sage, 1995), p. 50.

43 Personal interviews: Tarek Rashed (Cairo, 5 September 2012), Omar al-Moghazy, Matrix (Cairo, 8 September 2012).

44 Tarek Rashed Studios signed for animation production with producers from Kuwait for creating *Youmiyyat Bou Qatada wa Bou Nabeel*, with Omani producers for producing *Youm wa Youm*, and with Emirati producers for *Khousa Bousa*.

45 Computer Graphic Studio was subcontracted to Dargaud Media for producing series of *Garfield* and *Bali*. It also collaborated with Planet Nemo Studio on productions aired on Disney Channel and with Cyber Group Studios for producing *Mademoiselle Zazie*, aired on France Télévisions.

46 *Pink Panther and Pals* was a co-production with MGM Studios aired on Cartoon Network. They also did animation work for the production of *Postman Pat: The Movie* and *The Life and Adventures of Santa Claus*.

47 Kenton T. Wilkinson, 'Where Culture, Language and Communication Converge: The Latin American Cultural-Linguistic Market', Phd Dissertation (University of Texas, 1995).

48 Waisbord, Silvio, 'McTV: Understanding the global popularity of television formats', *Television & New Media*, 5/4 (2004), p. 359.

49 Straubhaar, Joseph, 'Beyond media imperialism: Asymmetrical interdependence and cultural proximity', *Critical Studies in Mass Communication*, 8 (1991), pp. 39–59.

50 Sakr, *Arab Television Today*, p. 2.

51 Alexandra Buccianti, 'Dubbed Turkish soap operas conquering the Arab world: social liberation or cultural alienation?' *Arab Media and Society*, March (2010).

52 Mustafa al-Faramawi directed the series, *Stories in the Quran*. Animation was done by Egypt's Cartoonile and distribution by Cedar Arts Production. After the success of the first series, two more were produced. *Human Stories in the Quran* debuted in 2012, while *Women's Stories in the Quran* was aired in 2013.

53 Avi Santo, '"Is it a camel? Is it a turban? No, it's The 99": Branding Islamic superheroes as authentic global cultural commodities', *Television & New Media*, 15/7 (2014), pp. 679–95.

54 Sakr, *Satellite Realms*, p. 66.

55 Joseph Straubhaar, *World Television: From Global to Local* (Thousand Oaks, CA: Sage, 2007).

56 See Chapters 4 and 8 in this volume.

5

Rebranding Al-Jazeera Children's Channel

The Qatarization Factor

Naomi Sakr and Jeanette Steemers[1]

Attaching the Al-Jazeera brand name to a children's channel may not have seemed a controversial choice when Al-Jazeera Children's Channel (JCC) was launched in September 2005. In January that year, *Brandchannel* magazine's annual survey to name the world's 'most influential' brand had put the Doha-based Arabic-language news channel Al-Jazeera, financed by the Qatari ruling family, in fifth place after Apple, Google, Ikea and Starbucks.[2] Although JCC was a project of Qatar's first lady at the time, 90 per cent owned by her Qatar Foundation for Education, Science and Community Development and housed in Qatar's Education City, 10km away from Al-Jazeera's Doha studios, JCC was initially linked by name to Al-Jazeera, even though the latter owned a mere 10 per cent stake. Several years later, after sweeping management changes at JCC, the organization made two big decisions that reversed these early features in a somewhat paradoxical way. In June 2012 a rebranding of JCC was initiated, which removed the overt reference to Al-Jazeera. With the removal of the name, however, came the introduction of Al-Jazeera oversight. In June 2013 a JCC official revealed that JCC ownership arrangements were being changed. Qatar Foundation would cede its 90 per cent share and JCC would be formally incorporated into the Al-Jazeera Network.[3]

What happened in the intervening period to prompt this turnabout? One interpretation could be that the actions of 2012–2013 demonstrated recognition by the channel's new management that mistakes had been made when the channel was set up. That they were made despite feasibility studies being conducted for two years before the launch suggests that the studies may have paid limited attention to the question of channel identity. One mistake, admitted by JCC's first managers, was the creation of a single channel intended to reach children from the ages of 3 to 15 years. As was acknowledged in 2009, when the preschool channel Baraem (Buds) was split off from JCCTV, 'targeting kids from 3 to 15 is difficult to achieve'.[4] Baraem was duly given its own logo and visual identity. In contrast, its companion channel, aimed primarily at 7- to 12-year-olds, retained the existing association with the Qatari news channel and, by implication, the latter's reputation for political controversy. The link was signalled visually through a version of the distinctive pearl-drop-shaped Al-Jazeera logo and verbally by linking the name 'Al-Jazeera' with 'children'. Al-Jazeera Children's Channel was the one rebranded as Jeem TV.[5]

This chapter explores several aspects of the rebranding to understand what it reveals about the evolving JCC project as a whole. Haya bint Khalifa Al Nassr, then JCC's Qatari Acting Executive General Manager, was explicit about the salience of brand when she announced what was effectively a relaunch of JCC and its component parts in 2013. 'JCC is leading a change at the heart of the business', she said. 'We wanted to integrate a child-centric brand that caters to the modern needs of Arab children and a generation of new media adopters, and a brand that offers a full scale proposition over multiple platforms'.[6] That narrative, albeit relevant to the present study, represents only one perspective on a complex set of events. For that reason the chapter starts by reviewing ideas on branding in the television industry, nation branding and the branding of children's programming. It goes on to explore the nature and context of organizational and programming changes that took place in JCC in 2011–13 and the branding and rebranding processes associated with various stages in its development. It concludes by considering channel identity issues that the rebranding process revealed and was supposed to resolve.

Branding TV, Nations and Children's Media

Television branding dates from the early days of television, at least in practice if not in the terminology used to describe the practice, in the sense that graphic designers soon responded to a need for snappy visual clues to channel identities and programme titles. In the 21st-century digital world, the skills of broadcast promotion and design combined in a 'fast moving and nebulous field' of 'promotional screen industries', involving complex networks and interactions among an array of companies and occupations in advertising, media sales, broadcasting, production studios, digital design and communication.[7] Yet research on the management of media brands remained scarce, paying only rare attention to the strategic nature of media branding, even though brands may be considered as part of a 'company's strategic intellectual capital' and brand management affects a company's business performance.[8]

As media branding and promotional screen industries have developed, so has the idea of branding nations, despite the dissimilarity of nations and companies. Melissa Aronczyk recalls that her research on nation branding was still seen as novel in 2003, whereas 10 years later the notion that territorial places should not only have a brand but should devote resources to developing one had become a 'commonplace assumption'.[9] For most of those 10 years a preponderance of instrumentalist 'technical-economic' studies on nation branding treated national identity as an asset or liability to be managed by experts, while only a small number of cultural studies questioned the practice, probing the ways it limits the range of possible national identity narratives.[10] In a research agenda for future work on nation branding, Nadia Kaneva urged scholars to examine its constituent practices from a political economy perspective, looking at the branding consultancies, national agencies, ruling elites and global institutions that are implicated in perpetuating nation branding projects and at the benefits they stand to gain.[11] Subsequent work in line with this agenda has shown that branding consultancies may have rather different motives, depending on whether they are national or international, and based inside or outside the country which is the subject of a branding campaign.[12]

According to Mehran Kamrava, media branding and nation branding came together in Qatar in 1996 with the launch of the Al-Jazeera news channel. This move, intended to 'brand Qatar as a pioneer', put it on the road to becoming a ' "brand state" par excellence'.[13] Kamrava associates Qatar's 'concerted' branding activity with what he calls 'diplomatic hyper-activism', reflecting the authorities' determination to project an image of the country as a 'serious regional and global player'.[14] There are many examples of this Qatari aspiration to a global role in all fields, including sport, through events like the Asian Games and Asia Cup that long pre-dated Qatar's bid to host the Football World Cup in 2022, and education. The Qatar Foundation (QF), formed in 1995, a decade before it launched JCC, sought early on to position itself as a global player in education. Its Education City, opened in 2001, was described in 2008 as the 'largest enclave of American universities overseas'.[15]

Against this background, Qatar Tourism Authority's 2003 decision to commission Tarik Atrissi Design to brand Qatar can be seen as a relatively early move in explicit global attempts at nation branding but not especially early in terms of Qatar's own development as a branded state. Atrissi says he was given a brief to 'create an identity that reflects the country's strategy and long term vision'.[16] In contrast, the United Arab Emirates (UAE), home to brand-conscious airlines Emirates and Etihad, waited until 2012 to adopt a country logo, which the website setting out the five designs shortlisted for adoption said were intended to 'promote a unified identity for the UAE and express its unique aspects'.[17] The combination of unity and uniqueness essential to all nation branding is recognized by Aronczyk as serving to 'model' national distinctions internationally, in a way that leaders hope will generate positive foreign public opinion that will 'boomerang' back home, fostering 'domestic consensus' and 'pride and patriotism within the nation's borders'.[18]

Miriam Cooke, who highlights Gulf nations' branding activity in the subtitle of her book *Tribal Modern*, uses words like 'authenticity' and 'leadership' to pinpoint the qualities envisaged by Qatari leaders in creating spectacular buildings like the Qatar Museum of Islamic Art. Cooke sees authenticity as a trope that connects young and affluent Gulf populations with a distant cultural heritage, enshrined in the Qatar Museums Authority's promise of a dialogue about 'rapid change and modernization', in which the museum building is said to give 'concrete expression to the identity of a nation in movement'.[19] Aronczyk notes that nation branding often marries 'tropes of heritage and modernization, domestic and foreign concerns, and market and moral ideologies in the projection of national identity'. Thus, she continues, a nation's brand is meant to offer a 'version of nationalism rooted in the unifying spirit of benign commercial "interests" rather than in the potential divisions of political "passions"'.[20]

Ultimately, given that nations are too complex, with too many internal contradictions and disparities, to be captured by colours and a typeface, some argue that what is being branded is 'not a nation but a marketing-driven entity circulating amid flows of labor, capital and image'.[21] In Qatar's case, writes Shannon Mattern, what is branded is a 'simulacrum of a nation, complete with imported, prefabricated universities, science parks, and cultural institutions'; the brand effectively depoliticizes the state, erases the nation and 'puts in its place a multinational corporation'.[22] The idea of depoliticizing the state is supported by evidence of the Qatari authorities' own suppression of the term 'politics' in relation to local affairs. When Northwestern University-Qatar, which is based in Education City, surveyed media use in eight Middle Eastern countries in early 2013, the Qatar Statistics Authority asked for survey questions to be worded differently when asked in Qatar, so that words like 'social' or 'public' would replace the term 'political'.[23] Some questions with political implications, such as one asking whether 'you think things in your country are generally headed in the right direction', were omitted altogether in the Qatari survey.[24]

The Qatari government's concern to establish recognizable brand identities for the country and its institutions, including media outlets, raises interesting questions about its branding of a children's channel, in light of the way global players such as Fox Kids and Disney Channel use brand promotion to create a sense of identification and belonging among child audiences.[25] Research shows that their promotions and interstitial content seek to transform the space of a television channel or website into an 'authentic' place where children may play, make friends, participate in games and interact with characters and one another.[26] These places, where an 'alluring consumer identity for children' is 'explicitly constituted in children's terms', are intended to make children feel 'liberated from social constructions, such as gender, race, and/or class, that would make them feel left out or marginalized' and from 'those aspects of peer culture that might also destroy their confidence in the power of consumption'.[27]

103

In view of the focus on heritage and cultural identity within Qatar's efforts at nation branding, it seems unlikely that JCC branding would seek to liberate Arab children from what the Qatari authorities consider to be local cultural values and traditions. The latter have sought to present the country as a pioneering Arab and Muslim player with 'authentic' (but ostensibly apolitical) cultural traditions, a strong focus on education and a leadership role. The remaining sections of this chapter explore whether JCC was intended to form part of a Qatari claim to cultural leadership, and whether it became enveloped in the ethos of a depoliticized corporation-nation. At the same time, given the role of intermediaries from promotional screen industries outside Qatar in the branding of JCC, the analysis explores the constituent practices of nation branding and media branding in this case, as well as crossover between them, paying attention to the ways they took account of local perceptions about children's media needs.

Background to Changes at JCC, 2011–2013

There are at least three levels on which to assess policy changes affecting JCC in the period before, during and after its re-launch in 2013. One is policy as expressed by JCC's internal management, both the managerial team that held office until September 2011 and those who took over after that date. The second relates to policy within JCC's first majority owner, QF, and within the Al-Jazeera Network after it took JCC over from QF. The third is the level of Qatari internal politics and foreign policy as they affect both QF and the Al-Jazeera Network. To start with the third and last of these levels is to set the context for the other two. A recurring theme across all three levels is the issue of resource allocation, given the fiscal demands created by Qatar's regional and global ambitions coupled with the finite and unpredictable stream of revenues from oil and gas. Another theme is Qatarization, the policy of appointing Qatari nationals to posts previously held by expatriates.

The period 2011–2013 was something of a turning point for Qatar in its self-appointed role as regional trendsetter and mediator. Marked at the beginning by the Arab uprisings and toppling of dictators in Tunisia, Egypt and Libya, and at the end by the June 2013 accession and early months in office of a new Qatari Emir, this three-year period saw Qatar's rulers make – and then undo – a series of what came to be seen as 'mis-calculations'.[28] In April 2011 US President Barack Obama acknowledged what he called the 'leadership' of Qatar's Emir, saying it had been essential to shaping the coalition of NATO and Arab countries in 'trying to promote a peaceful transition in Libya'.[29] In this perceived leadership role, Qatar was emboldened to redouble its long-standing support for the Muslim Brotherhood across the region, expecting that post-dictatorship elections would bring Islamists to power, from which vantage point they would repay Qatar's support by safeguarding its interests in their countries. The plan seemed to be working when Mohammed Morsi was elected president in Egypt in 2012, but then came disastrously unstuck with his removal a year later, just days after the Qatari Emir, who had initiated the policy, abdicated in favour of his son, Sheikh Tamim. Although abdication is a 'well-established' practice among the ruling Al Thani,[30] on this occasion the combination of a region in turmoil with a 'failed bet of the highest magnitude'[31] is seen as having encouraged the incoming Emir, Sheikh Tamim, to widen the 'tiny apex of decision-making' that had previously mobilized 'different parts of the state apparatus in pursuit of a common objective'.[32] His more cautious approach to power and policy-making had implications for both QF and Al-Jazeera.

Sheikh Tamim, whose accession had been expected for several months beforehand, was by no means a newcomer to the making of domestic policy; he chaired internal development planning bodies for several years, including the Qatar National Vision 2030, which was launched in 2008. In this capacity he would have become familiar with calls from the IMF for greater efficiency in public spending[33] – calls that potentially contrasted with increases in salaries and benefits for Qatari civil service and military staff that had been announced in 2012, apparently as part of government moves to avert any internal unrest.[34] Indeed, in his foreword to the *Qatar National Development Strategy 2011–16*, published in March 2011, Sheikh Tamim noted both the 'stresses that accompany rapid progress' and the need for 'responsible use of resources'.[35] The Strategy document speaks explicitly of a new 'integrated approach' to allocating state funds, whereby spending will be more closely aligned with leadership priorities and implementing agencies will be asked to 'identify potential savings in other areas'.[36]

The Strategy document did not specify how the realignment of spending would affect institutions such as QF and Al-Jazeera. But it did highlight the role played by cultural investment in helping the government to 'improve branding of the country's global image' and 'promote Qatar's culture', thereby positioning the country to 'assume a larger leadership role within global society'; it also envisaged Qatari media taking a larger role in 'promoting cultural objectives', given the importance of media in 'shaping policies and identity'.[37] At the same time, however, the document suggested that information was lacking about the social and economic impact of some cultural activities.[38] Doubts on this score were evident in QF's withdrawal from international football sponsorship only three years after it entered the field in December 2010. The sponsorship deal, worth a reported €170, was originally for five years and made QF the first entity ever to pay for its logo to appear on Barcelona Football Club shirts. Since 2006, Barcelona had donated to UNICEF to carry the UNICEF logo.[39] In November 2013, however, QF ceded its place to Qatar Airways for the remaining period, changing its own status to Barcelona's Official Human Development Partner. This ended a situation in which QF, a nonprofit organization, paid a spectacularly large sum to advertise itself.[40]

Meanwhile, QF, which set out its own 10-year Strategic Plan in May 2013, had acquired a Qatari president in place of the Egyptian professor of parasitology, Mohammed Fathy Saoud, who had occupied the post since 2007. Promoted to his new role in September 2013, Saad Al Muhannadi, who previously oversaw construction projects in and around Education City, stressed his intention to ensure that the opportunities afforded by QF would be 'available for the collective benefit of the local population'.[41] His words resonated with the QF pledge in 2011 to increase its proportion of Qatari employees to 50 per cent by 2016, based on the 2011 headcount.[42] QF Annual Reports at this time frequently alluded to Qatarization. In another example of the policy in action, Doha International Family Institute, a QF member, saw its Executive Director, Richard Wilkins, a socially conservative American lawyer, replaced by a Qatari, Noor Al Malki Al Jehani, in early 2012.

Over at the Al-Jazeera Network, the appointment of a Qatari in place of a non-Qatari at the helm took place in September 2011, attracting a great deal of international media attention. Qatar's foreign policy choices in 2011 were being conspicuously played out in reporting by the Al-Jazeera

Arabic news channel, which played cheerleader to the uprisings in Egypt, Libya and Syria but not in Bahrain, Qatar's neighbour and co-member of the Gulf Cooperation Council (GCC). Wadah Khanfar, a Palestinian, stated that he was stepping down as Director General of the Al-Jazeera Network of his own accord, having met his targets for the network; he was replaced by Sheikh Ahmed bin Jassim Al Thani, an executive at Qatargas and a member of the Qatari ruling family. Some news reports suggested that leaked US diplomatic cables revealing past consultation over Al-Jazeera coverage among Khanfar, the US Defense Intelligence Agency and Qatar's Ministry of Foreign Affairs played a part in Khanfar's departure. Other commentators found it logical that a local businessman should take charge of a network that had grown to encompass 20 channels, over 65 international bureaux and some 3,000 staff, including 400 journalists.

Documentary evidence of Qatari foreign ministry involvement in Al-Jazeera's editorial decisions in previous years gave credence to an assumed link between Qatari foreign policy and Al-Jazeera's explicit support for Islamists after the uprisings, in particular the Muslim Brotherhood in Egypt and its Doha-based cleric Yousef al-Qaradawi. The regional polarization this reflected came to a head in 2012–2013, leading to large-scale resignations from the network, negative publicity internationally and imprisonment of Al-Jazeera journalists by the Egyptian government. After the accession of Sheikh Tamim in June 2013, however, a gradual shift appeared in the policy of determined support for the Muslim Brotherhood. Sheikh Ahmed bin Jassim moved from his position at Al-Jazeera to become Minister of Economy and Trade. In his place came Acting Director General Mostefa Souag, a former professor of literary theory at the University of Algiers with media experience gained inside and outside the Al-Jazeera Network. In November 2013 Qatar signed an agreement in Riyadh with Saudi Arabia and Kuwait to refrain from backing 'hostile media outlets'. The deal got off to a shaky start as Saudi Arabia, Bahrain and the UAE withdrew their ambassadors from Doha in March 2014 in protest at what they saw as continued interference by Al-Jazeera. But eventually Qatar undertook to abide by the Riyadh agreement and demonstrated this in December 2014 by suspending Al-Jazeera's Mubasher Misr (Direct from Egypt) channel. The reward came in June 2015 with an order by GCC ministers to their media to support Qatar's holding of the football World Cup in 2022.[43]

Meanwhile Sheikh Tamim assigned Palestinian academic and politician Azmi Bishara to create a new satellite channel based in London as one of a group of Qatari-backed media ventures that seemed intended to deflect attention from Al-Jazeera network. Opinion was divided on how the London-based Al-Araby al-Jadeed outlets that emerged in 2014 would differ from Al-Jazeera, either in terms of ownership or content. However, with Al-Jazeera Sport already rebranded as BeIN Sports in December 2013 and Jeem TV having replaced what was previously known as Al-Jazeera Children's Channel in June 2013, the Qatari ruling family seemed to be downplaying the Al-Jazeera brand. That process continued with the 2015 closure of Al-Jazeera America and an announcement by BeIN Media Group that it would expand into movies and entertainment, including a partnership with Turner, a division of Time Warner, to offer Turner-owned channels such as Cartoon Network, Boomerang and others through BeIN's distribution network.

Reshaping JCC Management, Strategy and Programmes

The Qatar Foundation for Education, Science and Community Development divides its projects according to the three categories identified in its title. Al-Jazeera Children's Channel and Baraem, together with their associated educational video-on-demand portal, Taalam.tv, and children's choir, Siwar, were classified by QF as 'community development', as distinct from education or research. Signs of a major project overhaul emerge from a comparison of the entries on JCC in the QF annual reports for 2010–2011 and 2011–2012, followed by the absence of any entry in the *Annual Report 2012–13*, reflecting JCC's move from QF to Al-Jazeera. What cannot be gleaned from this comparison on paper is the scale of the change in reality, in the shift from non-Qatari Arab managers to Qatari ones, in the number of employees affected, the effect on their lives and the impact on JCC's role as commissioner of, and outlet for, children's content produced by Arabs in Arabic.

In setting out JCC's goals, the QF *Annual Report 2011–12* repeated elements that dominated JCC promotional material from the outset in 2005: the intention to educate, entertain and inspire young minds; to set high standards in content, creativity, originality and production values; and to commit to preserving 'Arabic culture and heritage.'[44] Newly introduced, in contrast, was the 'vision' to create a '360-degree media proposition.'[45] This signalled a multimedia revenue-maximizing approach in which digital screen content is repurposed for online games, computer apps, toys and other forms of merchandizing. The commercial implications of this vision are echoed in the stated aim to 'develop a robust revenue diversification plan' and implement a 'merchandizing strategy', as well as the stated achievements, which include developing and executing a 'budget and manpower optimization plan.'[46] Rebranding was presented as part of this process, with a 'new brand, logo and identity' to be launched 'across diverse platforms' and staff to attend workshops on 'brand immersion.'[47]

Compared with the original plans for JCC, those described above represent a fundamental departure. In its first incarnation, JCC was a non-commercial, fully funded project with specific quantitative targets for in-house production. It started with a self-declared 'public service mission' and an annual budget of $50 million provided by QF.[48] By 2009 this had doubled to $100 million, with 40–60 per cent of output said to be locally produced. The aim was to teach children about their 'lives, rights, education, health, environment and the world', so as to offer an alternative to other Arabic-language children's channels, which were seen by Mahmoud Bouneb, JCC's Tunisian-born executive general manager at the time, as promoting 'materialism' among children and treating them as 'mini-consumers.'[49] By producing talk shows and game shows locally, JCC believed it could meet its objective of listening to children, which Bouneb felt was something new in pan-Arab television.[50]

Whether this approach was implemented in a way that generated large and loyal audiences cannot be known for sure because of questions over the credibility of pan-Arab viewership data among the relevant age groups. But the Qatari senior managers who took over suddenly and unceremoniously at JCC in September 2011 were doubtful. According to Saad Al Hudaifi, who in 2013 succeeded Haya bint Khalifa Al Nassr as Acting Executive General Manager, one of the new managers' first actions was to conduct a dozen workshops with children of 20 different nationalities living in Qatar 'to understand their needs' because 'if you don't listen to them you can't produce programmes for them.'[51] At the time of the management change young viewers had a number of alternatives to JCC, all of them showing dubbed imported cartoons. One was the decade-old Syrian-owned Spacetoon Arabic. Another was MBC3, set up as part of the Saudi-owned MBC Network in 2004. Then there were the regional Turner Broadcasting channels, Cartoon Network Arabia and Boomerang. Nickelodeon content, aired for a short period as Nickelodeon Arabia, was acquired by MBC3 in 2012. Under Al Nassr and Al Hudaifi, JCC indicated its intention to compete with MBC3 on MBC3's own terms by signing a multi-year deal with Disney in March 2013, for the exclusive right to acquire and dub a large number of Disney cartoon series for both its Jeem TV and Baraem channels, thereby denying these shows to MBC3. Other purchases of foreign content included 180 hours from the BBC in November 2012 followed by three series of the BBC's *Dr Who* in 2013. JCC's Haya bint Khalifa Al Nassr described the acquisitions as the 'start of an exciting content transformation'.[52]

The bulk import deals and recruitment of staff from outside JCC to head new 'Ad Sales and Sponsorship' and 'Licensing and Merchandizing' departments went hand-in-hand with a deliberate pitch to increase both audience share in, and advertising from, Saudi Arabia and Egypt. This was to be achieved by inviting more guests from these countries to feature on Jeem TV shows.[53] It also accompanied the development of separate feeds for different parts of the world, building on existing transmissions to Europe via the Hotbird satellites. With JCC's incorporation into the Al-Jazeera Network, it anticipated reaching an estimated 8 million Arabic speakers residing in the US,[54] following the August 2013 launch of the US cable and satellite news channel Al-Jazeera America. This aim was to become a casualty of the latter's closure two years later.

In terms of staffing, however, the sudden Qatarization of JCC's top management in and after September 2011 remained unexplained. Tunisian journalists, shocked at the treatment of executive general manager Bouneb, attributed it to a dispute within the ruling family, involving QF head Sheikha Moza, wife of the then ruler Sheikh Hamad, and the offspring of another of Sheikh Hamad's wives.[55] Whatever the trigger, it marked a watershed not only in the JCC ethos and business model but also for its workforce. In contrast to ample anglophone trade press coverage of JCC's new deals with foreign content suppliers, very little emerged in public about the fate of expatriate Arab professionals, or even independent

UK producers and consultants, who had worked to build up JCC over the previous six or seven years.[56] When Bouneb came to his office on 20 September with news of Khanfar's departure as Director General of the Al-Jazeera Network, it apparently prompted his Moroccan wife, Malika Alouane, JCC Director of Programmes, to wonder out loud when it would be their 'turn to be dismissed'.[57] Their turn came a few days later, just as they were about to attend MIPJunior, the international market for children's shows, in Cannes on 1–2 October 2011. Bouneb, Alouane, Cost Control Manager Haitham Qudaih (a Palestinian) and several other non-Qatari members of staff were fired from JCC but denied visas to exit the country, which – under Qatar's *kafala* employment sponsorship system[58] – expatriate staff employed by Qataris require for any foreign travel. In all, up to 30 JCC senior managers were laid off in that round of departures and, on 5 October, Qatar's public prosecutor threatened to sue Bouneb and seven others for mismanagement.[59]

A second round of terminations of non-Qatari staff took place on 3 December 2011, after which some reportedly faced a prolonged and confusing sequence of denied exit permits, cancelled residency permits and financial uncertainty, whereas sacked colleagues with Australian, Belgian and French nationality were allowed to leave Qatar before the end of the month.[60] With further sackings after that, some former JCC employees estimate that a total of 120–180 staff members quit the organization. All freelance contracts ceased. JCC co-production partners received emails stating that their projects would not proceed because they did not 'meet or comply with JCC's artistic vision and strategic production plans for the future'.[61] Co-production of a series called *Discover Science* with Japan's public service broadcaster NHK was halted, leaving NHK to link up with other partners in Germany, South Korea and South Africa for subsequent seasons.

JCC's incoming Qatari managers refused to comment on the change in personnel. Formal charges of financial mismanagement, relating to a sum of QR3.1 million (US$851,500) over eight years, were eventually filed against Bouneb, Alouane and Qudaih in December 2012, by which time two separate investigations by the Qatar National Audit Bureau and auditors Ernst and Young had both concluded that there were no grounds for criminal prosecutions.[62] In November 2014, with no verdict reached, a Qatari court announced that it would widen the scope of investigation by asking a Qatar Media Corporation committee of three people to review 3,000 hours of programming to assess whether JCC funds had been 'over-spent' during Bouneb's term in office.[63] Eventually, in March 2015, the charges were dropped, in return for which Bouneb undertook not to speak negatively of Al-Jazeera or QF.[64]

The Evolving Brand Identities of JCC Channels

Although JCCTV's rebranding as Jeem TV in 2013 was accorded high visibility, the work of building up brand identities for the JCC project had actually started many years earlier. An account of successive phases of the branding process can help to shed light on developing aspirations and expectations behind the channels at various points in their evolution. The consultants and designers include Fitch Middle East, part of a multinational operation, UK-based companies Radiant and Kids Industries, and Netherlands-based Tarik Atrissi Design.

Fitch, acquired by multinational marketing communications company WPP in 2003, is a retail and brand consultancy with studios across the globe, from Seattle and Atlanta to Singapore and Beijing. Fitch's Doha studio, its first in the Middle East, started out in 2004 in the Qatar branch of Virginia Commonwealth University (VCU) through a collaboration with Qatar Foundation that the company's public relations material described as 'unique'. VCU-Qatar was the first American university in QF's Education City, offering degrees in Communication Arts and Design, Fashion Design and Merchandizing, and Interior Design. Fitch worked jointly with VCU-Q at QF's invitation to design and brand the Doha Asian Games in 2006.[65] By 2011, as testified in a promotional video featuring QF's director of Human Resources, Fitch was considered 'an important part of Qatar Foundation',[66] a status that reflected the extent of its work not only for QF institutions but also for other Qatari bodies such as the Supreme Council of Health, Katara cultural village, Qatar Football Association and others. Speaking on the video, Fitch Middle East's Managing Director at the time situated Fitch at the heart of local brand developments, stating that it was helping the 'brands of the region to emerge and to succeed'.[67]

In light of the Doha Asian Games 'potential TV footprint of 1.5bn people', highlighted by Fitch's London Client Director,[68] and the array of design needs for uniforms, merchandizing, marketing and digital communications arising from the games, the company's role places it squarely in the promotional screen industries. From its vantage point within QF, Fitch was well placed to brand QF's media initiatives, including the televized Doha Debates and JCC, launched in 2004 and 2005 respectively. By its own account, the company's preoccupation with JCC was twofold: to develop a brand that would interact with the target age group by being 'relevant in the marketplace' and to establish a 'new brand language' that would reflect JCC's 'edutainment mission', designed to encourage interest in science, health, technology, sports and culture.[69] But the branding team could not compete with the opportunities for building brand recognition available to major US content providers for children. Nickelodeon, for example, could benefit from the range of distribution platforms and consumer goods managed by other Viacom subsidiaries, thereby putting itself 'on the radar' as a 'fun place to be' in a way smaller operators could not emulate.[70] Instead, the Al-Jazeera mark was kept as part of the JCC logo to establish a connection with the Al-Jazeera network, while, according to Fitch's website account of the project, the JCC brand language used brightly coloured paint splashes, with 'fun shapes and cut-outs'.[71] These were not dissimilar to the orange splatter – or 'splat' – logo associated with Nickelodeon from the mid-1980s to around 2009.

The Al-Jazeera mark was decidedly not present in the logo for the pre-school channel Baraem, which was spun off from JCC in 2009. Few people know for sure whether Bouneb was hoping to drop the Al-Jazeera link altogether at some point; certainly Bouneb himself was still convinced in June 2011 that rebranding of JCCTV was 'not up for discussion'.[72] The Baraem branding contract was assigned, in 2007, to a UK company, Radiant Studios. Radiant was asked to handle the entire process for Baraem and to refresh the branding of JCCTV in readiness for its separation from pre-school content. The London-based company had previously entered the Al-Jazeera orbit by being involved with the launch of Al-Jazeera English in 2006, and its senior staff had experience with other big clients in the spheres of both media and sport. For its work on Baraem, Radiant was not called upon, as branding consultants sometimes are, to help articulate brand values, because JCC management had already defined these.[73] Instead the company collaborated day to day with JCC managers responsible for strategy, marketing and design. The vision, as Radiant executives understood it, was for Baraem to be a pan-Arab channel with global distribution, no overt attachment to Qatar and a colour palette that would stand out in its own right by avoiding the distinctive orange of Nickelodeon and green of MBC3.[74] In order to inject on-screen movement into the 'buds' featured in the channel's name, Radiant turned them into birds and butterflies to produce an identity package of logo, character design, broadcast idents, set design and promotional material. It initiated the channel website and, even though pre-schoolers are not expected to read text on screen, it recommended that JCC should commission a new Arabic font.[75] As a result, Nadia Chahine, an award-winning typographer specializing in Arabic fonts for Linotype, designed a font bearing the name Baraem, clear enough for young children but still 'embedded within the tradition of Arabic calligraphy'.[76]

Radiant Studios returned to refresh the Baraem brand after it had been established for two years, which meant there was no need for further input as part of the overhaul of JCCTV's image in 2012–2013. The new post-2011 JCC managers anyway did not approach Radiant for the latter task. Instead, it seems a number of companies contributed, in line with a practice noted by several Western expatriates working for Qatari institutions, whereby foreign contractors are played off against each other and non-Qatari employees of those institutions avoid being linked too closely with something that a Qatari boss particularly dislikes. In what seems to have been a fairly typical experience, a company hired to do a job in the mid-2000s discovered that the same job had been spread across three separate agencies in different countries, with no clarity as to who was running what. The risk of this approach for Qatar is that it may have the effect of diminishing the sense of ownership and accountability felt by non-Qatari agencies. The risk for agencies is that their fees are paid late, or only in part, or not at all.[77] Qatar had already earned notoriety in the construction industry by 2013 for its alleged 'culture of non-payment' of architects' and consultants' fees.[78]

One of the figures involved in the 2012–2013 rebranding exercise that produced Jeem TV was Lebanese-Dutch designer Tarik Atrissi, who set up his studio in the Netherlands in 2000 and had a track record with the Qatar Tourism Authority for having created a visual identity for Qatar. Atrissi blogged about his role in Jeem TV in April 2013, saying that he had been involved right from the 'brainstorming phase' to find the channel's new name, 'all the way to fully designing the logo of the new brand' as well as custom-made bilingual Latin and Arabic typefaces.[79] In the blog, Atrissi gave credit to two UK-based companies, Jump Design and Kids Industries, for work on motion graphics and market research respectively. Kids Industries had already been contracted to do marketing work on Baraem. But, in Kids Industries' approach to the business, marketing is an all-embracing term. Describing its offer to clients, Kids Industries declares that 'effectiveness' requires integration of 'brand insight, strategy and content', and integration 'is what we do'.[80] Thus it is hard to narrow down the company's precise role on either Baraem or Jeem TV; for example, within JCC there was a perceived link between Kids Industries and a UK coaching and consultancy practice called The Creative Garden, which says it promotes creative thinking in broadcasting and new media through workshops, mentoring and strategy forums.[81]

On its website, Kids Industries lists strategy and content as the two areas in which it assisted Jeem TV.[82] It says the JCC leadership team had decided it was time to respond to Arab children's 'adoption of the digital age' and provide them with 'better content, and a stronger experience'. Director Gary Pope says he felt privileged, given his background as a schoolteacher, to be given the opportunity to 'help an entire culture to learn about itself, to move forward, to improve education'.[83] His company compiled a limited-edition glossy oversized hardback book documenting the birth of Jeem TV, through the original brand wheel and experiments with characters, moods, humour and ways of interacting with the logo. They opted for colours like orange and turquoise, deemed sophisticated and gender-neutral, taking care to reference shapes and forms from Qatari culture and to include allusions to football in anticipation of the 2022 World Cup; there is a 'lot of national identity and national pride that comes through in their direction to us', Pope said.[84]

The rebranding process was followed through with live launch events at malls in Egypt, Saudi Arabia, Morocco and the UAE in March 2013 that required considerable and sometimes challenging levels of coordination with JCC offices in Doha. Alongside high-profile acquisitions from Disney and the BBC, Jeem TV also announced that it had developed new in-house shows: a five-minute newscast, a technology programme called

Shashatech ('Screen Tech', which in Arabic also means 'Your Screen'), and *Noun*, a programme said to be for 'girls and families' to 'get the chance to explore new ideas'.[85] The puppet and magazine show *Anbar* was revamped. Kids Industries helped with ideas for the new locally made Arabic content in the expectation that this material would eventually start to replace the imports that had suddenly been boosted as part of the rebranding. The proposed strategy was to use Disney content for a short period to recruit audiences and retain them, allowing JCC meanwhile to build up indigenous content.

Conclusion

In light of Qatar's early experiments in branding the nation and its institutions, it was to be expected that JCC channels would be the subject of branding projects from the time that Al-Jazeera Children's Channel was launched in 2005. But the evidence reviewed here indicates that the attention paid to branding within JCC intensified in stages over time, reaching a peak with the development and launch of Jeem TV, and that the underlying brand values also shifted decisively at that same moment. Interpretations as to how they shifted depend on whether management rhetoric is privileged over narratives of those involved at various stages in the branding process, or vice versa. On one hand senior executives said they were pitching to re-establish a position with pan-Arab audiences and to meet the needs of children as early adopters of new technology. The JCC press release announcing that the company would co-sponsor the Big Entertainment Show in Dubai in 2013 highlighted the importance of 'Arabic content and offerings' that support the 'values and culture of Arab families across the MENA region'.[86] On the other, in parallel with its heavy emphasis on content imported from Disney and the BBC, and its move away from educational content or any explicit reference to a link with Al-Jazeera, Jeem TV seemed to place declining emphasis on Arab culture and a growing, albeit subtle and indirect, stress on closer identification with Qatar and its relationship with the global economy. Such ambivalence between pan-Arab ambitions and national identity was not out of keeping with broad but relatively undefined objectives for investment in cultural leadership outlined in the Qatar National Development Strategy released in 2011.

A certain lack of coherence between brand rhetoric and reality is not surprising in view of the number of different non-Arab players engaged to help with all aspects of branding JCC ventures, a phenomenon accentuated by the middle-management roles played by risk-averse Arab expatriates in Qatari institutions such as JCC. These players' profiles make it unsafe to attribute critical decisions about branding, brand values and cultural leadership to strategy emanating directly from Qatari ruling family. Although Qatari state institutions are linked to the ruler's power base, and plans for JCC can in theory be traced to wider elements of the Qatari government's foreign and fiscal policies, it is hard to discern coherence because, although expatriate employees and foreign consultants may be paid to advise on strategy and implementation, this does not mean their advice is taken. As demonstrated so forcefully by the abrupt removal of so many expatriate staff from JCC in 2011–2012, transparency and continuity have been lacking in this children's media project, undermining the chance of establishing brand coherence.

Instead, following observations by Mattern, Aronczyk and others on the depoliticization that goes with nation branding, it could be said that JCC's interest in rebranding Jeem TV was a matter of form and image more than editorial substance. To that extent its beneficiaries were the executives who made the decisions and won the contracts rather than the children at whom Jeem TV was aimed. The effort that went into creating an image for Jeem TV, through a logo, typefaces, idents, set design and so on, was not matched by any burst of spending on creating the levels of Arabic-language content that had been envisaged when JCC first came on the scene.

Notes

1 Research for this chapter was conducted as part of a project funded by the UK's Arts and Humanities Research Council (see the Acknowledgements section of this volume).

2 Stephen Brook, 'Al-Jazeera is world's fifth top brand', *Guardian*, 1 February 2005.

3 Doha News Team, 'Official: JCC to leave Qatar Foundation for Al-Jazeera', *Doha News*, 15 June 2013.

4   According to Mahmoud Bouneb, first JCC Executive General Manager, inter-viewed by *The Channel*, 2, 2009, p. 15.

5   *Jeem* is the name of the first letter of the Arabic word *jazeera*, which literally means 'island' but can refer to the Arabian Peninsula.

6   Quoted by Louise Duffy in 'JCC reveals organisational restructure, launches Jeem TV', *RapidTVNews*, 2 April 2013.

7   Catherine Johnson and Paul Grainge, 'From broadcast design to "On-Brand TV": Repositioning expertise in the promotional screen industries', in M. Banks, B. Conor and V. Mayer (eds), *Production Studies: The Sequel!* (Abdingdon: Routledge, 2016), pp. 46–47.

8   Nando Malmelin and Johanna Moisander, 'Brands and branding in media management: Toward a research agenda', *International Journal on Media Management* 16/1, 2014, pp. 10, 16–18.

9   Melissa Aronczyk, *Branding the Nation: The Global Business of National Identity* (New York: Oxford University Press, 2013), p 4.

10 Nadia Kaneva, 'Nation branding: Toward an agenda for critical research', *International Journal of Communication* 5 (2011), pp. 119, 122, 128.

11 Kaneva, 'Nation branding', pp. 128, 132.

12 Göran Bolin and Per Ståhlberg, 'Mediating the nation state: Agency and the media in nation-branding campaigns', *International Journal of Communication* 9 (2015), p. 3077.

13 Mehran Kamrava, *Qatar: Small State, Big Politics* (Ithaca, NY: Cornell University Press, 2013), pp. 91–92.

14 Kamrava, *Qatar*, pp. 90, 92.

15 Tamar Lewin, 'In oil-rich Mideast, shades of the Ivy League', *New York Times*, 11 February 2008.

16 http://www.atrissi.com/qatar-nation-branding/.

17 Quoted by Derek Baldwin in 'Vice-President urges public to take part in UAE National Logo selection', *Gulf News*, 24 June 2012.

18 Aronczyk, *Branding the Nation*, p. 16.

19 Miriam Cooke, *Tribal Modern: Branding New Nations in the Arab Gulf* (Oakland, CA: University of California Press, 2014), pp. 13, 80–84

20 Aronczyk, *Branding the Nation*, p. 17.

21 Shannon Mattern, 'Font of a nation: Creating a national graphic identity for Qatar', *Public Culture* 20/3, 2008, p. 481.

22 Mattern, 'Font of a nation', pp. 481 and 494.

23 The Qatar-specific rewording is shown in the 'Questionnaire' section of the study at http://menamediasurvey.northwestern.edu/#. The statement that Qatar Statistics Authority asked for the changes is made by Charles Rollet in 'In Doha, a climate of fear', *The Northwestern Chronicle*, 14 February 2014, http://www.nuchronicle.com/in-doha-a-climate-of-fear/. Rollet sources his statement from an early version of the report.

24 See p. 26 of 'Questionnaire', as above.

25 Cindy L. White and Elizabeth Hall Preston, 'The spaces of children's programming', *Critical Studies in Media Communication* 22/3, 2005, p. 240.

26 White and Preston, 'The spaces of children's programming', p. 240.

27 White and Preston, 'The spaces of children's programming', pp. 247–248.

28 For example, Lina Khatib, *Qatar and the Recalibration of Power in the Gulf* (Beirut: Carnegie Middle East Center, 2014), p. 3.

29 The text of Obama's speech during a US visit by the Emir was contained in a White House press release, 14 April 2011.

30 Rosemarie Said Zahlan, *The Making of the Modern Gulf States* (London: Unwin Hyman, 1989), p. 87.

31 Kristian Coates Ulrichsen, *Qatar and the Arab Spring* (London: C. Hurst & Co, 2014), p. 171.

32 Ulrichsen, *Qatar*, p. 175.

33 International Monetary Fund, *Qatar: Staff Report for the 2011 Article IV Consultation* (Washington: IMF, 2012), p. 26.

34 http://english.alarabiya.net/articles/2012/05/29/217311.html.

35 Qatar General Secretariat for Development Planning, *Qatar National Development Strategy 2011–16: Toward Qatar National Vision 2030* (Doha: Qatar General Secretariat for Development Planning, 2011), p iii.

36 *Qatar National Development Strategy*, p. 268.

37 *Qatar National Development Strategy*, pp. 209–210, p. 205.

38 *Qatar National Development Strategy*, p. 209.

39 Mark Mulligan and Roger Blitz, 'Barcelona agrees €170 sponsorship contract', *Financial Times*, 10 December 2010.

40 David Conn, 'How Qatar became a football force: from Barcelona to PSG and World Cup, *Guardian*, 18 November 2013.

41 Quoted by Shabina Khatri, 'Sheikha Moza appoints new president to Qatar Foundation', *Doha News*, 24 September 2013.

42 *Qatar Foundation Telegraph*, 102/9 January 2014, p. 1.

43 http://www.arabianbusiness.com/gcc-ministers-instruct-regional-media-support-qatar-2022-tournament-595716.html.

44 Qatar Foundation, *Annual Report 2011–12* (Doha: QF, 2013), p. 213.

45 QF, *Annual Report 2011–12*, pp. 213 and 214

46 QF, *Annual Report 2011–12*, pp. 213 and 214

47 QF, *Annual Report 2011–12*, pp. 213 and 214

48 Naomi Sakr, *Arab Television Today* (London: I.B.Tauris, 2007), p. 155.

49 Kate Hahn, 'Arab network reaches out to next generation', *Variety*, 22 September 2009, http://variety.com/2009/tv/news/arab-network-reaches-out-to-next-generation-1118008981/.

50 David Lepeska, 'How Al Jazeera Children's Channel grew up', *The National*, 8 January 2010.

51 Interviewed by Sakr, Dubai, 18 November 2013.
52 Nick Vivarelli, 'Disney content to air on Al-Jazeera kids' channel', *Variety*, 11 March 2013, http://variety.com/2013/tv/news/disney-content-to-air-on-al-jazeera-kids-channel-1200006822/.
53 According to Acting Executive General Manager Saad Al Hudaifi interviewed by Sakr, Dubai 18 November, 2013.
54 Al Hudaifi, interviewed by Sakr.
55 AFP, 'Manifestation pour la libération d'un candidat aux élections retenu au Qatar', 9 October 2014, http://www.huffpostmaghreb.com/2014/10/09/tunisie-mahmoud-bouneb-qatar_n_5959398.html.
56 See Naomi Sakr and Jeanette Steemers, 'Co-producing content for pan-Arab children's TV: State, business and the workplace', in V. Mayer, B. Conor and M. Banks (eds), *Production Studies: The Sequel!* (Abingdon: Routledge, 2016), pp. 238–250.
57 Recollection of a former JCC employee interviewed by Sakr in Doha on 23 November 2013.
58 The system has been challenged by the International Labour Organisation and human rights bodies.
59 DigitalTVEurope, 'Jazeera dismisses kid's channel chief and senior staff', 11 November 2011, http://www.digitaltveurope.net/17567/al-jazeera-dismisses-kids-channel-chief-and-senior-staff/ (accessed 25 November 2011).
60 Recollections of a former JCC employee interviewed by Sakr and Steemers, Kuala Lumpur, 10 September 2014.
61 DigitalTVEurope, 'Jazeera dismisses kid's channel chief'.
62 Human Rights Watch, 'Qatar: Abolish exit visas for migrant workers', 30 May 2013, http://www.hrw.org/news/2013/05/30/qatar-abolish-exit-visas-migrant-workers (accessed 28 June 2014).
63 Peter Kovessy and Riham Sheble, 'Qatar Media to review 3,000 hours of programming as JCC trial continues', *Doha News*, 26 November 2014.
64 Riham Sheble and Peter Kovessy, 'Charges against JCC executives officially dropped in Qatar court', *Doha News*, 12 March 2015.
65 VCU press release, Richmond VA, 9 May 2004.
66 https://www.youtube.com/watch?feature=player_embedded&v=xj2m5WOZTLI.
67 https://www.youtube.com/watch?feature=player_embedded&v=xj2m5WOZTLI.
68 Anthony Ryman interviewed by Charlie Jackson, 24 July 2007, http://anthonyryman.blogspot.co.uk/2007/07/country-branding-qatar-interview.html (accessed 4 January 2015).
69 Fitch webpage headed 'Delivering fun and education to the Arab child'. Available at http://www.fitch.com/case-study/a-state-of-the-art-pan-arab-edutainment-channel/ (accessed 4 January 2015).
70 Kevin S. Sandler, '"A kid's gotta do what a kid's gotta do": Branding the Nickelodeon experience', in Heather Hendershot, *Nickelodeon Nation* (New York: New York University Press, 2004), pp. 55, 64.

71 Fitch, 'Delivering fun and education'.
72 Conversation with Sakr, Doha, 22 June 2011.
73 According to Radiant sources, interviewed by Steemers and Sakr, London, 2 March 2015.
74 Radiant sources, London, 2 March 2015.
75 Radiant sources, London, 2 March 2015.
76 See the item entitled 'Baraem' in the German design magazine *Novum*, September 2009, p. 52.
77 Sakr and Steemers conducted off-the-record interviews with consultants and companies whose names are not mentioned in this article. One respondent, interviewed jointly in London on 15 September 2015, reported non-payment by JCC over a period of three years.
78 Construction Week staff, 'Qatar's culture of "non-payment" has to change', *Construction Week Online*, 6 January 2013.
79 Tarek Atrissi, 'Logo and typography design for Jeem TV; the new branding for Al Jazeera Children Channel', 23 April 2013, http://blog.atrissi.com/logo-and-typography-design-for-jeem-tv-the-new-branding-for-al-jazeera-children-channel/ (accessed 17 June 2013).
80 http://www.kidsindustries.com/ (accessed 3 February 2016).
81 Sakr's interview with former JCC employee, Doha, 23 November 2013.
82 http://www.kidsindustries.com/our-work/case-studies/jeemtv (accessed 3 February 2016).
83 Interviewed by Steemers and Sakr, London, 13 February 2015.
84 Gary Pope interview, 13 February 2015.
85 JCC press release, Doha, 28 March 2013.
86 JCC press release, Doha, 17 July 2013.

6

A Channel for Every Child

Exploring a Parallel Arab Children's Television Universe

Tarek Atia

Although the vibrancy of Egyptian media only captured the world's attention in 2011 after the January 25 Revolution, the media landscape in Egypt had actually been experiencing rapid growth and diversification since the mid-2000s. More newspapers, websites and satellite TV channels were emerging in Egypt just as the digital revolution was acting as a catalyst for media fragmentation and change worldwide. It could be argued that, in the aftermath of January 2011, Egyptian online media outlets expanded exponentially in a process that has continued to provide a rich, if noisy, spectrum of options for young and old media consumers alike. At the same time children and young people were becoming increasingly active participants in this outpouring of media activity. They created all types of content, including accounts of how the revolutionary events were affecting them, while simultaneously exploring and benefiting from all the new digital tools that were making expression and media production easier and more accessible. This lively and, for the most part, unstructured outpouring of media production spanned the spectrum of subjects and styles, from imitations of foreign formats to home-grown and popular political satirical programmes and animations.

It was about time. There is plenty of evidence to show that children's participation in the media production process was traditionally rather limited in Egypt. When government authorities reported to the Committee on the Rights of the Child in Geneva on their efforts in 2001–2008 to comply with the Convention on the Rights of the Child (CRC), their report highlighted the slow process of raising awareness of children's rights in Egyptian society and the need for a 'shift in attitudes'.[1] The report had nothing at all to say about children's freedom of expression, referring only to Article 17 of the CRC on access to appropriate information, and state efforts to provide books and libraries for children and media content aimed at children.[2] Responding, the Committee noted a direct link between the physical and mental health of children and adolescents and their need to impart and receive information. It recommended in particular that Egypt should enforce Article 3(c) of the country's own Child Law of 2008 concerning children's right to freedom of expression and urged the authorities to 'encourage children's active involvement in the media', thereby consolidating their 'position in society' as holders of rights.[3] The Committee said it remained 'seriously concerned' that the practical application of children's right to be heard had not been systematically integrated into the development of public policies and programmes, and called for schools and other educational institutions to be given sufficient resources to 'equip children with the skills and opportunities to express themselves freely'.[4] Perhaps unbeknownst to either the Committee, or Egyptian officials, technology was already opening spaces for children to express themselves in ways never previously imagined.

If, as indicated by the CRC's feedback, Egypt was lagging behind in terms of children's free expression, one of the main reasons may lie in longstanding patriarchal traditions that tend not to encourage children's curiosity, independent thinking or creativity, either at home or at school. Yet not only was that paradigm in stark contrast to the natural inclination of children everywhere to create and express themselves, it was also directly antagonistic to the overall opening up that was under way in Egypt in 2011, facilitated by growing ease of access to global content. When Arabic content for children online proved wanting, as, for example, in the limited subject matter and production values of a channel like Tuyur al-Jannah, available via YouTube as well as satellite, Egyptian children were naturally keen to find alternatives, including by creating content of their own. Perhaps inevitably, the results were sometimes controversial, as the examples discussed in this chapter will show. The controversy, however, stemmed more from structural and environmental factors than the children themselves.

Screen Time, Creativity and Corporate Commerce

Many people lament the dynamics that govern contemporary childhood in a modern, technologically advanced world. A popular meme that has circled the internet over and over testifies to this angst. It features two photos: one, showing children playing wildly in a park, is captioned 'This is Childhood'; the other, showing children sitting indoors, each one staring into a different screen to access games, music, telephony and so on, bears the caption 'This is Shit'. Variations on the theme are well established. Images circulate of a family together at the dinner table all staring at screens. Cartoons contrast the supposed activities of children in a pre-digital era with the alleged passivity of children entertaining themselves with a digital device. It is a characteristic of every generation that adults worry that children today are not experiencing childhood as the previous generation did, or that they are spoiled and lazy. On one hand online access gives today's children and young people a wide choice of entertainment at the touch of a button: from music to movies to video games and books, all either downloaded or embedded in their devices or just a simple internet connection away. On the other, it must be questionable that this makes them lazy, or represents a lesser quality of 'life experience'. Evidence suggests that the digital revolution has opened up unprecedented opportunities for children and young people to create their own entertainment, their own content and their own media, to express themselves in a different way and with perhaps more possibilities than any other generation before them. To take advantage of these opportunities is the opposite of being lazy or spoiled. Children in the vanguard of this trend spend a great deal of their time working hard to create media that their contemporaries, nationally and internationally, will want to watch and enjoy. As the boundaries between consumers and creators of media become increasingly blurred, the process of creating media will become as simple as consuming it for anyone, even the youngest child.[5]

Age thresholds for children's use of digital technology are lowered every day, as toddlers insist on experimenting with smart phones and tablets, and adults stop resisting, seeing the gadgets as learning tools, fun activities and effective babysitters. Parents see a benefit in giving cell phones to small children, for ease of two-way communication if not surveillance. Ownership of a desktop or laptop computer is widely seen as an essential part of school life. The spread of digital devices may not translate directly into children creating their own media, but it does mean a huge increase in the potential to do so. A baby monitor that connects a newborn in Paris with a parent attending a meeting in London, or parents' desire to share an infant's every milestone with friends on Facebook – practices like these offer a window onto the ubiquity of being televised and imply a likely multiplier effect in the years ahead in terms of the norms of content creation. With that in mind it behoves researchers to consider potentially ethically suspect scenarios whereby children who create audio-visual content are enticed into a world of adult commerce. This chapter, in looking at some pioneers of video made and shared by children and at the ecosystem emerging around them, highlights the way corporate interests have co-opted the phenomenon in ways that also seem certain to increase. Inevitably, in capturing a moment in time, the study describes people who have since moved on to new platforms and new experiments and companies that have since disappeared. But the focus is on the phenomenon of children and young people creating online content and the economic, political and social ramifications of that activity.

Wayne's World in Egypt

Children are naturally curious and in recent years manufacturers of software and games for children have incorporated that curiosity into online activities that seem to have worldwide appeal. Arab children, like their counterparts in Asia, Europe or North America, enjoy immersive online gaming technologies like *Poptropica*, *Club Penguin* and *DragonFable*. These three examples, although different in their specific approach, all share a particular combination of characteristics: a virtual world or community, where participants can make their own virtual spaces, or populate them with friends, purchase supplies and compete for virtual prizes. The main goal is achievement: performing an action and getting rewarded for it with elements essential to succeeding inside the game. Games like these serve as a rapid-fire introduction to the media creation and sharing concept that is such an integral part of the way everybody uses digital technologies. In this way they are the building blocks upon which children who go on to create their own content could be said to cut their 'virtual teeth'.

From *Poptropica* and the like, children tend to graduate into *Minecraft*, a highly immersive game where players build entire worlds and populate them with characters and adventures. This and the other games mentioned above usually involve children meeting each other's virtual characters and interacting or competing with them in closed digital worlds. For some children, the experience does not stop there. As they get older, there is an impetus to broadcast their game-playing experiences to a wider audience, mostly made up of other children. Indeed, gaming videos have proved to be one of the most popular genres in which children create their own content on YouTube and other digital platforms. As we shall see, in 2015 it was the most popular and lucrative of all types of content creation by children in the Arab world. But it was far from the only form of video-based digital self-expression gaining traction in the region.

It is here that the opening to adult commerce can best be explained by reference to the 1992 Hollywood comic hit movie *Wayne's World*. Although released a year before the first internet browser, and predating by at least 13 years the outpouring of individual home-grown talent appearing on YouTube and other new media platforms, *Wayne's World* presented a scenario in which two 20-somethings, Wayne and Garth, produce their own TV show in Wayne's basement and broadcast it on public access cable TV. In many countries public access TV provides space for independent entities and ordinary citizens to produce and broadcast their own shows, however idiosyncratic. Egypt, however, has no tradition of public access or independent non-commercial broadcast production. In Egypt, therefore, the digital revolution actually skipped right over what would elsewhere have been a natural evolution in the distribution of non-commercial content; it unleashed a great number of hidden talents that had no previous public outlet and gave them access to smaller screens, on computers, tablets and mobile phones.

There are hundreds, if not thousands, of children in the Arab world who are currently creating their own video content online. For various reasons it is impossible to count accurately how many. They are not all using the same platform and there is no easy way to search for content creators by age group. Children in particular will often become very active at creating and uploading videos but then move on to other passions and delete what they made, or switch to one of the new platforms that are constantly emerging. What is possible, however, through conversations with young people who are part of this phenomenon, as well as adults within the emerging ecosystem that is monitoring and sometimes exploiting it, is to paint a clearer picture of its scope and depth.

The speed with which the phenomenon took hold in Egypt was highlighted by a popular mainstream TV series broadcast during Ramadan 2015. An entire episode of *Lahfa* ('Yearning'), starring Donia Samir Ghanem, was dedicated to the idea of young people becoming famous for videos they produced for YouTube. Two years earlier, in contrast, children who had begun creating videos and even entire channels on YouTube were still a limited group of first-movers. At that point many of the social media platforms that have since emerged and become popular for such video creation had not yet been invented, or had not yet achieved the critical mass or popularity they have now. However, through many years of work in digital media development and because I had access to young teenagers aged 12–14 years old, who were close to my family, I came into contact with a group of people who were beginning a new trend in Egypt: teenagers starting their own YouTube channels. I supplemented my study of this activity by interviewing individuals who worked for YouTube in the Middle East.

Being, myself, a journalist at the cutting edge of this field, it seems almost natural that my son would travel down the same road, and end up being a pioneer of these new forms of expression. Fourteen years old in 2013, Omar had been creating videos since he was 12 and established two YouTube channels. Clearly influenced by the big budget ecosystem of Hollywood style video, Omar called his first channel OmarAtiaProductions. On it, he uploaded a series of homemade skits involving himself or friends and family, as well as early attempts at exhibiting professional video editing techniques. For instance, *Geek Bullet* was a short film about an angry reaction to a child's playing ball, filmed from multiple perspectives and featuring editing techniques mimicking cinema. Another well edited short piece was a skateboard race between a boy and a tiny plastic army man toy. Again the highlight for an adult observer was the use of interesting camera angles and fast-paced editing. His other channel, called TheSuperTahrir, with the tagline 'Political cartoons and animations', carried Omar Tarek's own cartoon version of the Harlem Shake video, in his case featuring unpopular politicians. The video demonstrated Omar's familiarity with the global YouTube scene, in which similar Harlem Shake videos, using a 2012 song, had been uploaded in a viral trend around the world.

The satirical element continued after 2013. At the time of writing, two years later, the channel carried several satirical videos about Egypt's deposed president Mohamed Morsi, who pursued the interests of the subsequently banned Muslim Brotherhood. It is clear that Omar's video experiments reflect the moment, both nationally and in his own life. Immediately after January 2011 he was influenced by an outpouring of political expression and a general shift away from previously held taboos regarding criticism of political leaders. In 2015 he would often produce in bursts, uploading several short works, and then later taking them down. This may be because, as he says, he created the channels as a test to see how YouTube worked. It allowed him to understand the practicalities of online video content creation tools like editing, annotations and tags, all of which are important for anyone wanting to grow their audience on YouTube or other social networks. 'It was summer and I was bored', he says of the experience. Back at school in the fall, it became clear that he was not the only one experimenting. His friends started talking about the channels they had created, or had come across. These included both video blogs and gamer channels. It also emerged that a professional production company had approached some of these young people and begun offering official YouTube partnerships with its promise of potential revenue generation – something the children were unable to attain on their own.

The Promise of Making Money

Baraka One Web was an attempt by a producer of traditional television series in Egypt to tap into this emerging field. As a digital marketing agency, linked to a production company, it dangled the offer of a YouTube partnership in front of the young video creators, which also promised to unlock additional technical features like the creation of a marketing banner for the channels and custom thumbnails. These features later became available to everybody with a YouTube channel, and not just the larger production companies, which in turn meant that individuals no longer had to be part of a network to begin earning revenues from YouTube. That is why other content creation platforms would later begin eclipsing YouTube as venues for children creating content, because they simplified things that were too complicated on YouTube. These would include platforms such as Vine, Dubsmash, Snapchat, Instagram, Facebook, Periscope and a bevy of other now ubiquitous social media platforms that diversified and simplified the entire process by allowing users to record directly onto the platform, or even to live stream. Despite constant changes in the field, YouTube had hitherto required videos to be created using standard broadcast tools like editing suites and professional cameras and graphic effects before being uploaded onto the platform.

Back in 2012 and 2013, in the face of these complications, many of the children creating content jumped at the opportunity to become part of what Baraka One Web was offering. The production company began hosting offline events, like gaming tournaments, as a way of creating a community and bringing in additional revenue. The teenage content creators were charged a fee to attend the event, which they had to attend to benefit from the networking opportunity and become eligible to win a prize or obtain technical and other support from a real production company. Everything on offer seemed like a dream come true. When the video creators met and compared notes they were able to exchange information about production details and hardware and software preferences, but also how much money they were actually making and might hope to make.

Following the Baraka One Web lead, other production companies started getting into the game. One was BIG productions, the same company that produced the very popular show *Al-Bernameg* ('The Programme'), starring former cardiac surgeon turned political satirist Bassem Youssef, widely known as the Arab world's John Stewart. *Al-Bernameg* and Bassem Youssef were the biggest thing ever to have happened to independent content creators in the Arab world. From a YouTube show produced in his home, which gained 5 million views in three months, to the most popular

TV show in the Arab world generating millions in advertising revenue and attracting a weekly audience of some 30 million viewers, Youssef's rise was well documented by the global media. His success in political satire caused so much adverse pressure on him and the channel airing his material that he decided to quit in mid-2014. But his relevance to the young people starting to create their own media can never be overstated.

BIG, having brought a YouTube creator into the broadcast television mainstream, sought to leverage its credibility to replicate the process with others who were exhibiting talent on YouTube. This included children. Various events were held to spread the word. Although this may have been the first high-level business foray into the field, others then emerged, including the same group of people who worked with Bassem Youssef before he went off the air. Although he is older than the teenage creators discussed here, Youssef's widespread and rapid success has served as an inspiration to young content creators in the Middle East. His daring satire, often mixing sexual innuendo with harsh political commentary and song-and-dance routines, has been widely imitated.

It is easy to see why early adopters of the video creation trend were eager to partner with larger entities. One of my teenage respondents explained: 'There are a lot of people trying to make videos or entire YouTube channels, but many fail because they do not have the proper equipment – sound, lighting, quality of camera, creative ability, script-writing, marketing, advertising'. These are precisely the areas where the production companies sought to add value. For example, in 2014 an Egyptian teenager, who called himself Joe Kabbo, started making standard gaming videos and posting them on his own YouTube channel. He then saw the mistakes and faulty elements of others like him who were making poor quality videos. Inspired by the example of Bassem Youssef's *Al-Bernameg*, which makes fun of news and talk shows, Kabbo decided to make a web series where he would make fun of the gaming community. He joked about their production values, choice of games and ability to keep their audiences interested.

Kabbo started by using a computer webcam with no editing, talking about the faults in the gamer videos. In two days, his video had around 2,000 views. Seeing how much it angered the community, Kabbo apparently wanted to step up his initiative by working harder on the script and the quality of the show. He recruited a team of volunteer editors and cameramen and three months later was approached by BIG, the producers of Bassem Youssef's show. With this partnership the show became even higher quality in terms of the camera being used, the sound quality, the set and the editing. But Kabbo's story is not typical. A closer look at the progression of some of the early adopters in Egypt reveals varying levels of failure and success. In 2013, young Egyptian YouTuber Mokey uploaded 85 videos to his channel, which had 361 subscribers and a total of 19,542 views. Two years later he had 1,963 subscribers, 131,736 views, and had uploaded 229 videos. Mokey at that point was creating two types of videos: comments on games, and attempts at video blogs. Some of these were just the young man filming himself chatting to the camera while on vacation, or discussing some aspect of teenage life.

Mokey was constantly experimenting. One day he would talk about a new rule on a popular video game and go out into the street to interview people about it, including people who know nothing about the game, just to get a laugh or two. He would video random jokey conversations with people around him, including his family's driver. His style, confident and quirky, may or may not have served him well, being unfamiliar to some viewers. But Mokey became part of the global Maker Studios network, through which he began making revenue of somewhere between $14–$110 per month, according to Social Blade, a website that ranks and provides key data on the popularity and potential revenue of YouTube channels. However, because he was operating in the grey zone of copyright laws on YouTube, he soon found himself violating those laws by posting too much copyrighted content and had his channel removed by YouTube. On his new channel he explained how he started getting community guideline strikes because his old videos were full of copyrighted material. The new channel, called Moketeke, was established in December 2014, and within just over half a year had managed to get 4,954 subscribers and 270,885 views on 37 videos. It was clear from his experimental camera angles, enhanced editing techniques and attempts to insert comedy and audience interaction into the videos (which are still within the genres of gaming and video blogging) that Mokey was trying hard to be 'discovered', become famous, make lots of money and maybe become the next Bassem Youssef.

There was no knowing in 2015 whether Mokey would find the technical assistance he was clearly seeking, or get bored and move on to something else. In the meantime he opted to collaborate with some of the other early adopters, including Omar Tarek, with a division of labour among Mokey, the natural performer and Omar, the talented cameraman and editor. Together they were able to make videos of higher and higher quality.

Other young Egyptian YouTube early adopters include X the Pie, whose name is inspired by the most popular YouTube gamer in the world, Felix Kjellberg, known on YouTube as PewDiePie. PewDiePie had gained 33 million subscribers by the start of 2015 and made $7.4 million in 2014.[6] His Egyptian namesake, X the Pie, was reportedly making $9–$71 per month from Baraka One in 2015, having produced 227 videos (mostly gaming videos) that had garnered 3,949 subscribers and 277,000 views.[7] The first Egyptian girl to become prominent in this field, EgyGirlGamer, had 1,418 subscribers and over 25,000 views on 40 videos.[8] She started making comedy videos in 2013 but moved into gaming videos in late 2014. EgyGirlGamer has collaborated with others, like the sound engineer on Kabbo's Egyptian gaming parodies, and conducted interviews with another creator called Flamce00. Flamce00 has nearly 8,000 subscribers, 627,000 views[9] and is part of a big global network called BroadbandTV.

However, the Egyptian community turns out to be far smaller than its Saudi Arabian counterpart in the genre of gaming video creation, even though Egypt's total population at 85 million is nearly three times as big as the Saudi population of 31 million. There is an eager audience in Saudi Arabia for children and teenagers producing both gaming videos and 'unboxing' videos. The latter constitute a particular YouTube genre, featuring the unwrapping on camera of gadgets, toys and other items. Already well established in 2013, unboxing of toys proved especially popular with children, apparently as a way of knowing more about a toy but also often as a vicarious source of pleasure for children with no other access to the toys shown.[10] In affluent Saudi Arabia the YouTube traffic levels have been so significant that some of the children and teenagers who have proved most popular have been commissioned by big multinational game makers to make videos. Not only is the Saudi market attractive to multinationals, in terms of the numbers of people with high purchasing power, but the closed nature of the society also plays a part; with few other forms of activity and entertainment for young people, online video of gaming and unboxing fills a gap. One Saudi Minecraft video maker, named d7oomy_999, has over 1 million views on his videos.[11] As audience interests become even more specialized, the genre has expanded to include a video creator named z-pad on a network called Sekai, discussing anime and manga.[12]

The speed at which these trends become commercialized remains tied to market needs. Every day a new player enters the field and new genres and creators emerge. One is Shehab Abu El Fadl, a 13-year-old from Cairo who started a channel called Technowhiz2000 in October 2013, his launch video entitled 'Unboxing: Samsung Galaxy Note 3'.[13] He produced videos at a rate of around one a month, mainly in the unboxing genre, featuring technology items such as smart phones and describing them in a helpful and informative manner. Over the first four months Shehab convinced a friend to help improve his introduction, with the result that by the time of the fourth video he was achieving a more professional look. As a presenter in his early teens, he had a friendly style, but clearly needed advice on editing. His videos received hundreds of views and several comments, but he did not continue uploading, thereby demonstrating how children can be passionate or experimental in this field for a while but then get bored or frustrated or move on to something else.

In all of these cases, what was happening in the Middle East paralleled trends elsewhere in the world, except that it was happening just a little later. For example, YouTube carried the popular series *Kids React* and *Teens react* for years before the idea was copied in the Middle East in 2014. The series of short videos stars ordinary children, albeit telegenic or personable ones, who are filmed as they watch videos on YouTube and react to them. A young documentary filmmaker tried the very simple format for an emerging website called 'dotmasr' ('masr' means 'Egypt') but did not continue.

As these series indicate, there are infinite possibilities for children watching other children on YouTube, limited only by the video creators' imaginations. Practical constraints remain, however, not least in the form of legal risks. In 2013, three teenagers, aged 14–15 years, were detained by police in the Moroccan town of Nador and threatened with five-year prison sentences for posting pictures of a couple kissing on Facebook. They were eventually acquitted. But in 2015 four Egyptians aged 16–17 years were convicted of contempt for religion for making a sarcastic video about so-called Islamic State. Several adults have been jailed in the UAE for their use of social media; examples include the case of a 30-year-old American, Shezanne Cassim, and several friends, who made a satirical video about teenagers in the Dubai district of Satwa and uploaded it to YouTube. Cassim, brought up in Dubai and well aware of local customs,[14] was arrested in April 2013 and charged with various offences under the UAE's cybercrimes law, including violation of Article 28, which imposes jail sentences and a fine of up to UAE Dh 1 million ($272,000) for using information technology to publish caricatures that are 'liable to endanger state security and its higher interests or infringe on public order'. The video was posted one month before the law came into effect,[15] but Cassim spent nine months in jail. According to a BBC account, he was eventually released just a few days before a high-profile BBC interview in January 2014 between Jon Sopel and the ruler of Dubai and Prime Minister of the UAE, Sheikh Mohammed bin Rashed al Maktoum.[16] In that interview, Maktoum admitted that mistakes had been made. Yet the episode demonstrated that the space for free expression for young people in the Middle East, even in the realm of comedy, is still insecure.

Format Variations

In 2015, as creating content became ever easier, the phenomenon of video creation accelerated but the formats changed. With YouTube, it was all about creating something that looked like or at least mimicked broadcast. Hence, for example, gaming videos follow the style of traditional sporting commentaries. On newer platforms, in contrast, content creation is more confined to the properties of the platform. For example, creators on Vine are limited to a very short format for their content. This has not prevented young stars from emerging, including Shady Sorour, a talented and funny Egyptian who started creating short comedic videos when he was 16–17 years old. By late 2015 he was one of the kings of Egyptian video creation who were independent and not linked to a corporation. He managed to bring his short videos over and reformat them to YouTube, thereby beginning to significantly monetize his efforts.

A typical Sorour video would involve the young comedian playing the parts of a teenager, his mother, his father, and it usually involved very quick edits of manic reactions like the mother hitting him with a flip-flop, the father just sitting around watching television and the teenager singing and dancing in his room to pop songs. He sometimes juxtaposes different ways girls in the West and girls in Egypt may react to certain situations, such as dating or a friend being sad. The videos have to be seen to be appreciated and the viewer will usually experience an instant reaction of either love or hate for Sorour's kinetic wild style of physical comedy.

However, the fact that Sorour, and most of the other serious creators, do seem to be seeking out fame and fortune brings us to a crucial question: Is it business or is it just fun? It seems to be the intersection between creative expression by children and the elastic mix of fun and business that deserves further investigation. Motives and mediums will continue to blur in cases like this. For many of these child content creators, the aim was to be famous or make money. But according to Haitham Yehia, who was head of Google's YouTube product for Egypt and the Middle East for several years, children are creating content primarily as a form of free expression, using Western tools but with original formats.[17] He believes that, for children, YouTube has become the TV, since that is what they are watching. But because YouTube is more complicated than newer platforms when it comes to creating content, children have started moving their avenues for creative expression to the more nimble and simple platforms like Dubsmash, a karaoke-like tool for video creation that allows young people to imitate famous scenes from songs, movies and TV shows. Other platforms like Vine, Snapchat, Keek and Ask FM have also became increasingly popular. It is much easier to create and upload content on those platforms than YouTube, which accounts for their popularity with young age groups. Today's children want content creation and distribution tools that have to be available while they are on the move.

Haitham Yehia left Google to work with a start-up called Meem, focusing on discovering talent online, but trying to do so without making the same mistakes attributed to Tube Star Network, which tried to improve on YouTuber's experiments by formalizing them. In some cases this process eliminated what made the videos so interesting in the first place. Meem sees trying to reformat successful YouTube content for broadcast television as a 'dangerous game', because of the need to give raw creative talent free rein.[18]

Conclusion

It seemed likely at the time of writing that some of the children identified in this chapter would be future stars, or behind-the-scenes talent, of the media and entertainment industries. At the time they were experimenting, they were possibly unaware that they were exercising their right to free expression. Several of them told me they were doing it just for fun. But those who may have occasionally ventured into political satire, or annoyed someone in another way, risked learning the hard way that there are limits to freedom of expression online – especially in the Middle East. In Egypt, for example, controversy soon surrounded an application called Dubsmash, which allowed the content creator to take a well-known scene from a television series, movie or song and dub their own take of it. When Dubsmash took Egyptian children by storm, adult heads were soon shaking disapprovingly at the idea of children acting out potentially suggestive adult scenes.

Such reactions raise the question of how the authorities behind any future clampdown would seek to justify their action as being in children's best interests. Long-standing cultural norms are changing in society as a whole, which makes it harder to use the notion of tradition as a basis for censorship. The more such content is produced, and the easier distribution becomes, the more the sheer volume will impede efforts to detect alleged breaches or offences, especially given the very limited audience for so much of what is uploaded. Any attention drawn to something reaching only a few hundred people could rapidly turn the few hundred into a few thousand or more, as the content 'goes viral'.

It may be that the growing opportunities for young people to create their own content will at least improve Egypt's chances of avoiding criticism from the CRC Treaty Body similar to that received in 2011. Combined with efforts by government, civil society and corporations to incentivize, enhance and spread tools in educational institutions, cultural centres and youth camps, digital expression will almost certainly grow and unleash creative talents of all kinds from even the youngest children. Meanwhile, as discussed here, that growth will be met by societal rejection, authoritarian responses, commercialization and exploitation. Indeed, the more governments clamp down, the more children are likely to use these new tools as one of their few outlets for free expression. And when children are arrested for Facebook posts, they are likely to grow up thinking they want to emigrate to freer climates. Ethical questions will come to the fore, but the phenomenon will also provide unprecedented insights into what children and young people are interested in. Keep your eyes on the screen.

Notes

1 Egypt, *Third and Fourth Periodic Reports*, submitted under Article 44 of the CRC, UN, 4 September 2010, p. 12.

2 Egypt, *Third and Fourth Periodic Reports*, p. 33.

3 Committee on the Rights of the Child, *Concluding Observations: Egypt*, UN, 15 July 2011, p. 11.

4 Committee on the Rights of the Child, *Concluding Observations: Egypt*, UN, 15 July 2011, pp. 9–10.

5 For more on the issues raised in this paragraph, see the London School of Economics website *Parenting for a Digital Future* at http://blogs.lse.ac.uk/parenting4digitalfuture/.

6 Reece Ristau, 'PewDiePie: No. 1 in #Famechangers Digital Star Ranking', *Variety*, 22 July 2015.

7 http://socialblade.com/youtube/.

8 http://socialblade.com/youtube/c/egygirlgamer.

9 http://socialblade.com/youtube/user/flamce00.

10 Heather Kelly, 'The bizarre, lucrative world of "unboxing" videos', *CNN*, 13 February 2014, http://edition.cnn.com/2014/02/13/tech/web/youtube-unboxing-videos/.

11 http://socialblade.com/youtube/search/d7oomy_999.

12 For example, http://z-pad.net/sekai/anime-discussion-04/.

13 https://plus.google.com/108437037971675097663/posts.

14 See Cassim's own account of 9 February 2014 on *The Guardian*'s website, http://www.theguardian.com/commentisfree/2014/feb/09/shezanne-cassim-jail-uae-youtube-video.

15 Jillian York, 'US citizen charged under UAE cybercrime decree', *Electronic Frontier Foundation*, 2 December 2013 https://www.eff.org/en-gb/deeplinks/2013/12/us-citizen-charged-under-uae-cybercrime-decree.

16 Jonathan Frewin, 'Jailed US YouTuber seeks UAE pardon', *BBC News*, 17 July 2015 http://www.bbc.co.uk/news/33551338.

17 Interviewed by the author, Cairo, 17 February 2014.

18 Haitham Yehia, Interview.

7

Gender, Music Videos and Arab Youth

The Curious Case of *Mini Studio*

Kirsten Pike and Joe F. Khalil[1]

From the beginning of the 1990s, children in the Arab world typically have grown up in front of a screen. In the 1990s, 'screen media' almost always meant state-owned television. Today, screen media have evolved to be regional, international, multilingual, digital, interactive and increasingly responsive to commercial imperatives. If state-owned television channels dedicated limited hours for children's programming with specific ideological and/or educational objectives, channels today offer more children's programmes, in more languages, from more places and serve a myriad of goals. This increase in quantity of television programmes for children does not necessarily mean better quality. As each Arab generation emerges, time spent with screen media increases, but pervasiveness, quantity and time are just part of the story. The main story is content, beginning with cultural messages, representations, beliefs and behavioural models. As Arab media move into commercially oriented practices (sponsorship, product placement, ratings and so on), it becomes important to discern possible outcomes of the merging of media and commercial interests and their impact on the construction of gendered identities.

Television programmers and advertisers have a keen interest in understanding how screen exposure affects children's behaviour, and they have conducted numerous studies on the topic. However, the outcome of this research remains largely inaccessible to the academic community and the public at large.[2] At the same time, children's television in the Arab world continues to advance rapidly, making it challenging for scholars to keep pace with changing programme offerings, viewing habits and parenting strategies. One point is perfectly clear: screen media (including television, DVDs and online sources) are becoming the everyday experience of most children in the Arab world and this pattern, increasingly, is being controlled by commercial interests outside the purview of regulatory control.[3]

In this chapter, we focus on representations of gender and consumerism in a Lebanese magazine/variety children's television programme, *Mini Studio*, and consider how the show socializes children to gender and consumer norms. For more than 20 years, this programme has been at the forefront of integrating cultural and technological trends, and responding to advertising interests while achieving local and regional success. For many in the television and advertising industry, *Mini Studio* is held as an example of low-cost production, popular appeal and commercial success. For others, the show is representative of an encroaching commercialization of children's media.

In a culture increasingly defined and experienced through media, we recognize the increased drive towards marketization, through advertising and product placement, as an additional layer in children's gender socialization. We then ask: What does the balancing of local and global traditions and trends mean for the ways that gender is imagined and mapped on *Mini Studio*? Specifically, how are girls and girlhood represented on the show, especially in the show's music videos? How do these representations compare to *Mini Studio*'s representations of youthful masculinity? And what do these representations reveal about the ideological, cultural and commercial politics of gender in an unregulated and increasingly commercialized children's television industry in the Arab world? Grappling with such questions is fundamental to our understanding of the intricate and perhaps transformative aspects of Arab children's media in the 21st century. This chapter examines the show from two different perspectives: political economy and critical discourse analysis. It seeks to understand the various ways gendered identities, particularly those of girlhood, are constructed.

The Political Economy of a Long-Running Programme

Mini Studio is a daily half-hour children's show that includes a mix of musical numbers and commercials, entertainment and pro-social messages. A veteran female presenter of the show described it as 'an institution. It is much larger than the people involved in it. It has no permanent stars, no permanent characters, no permanent audience … It is constantly evolving and adapting'.[4] It debuted on Murr Television (MTV) in Lebanon in 1992 and began circulating throughout the Arab world on MTV in the late 1990s.[5] In 2002, *Mini Studio* moved to the Lebanese Broadcasting Corporation (LBC) where it was re-branded as *Kids Power*, but returned to MTV in 2012, where it continues to air throughout the Middle East.[6] While it has gone through various stages of development over the years, *Mini Studio* currently features a regular cast of characters and performers (princesses, a prince, costumed animals, hosts, singers and dancers) and includes audience participation from local children who attend recordings of the show. A female creative on the show suggests that 'it is a unique programme … it's like a magazine or a voyage into the children's world … we try to have everything they like: music, dance, storytelling, cartoons, information, games, etc'.[7]

Typical episodes include some or all of the following: in-house music videos, on-stage song and dance numbers by performers, clips from popular transnational media (especially youth-oriented music videos from the West), entertainment skits, storytelling, advertisements, branded content, pop culture news and games. Some episodes also showcase talented local children, including those who sing, dance or play musical instruments. The show is shot in studio with a live audience attending some segments. Location shooting is mostly restricted to reports and clips.

A significant factor in the development and evolution of any children's media relates to its funding model. A programme such as *Mini Studio* is a complex business that must be sustained economically; otherwise, it finds itself lacking a television platform. Throughout its 20-plus years, the financial and business model that funds *Mini Studio* has been consistent in playing off market forces (television stations and advertisers) and a public hungry for children's programmes. The model remained relatively stable throughout the 1990s. The brainchild of radio and television producer/ presenter Ghazi Feghali, *Mini Studio* secured MTV as its platform and became the channel's exclusive children's programme. The show was originally built around two main female characters, Kikki and Sam, with several other guest characters. At its inception, the show introduced theatrics to children's programmes. Whether through costumes, sets or music, the *Mini Studio* team (soon branded as La Grande Famille – the big family) invited children into its studios, making them members of the *Mini Studio* Club. Taking its cues from Disney and French children's icons (such as Chantal Goya), *Mini Studio* bonded well with its audience, inviting them to special events and the weekly filming of the show. Shot out of sequence and then compiled in editing, the show minimized its production costs as sequences were repeated (such as the show's music videos) or spread over several episodes (storytelling). As a result, the show was often referred to as *Mini Market* in advertising circles. It worked in sync with various below-the-line activities, meaning that it promoted products without necessarily using traditional spot advertising.

In addition to managing production costs and increasing advertising opportunities, maximizing non-television-related revenues is also crucial for producers and staff. The show's popularity paved the way for several ancillary operations that include (but are not restricted to) theatrical plays, event animation and sales of DVDs and music CDs. According to various individuals involved with *Mini Studio*, these activities support the design and manufacturing of *Mini Studio* characters' wardrobe, the construction of sets and purchase of props and also provide additional income for many of the show's staff. These activities are managed and often operate separately from the show but under the 'franchise' of *Mini Studio*. Because the various synergetic practices of *Mini Studio* are so pervasive in Lebanese children's daily lives, they naturally warrant critical examination.

An initial concern is the show's persistent reliance on easily accessible freelance staff. As one veteran female staffer explained, 'It was all about who is available and who is willing to be on air.'[8] Of course, some talent was sought and often maintained, such as the two main presenters, Kikki and Sam; the latter left the show for a period and then came back. Because of its longevity, many of the current team grew up watching the show and some were even part of the show at a very young age. For example Youmna, the executive producer's niece, was featured in the show's music videos as a toddler and continued throughout her teens. As the show's business model developed, the ancillary operations gained importance in helping to spot talent and provide additional income for the show's large talent pool, which is estimated at around 20 people. One of the current male presenters explained that he 'grew up watching the show … I dreamt of being part of it … I feel like I was part of the show before even working here … now I get to do what I want and get paid for it … not much though; it's like a hobby.'[9] While this attitude might explain the high turnover in the show's talent pool, it also demonstrates *Mini Studio*'s success in building a community that appeals to both children and adults.

A second area of concern relates to policy and regulation. Lebanese government policies regarding children's media are virtually absent, and there is little evidence of wanting to improve the media experiences of youth or children. The Audiovisual Media Law of 1994, for instance, requires commercial broadcasters in Lebanon to provide adequate programming for children without clearly stipulating number of hours or origin of material, or taking any supervisory role.[10] Furthermore, this law does not limit the amount or nature of advertising that can be placed during children's television programmes. Although there has been considerable press and religious pressure to control exposure to obscene content, religiously insensitive speech or any acts that encourage 'vice', the matter of what advertising content and quantity is appropriate during children's programming has yet to be addressed in any serious way. One reason for this is that the Lebanese government and other Arab media organizations are reluctant to create restrictive media policies. Another is the absence of coordination among various concerned groups. A third is the widespread reluctance to continue financing children's programmes; this reluctance has been an ongoing issue, with few parties wanting to pay for quality content. To fill this funding gap, commercial television channels backed by deep advertising pockets are increasingly stepping up to claim a growing, attentive audience whose parents are willing to forgo their concerns about advertising content rather than search for an alternative, if available.

Gender Socialization

Gender socialization refers to the process by which cultural norms and expectations for males and females are passed along to children.[11] Traditionally, children learned gender roles through observation of males and females in their families, and later from friends, peers and community members. The transformation of Arab families from extended to nuclear families, alongside changes in economic welfare, impacts of migration and the introduction of cheaper technologies, have pushed media, particularly television, into a newly prominent role in gender socialization. Arab children today are familiarized with gender roles as soon as they are old enough to sit in front of a screen. As a result, children are exposed to gender norms and expectations that may or may not be like those available in their own families or immediate social circles. With satellite television in particular, Arab children are exposed to American, European (particularly French and British), Indian, Japanese and other characters featured in cartoons and children's variety shows. Arab children's increased exposure to programming coming from Arab countries other than their own is particularly interesting. Whether such programmes are based in the Gulf, the Levant or Egypt, children interface with an array of different dialects, terms and cultural practices. The underlying concern is that media's worldview is a distortion of reality and often disconnected from children's local linguistic and cultural experiences.

For *Mini Studio*, this reality is often seen as being designed for a specifically Lebanese, multilingual, middle-class target audience. In fact, the female presenter mentioned above suggests that 'our audience is mostly girls, especially pre-teens ... they tend to follow us faithfully and some of them became mothers and now their children are watching the show.'[12] As a gendered institution, *Mini Studio* has somehow maintained a nostalgic appeal for its 1990s viewers who in turn are introducing their children to the show. On a par with family and school, *Mini Studio* becomes an easily trusted edutainment institution. It reflects Lebanon's cultural diversity, colonial history and connectedness to global youth cultures by featuring songs in English, French and Arabic. In fact, many of the show's in-house music videos include songs with verses sung in all three languages – a move that not only validates the importance of Lebanon's multilingual heritage but also offers Arab children diverse cultural entry points into the show.[13] As one of the show's male presenters admitted, 'Language is very important to us ... We talk to them as adults, as mature people ... We also use a language that everybody can understand ... We do not shy from using foreign languages because this is how children speak.'[14]

While *Mini Studio* tries to impart values deemed important in (or for) Arab culture, including healthy living, reading and respect for parents and elders, it also aims to appeal to children who are receptive to Western youth cultures, trends and production techniques. Thus the show typically combines local messages with more global entertainment-oriented ones, such as Western celebrity gossip and clips from transnational media, especially music videos, movies and/or TV shows produced in the US, Canada and Europe (although popular videos from other regions, such as Asia, are also occasionally showcased). As several scholars of Arab media have noted, the balancing of local and global forms in Arab entertainment media has an array of economic, social and political motivations – from the potential for increased profits to cultural innovation through new ideas and expressions of identity, including more open displays of female sexuality.[15] In fact, *Mini Studio*'s audience is not restricted to Lebanon. It extends to the Lebanese diaspora, particularly in North America, Europe, Africa and the Gulf region. The producers realize their programme's appeal to parents and children in these countries and see *Mini Studio* as a way to connect the diaspora, which is also ready to invest in theatre tickets, events, DVDs and CDs, with the home country.

However, there was an immediate tension between the show's interest in appealing to broader demographics than the Lebanese audience and its ability to address that audience. In the process of appealing to Arab audiences, Lebanese essentialism – whether in language, dress or mannerism – had to be altered. The show's move to LBC required a revamping of the show and a change of name. Renaming it *Kids Power* was also to avoid legal battles over the copyrights of *Mini Studio*. In addition to Arabic, English became the show's lingua franca. A female creative on the show explained: 'We had to change because our audience lived then in Arab countries where English is the main and sometimes the only language other than Arabic.'[16] At the same time, the producers see the show as depicting a wide variety of roles for and attributes of girls and boys, women and men, as witnessed in the 'real world'. However narrow this reflection of reality may be, the producers see it as expanding the gendered aspirations and expectations of male and female youth. Producers cite how kids are invited to the show to display and share their talents. From martial arts to musical performances, children are featured regularly as 'role models' for others to follow.

Because of the significance of music and music videos in youth culture and the crucial role they play in socializing young people to gender norms,[17] music-oriented programming provides fertile ground for exploring the gendered politics of Arab children's television. And while there are several music-oriented children's programmes in the Middle East, *Mini Studio* offers a particularly useful case study within this genre. Not only does it circulate broadly in the region and strike a chord with pre-teens, but its efforts to target both girls and boys enables a comparative exploration of the show's gendered messages. Furthermore, given the prominent role of women and girls on the show, a close analysis of *Mini Studio* can help to fill what American scholar Ilana Nash has referred to as a 'girl-shaped gap' in cultural and historical research on female youth in popular culture.[18] This gap is arguably even larger when it comes to scholarship on media representations of girls in the Arab world, although recent studies are beginning to address the topic. One such work is a collection edited by Maya Götz and Dafna Lemish under the title *Sexy Girls, Heroes and Funny Losers: Gender Representations in Children's TV around the World*, which includes children's TV shows from Syria and Egypt in its sample of global programming.[19]

Representations of Gender and Consumerism on *Mini Studio*

In some ways, *Mini Studio* projects an image of a harmonious world where Lebanese girls and boys coexist on an ostensibly even playing field, an image largely disconnected from their future as adults.[20] For instance, the show regularly features both female and male adult hosts (for example, Kikki and Elie), and girls and boys appear in seemingly equal numbers as audience members, game contestants and talent performers. The show also celebrates girlhood fun, friendship and solidarity through segments starring girls, including Karen, a young teen who leads other girls in dance routines, and the 'princesses' – a troupe of female performers in their late teens and early twenties who sing, dance and act together in sketches. Although girls appear more regularly than boys in group dances, boys do perform in some numbers, importantly situating dance as an activity open to and enjoyed by both male and female youth. The show also highlights youthful masculinity in sketches involving male performers (for example, François and 'Prince' Philippe), and boys and girls are both positioned as powerful players in global consumer culture through product place-ments and advertising (a point to which we will return). Thus *Mini Studio* attempts not only to validate both girlhood and boyhood experiences, but, through the show's strong female presence, also refreshingly challenges the dominance of male characters in children's programming.[21]

However, while girls are highly visible on *Mini Studio* and some rep-resentations seem to hint at gender parity, closer inspection of the series reveals an array of gender stereotypes and contradictions. To begin, it is useful to compare the design of children's leisure spaces on the set. The space for girls is called the 'Princesses' Room'. The vividly pink room, which is where the princesses go to chat and perform sketches, prominently fea-tures a make-up table with a heart-shaped mirror surrounded by lights – a prop that tellingly places girls' surveillance of themselves at the heart of princess-themed 'fun'. In contrast, *Mini Studio*'s blue, red and yellow 'Boys' Room' boasts a large map of the world and two flat-screen TVs. Not only does this decor convey a more masculine sensibility, but it also suggests that boys like to survey the outside world (unlike girls, who presumably prefer to scrutinize themselves). It seems as if gender socializing of young boys and girls focuses on the assumption that males work outside while females stay at home in their sacred sphere, the domicile. Somewhat paradoxically, the 'Boys' Room' label suggests a more open gendered space, given that it would seem to be for anyone who is male. However, because the room for girls is named for 'princesses', many other kinds of girls – from athletes and tomboys to brainy girls and bug collectors – would appear to be left out of the show's vision of feminine fun.

As we might guess from their girly pink digs, the 'princesses' – including Jessica, Youmna, Vanessa, Chloe and Tatiana – are hyper-feminized. What is more surprising, perhaps, is that they tend to fluctuate uncomfortably between a sexualized and infantilized performance of youthful femininity.

Take, for instance, a music video featuring the girls singing and dancing to the English-language children's song 'A-B-C' in the episode that aired on 15 September 2013. As is customary on the show, the princesses (all of whom conform to feminine ideals of slimness and beauty) wear extremely girlish attire, including short ruffled skirts, fingerless gloves and sparkly accessories, from vests and jewellery to giant hair bows and tiaras. While the girls' cutesy facial expressions seem designed to convey childhood innocence, their pulsating moves and womanly features – accentuated through tight tank tops, high heels, voluminous hair and made-up faces – point to a sexiness that belies their girlish performance. What is more, each girl dances in her own life-sized and individually name-branded Barbie doll box (complete with a punch hole tab on top that makes it look like a real consumer product ready to be hung on a store rack); packaged as hyper-feminine dolls who are visually and metaphorically 'boxed in,' the show reifies their status as objects to be looked at and consumed while implying that, as play things, they should not be taken too seriously. Thus, even though the 'A-B-C' song aims to teach tots the English alphabet, its educational bent is overpowered here, as the lyrics seem secondary to the video's production of hyper-feminine spectacle.[22]

Other techniques utilized in the 'A-B-C' video, including medium close-ups of bouncing upper bodies, low angle shots that highlight the girls' legs and long shots that depict enormous plumes of smoke bursting between the girls as they dance, are oddly reminiscent of male rock videos from the 1980s in which scantily clad women were part of larger on-stage spectacles aimed at creating visual pleasure for (predominantly) male onlookers.[23] To this end, 'A-B-C' taps into a broader historical pattern in music videos that 'capitaliz[es] on [women's] sexuality while insinuating that a woman's worth is based ... on her physical appearance and sexual appeal.'[24] As young mothers who have grown up in the 1980s and 1990s are watching along with their children, these videos could be appeasing an older generation of parents for whom such images are already normalized.

The princesses' performance in 'A-B-C', when considered alongside the video's elaborate set design and visual effects, suggests that glamorous displays of hyper-femininity are not just desirable, but attainable, especially given that each girl plays the part of a consumer doll who replicates ideals of feminine beauty. If performers such as Jessica, Youmna, Vanessa, Chloe and Tatiana can be like Barbie, the show implies that by extension young Arab girls can be like her too. Indeed, this point is made clear when local girls appear on stage in skimpy costumes to celebrate their birthdays with great fanfare, such as when a tiny 10-year-old shimmies in a barely-there belly shirt (similar to that worn by Rio de Janeiro Barbie) during a Rio-themed rendition of the 'Happy Birthday' song, as confetti cascades down on her from above.[25]

The message is also apparent and further reinforced through advertisements and product placements for Barbie dolls and accessories produced by Mattel. In *Mini Studio*'s 15 November 2012 'comeback episode', which marked the show's return to MTV, producers treated viewers to a flashy advertisement for Barbie Fashionista dolls and clothing, which cheerfully promoted glitzy, consumer-oriented activities for girls, such as 'walk[ing] that runway' and 'shopping with … friends' for fancy clothes. Afterward, the female hosts Ghinwa and Manal, seated at a pastel pink table brimming with beautifully attired blonde Barbies, demonstrate how to use Mattel's fashion design kit to make a stylish, micro-mini dress for Barbie. The hosts' two-minute pitch goes beyond mere demonstration when they encourage viewers to make and photograph their own Barbie dresses, and then mail the photos to *Mini Studio* for a chance to appear on the show and 'win a really nice prize from Barbie'.[26]

While the Barbie promo is but one of many touted on the show, it offers a powerful indication of how gendered ideologies endorsed by the princesses are parlayed into lifestyle lessons that encourage girls not only to shop and consume, but also to cultivate the ideals of Western, heteronormative (and here, largely white) feminine beauty.[27] This pattern not only demonstrates how 'children's television is a partner with other industries in perpetuating an unattainable beauty model, particularly for girls', but also how this 'mostly young, thin, attractive, heterosexual, wealthy, and predominantly White' model of femininity bolsters Western beauty norms.[28] Indeed, just as Ghinwa and Manal encourage children to create trendy Western clothes for Barbie, the female voiceover in the ad implores girls to 'see what happens when you're a Barbie … fashionista', thus blurring the distinction between playing with Barbie and cultivating the kind of femininity that she endorses. Furthermore, by advocating Barbie play and framing Arab girls' playtime through the alluring lens of local celebrity and prizes, *Mini*

Studio's hosts position consumerism and fame as attractive modes of girl-oriented citizenship.[29] In the process, they give remarkable local validation to the globally circulated tagline in the 'Fashionista' ad: 'You're always a star wherever you are … wow!' – the final word exclaimed just as a dazzlingly bedecked blonde Barbie spins to face the camera for her final glamour shot (and consumer appeal). This practice of promoting heteronormative, largely white, feminine beauty and affluence ties in with an advertising industry that imagines its audience based on specific socio-economic and 'ethnic' markers, thus further socializing children to see these as the norm.

Interestingly, evidence of *Mini Studio's* success in marketing glamorous femininity, fashion and 'fame' to local girls can be found in a photo album labelled 'Birthday Celebration at *Mini Studio* CLUB House', which is posted on the show's Facebook page.[30] The album depicts an 8-year-old Arab girl's lavish makeover as part of her birthday party at *Mini Studio*. In line with the princesses' on-screen portrayals, the child's transformation (along with several pals) into heavy make-up, shimmery party frocks and ornate accessories culminates in an on-stage fashion show complete with a cat-walk and smoke and lighting effects similar to those used for the princesses in their music videos, albeit on a smaller scale. Additionally, the accessories modelled by the birthday girl appear to be the very ones donned by the princesses in their videos, including a sparkly blue vest like the one worn by Vanessa in 'A-B-C' and an enormous rainbow-colored hair bow like Youmna's in 'And We Said'. Thus, the birthday photos – which many children are likely to have seen, considering the hosts' constant appeals for them to visit their Facebook page – demonstrate how discourses promoted on the show are intertwined with Arab girls' real-life cultural and consumer experiences. They also suggest that even if local female youth fail to win a contest sponsored by the show, they can still have their girly day in the limelight by getting their parents to pay for a makeover party at home with the *Mini Studio* team.

Perhaps unsurprisingly, *Mini Studio's* male performers, including Elie, Philippe and François, are not overtly sexualized in their actions or costuming, unlike the princesses.[31] This gendered difference brings to mind Cara Wallis's finding that in contemporary music videos, 'the message given by and about women … seems to be that sexually suggestive behaviour is normal and appropriate for women but not necessarily for men.'[32]

This is not to suggest that male characters should be sexualized, nor to suggest that girls should be denied a sexual identity on children's television, but rather to highlight the show's narrow and uneven construction of gendered power. The celebration of sexiness and glamour for girls over other traits not only flattens female diversity in the Arab world (the programme does not feature women or girls who wear the hijab, for instance), but it also encourages young viewers to see beauty, consumerism and sex appeal as fundamental elements of female empowerment – thereby camouflaging how 'the discourse of the sexy little girl ... enacts the unequal power relations of the gender order'.[33] Even though the princesses' flirty performances would likely be considered tame compared to the sexually charged portrayals of women in today's adult-oriented music videos, they nevertheless underscore the boundaries that both frame and constrain youthful femininity on *Mini Studio*.

Mapping the Show's Local and Global Discourses of Femininity

What are the cultural and industrial forces that have helped shape this hyper-feminine and mildly provocative brand of youthful femininity on *Mini Studio*? Perhaps it goes without saying that sexualized images of women have long been used in Western music videos to pique audience interest and sell records, while critiques of sexual representations continue to inform scholarly work on the genre.[34] In recent years, erotic portrayals of Arab women have also become widespread in Arabic-language music videos – a pattern that intensified after the introduction of satellite channels to the region in the 1990s and the subsequent rise of local music television channels and videos as well as imports of international programmes on Arab channels.[35] Given the conservatism of many Arab societies, especially with regard to female sexuality, public morality and religion, music videos featuring sexually provocative Arab women have been highly controversial, prompting intense debates among cultural, religious and government authorities as well as citizens in the region and scholars of Arab media.[36]

Despite their critics, Arab female artists such as Nancy Ajram and Haifa Wehbe have achieved tremendous popularity and commercial success in the region. Writing in 2010, Elisabeth Cestor pinpointed Lebanese female artists, including Ajram, Wehbe and Elissa, as 'the role models for the new generation of Arab pop singers'.[37] Although this would seem to suggest a loosening of boundaries regarding 'acceptable' representations of Arab women in popular culture in the Middle East, it is important to note that Lebanon is also known for being more liberal and tolerant than other Arab countries, especially those in the Gulf region. According to Cestor, 'Sexually provocative behavior can most easily be introduced by Lebanese women' because Lebanon is 'less conservative' and has 'good relationships with the west'.[38] Lebanese female pop singers continue to have supporters and detractors, but their videos have undeniably touched a cultural nerve, in the process becoming a crucial site for the contestation and negotiation of gender politics in contemporary Arab culture.

While the princesses' sexy appearance on *Mini Studio* coincides with recent music video images of Arab women 'swaying provocatively and erotically to the tunes of Arabic songs',[39] it also dovetails with trends in postfeminist Western media culture, including the hyper-sexualization of girls in children's animated shows such as *Bratz* and *Winx*,[40] and Hollywood's fascination with 'womanly girls and girlish women' in films such as *13 Going on 30* and *Enchanted*.[41] Music videos on *Mini Studio* thus highlight how images of Arab female youth are bound up with hegemonic, patriarchal patterns of gender representation that – in an era marked by neoliberalism, global capitalism, cultural hybridity and consumerism – seem to defy local, national and regional boundaries. What is especially interesting about *Mini Studio*'s blending of local and global forms with regard to gender and national identity is that the show relies heavily on music video clips from the West to kick off episodes (presumably to attract viewers) but does not appear to air commercial Arab music videos from the Middle East during this or any other of the show's segments.

In the category of music videos, then, Arab female youth appear primarily, if not exclusively, in *Mini Studio*'s in-house productions, whereas young artists from the West dominate the commercial videos presented in the show's opening minutes. *Mini Studio* frequently features American female performers such as Selena Gomez, Miley Cyrus and Zendaya, as well as Canadian singer Justin Bieber (who is signed to an American record label) and boy bands like One Direction from the UK. The choice to showcase commercially successful non-Arab music videos, rather than Arab ones produced in the Middle East, is arguably driven by various social, cultural and economic factors. These may be assumed to include a desire to avoid public controversies that hit too close to home (namely, the firestorm surrounding provocative Arab female performers), the profit opportunities afforded by international stars, the cultural cachet that comes from being hip to global trends and a marketing strategy that positions *Mini Studio*'s own performers as the sole Arab 'stars' on the show. Several discussions with the creative team illuminated another dimension: logistics. Arabic pop videos are promoted by large companies with competing agendas, and the video release and airing is still relatively controlled. Still, the near absence of commercially successful Arab artists on *Mini Studio* leaves an unfortunate void; by not exposing children to the body of talent, diversity and innovation in Arab pop music clips, the show helps solidify the dominance and seeming spectacularity of Western music stars, products and trends on children's TV in the Arab world.

To provide an idea of the national breakdown of Arab and non-Arab media featured in the opening minutes of *Mini Studio*, we examined the 29 episodes that aired in March 2014, which are available for viewing on the show's website.[42] The male Lebanese presenter, Elie, hosted each opening segment, which typically ran four to five minutes in length and included celebrity news/gossip as well as a brief countdown to the 'video of the day'. In the month of March, *Mini Studio* featured 86 video clips in the show's opening, equivalent to three clips per day, aside from one episode that only featured two. All 86 clips came from non-Arab media, although one clip could be considered a French-Arab hybrid. Produced in France, the 2012 video 'C'est la Vie' featured the Algerian singer Khaled, who lives in France, singing in both French and Arabic. Perhaps unsurprisingly, most of the clips (97 per cent) were from Western media, especially music videos, although clips also included film trailers (such as *Maleficent*) as well as excerpts from TV shows and movies (such as *Kim Possible* and *High School Musical 3: Senior Year*). Approximately 86 per cent of the clips featured in March were produced in the US, followed by 6 per cent produced in the UK. Canada, France and Korea each produced 2 per cent of the videos, and one clip (less than 1 per cent) came from Japan (*Pokémon*). The Walt Disney Company produced 73 per cent of the 74 American videos shown. In fact, Disney content appeared in all 29 episodes. In light of the Walt

Disney Company's ubiquity and popularity in the Middle East as well as its status as a purveyor of childhood innocence and wholesome family values,[43] it would seem that *Mini Studio*'s producers view Disney media as a safe, convenient and affordable bet for quality international content (especially given that most clips appear to be streamed from YouTube).

Many of the Disney clips that aired on *Mini Studio* in March 2014 seem fairly innocuous, such as excerpts from Disney Channel TV shows like *Kim Possible* and *Sonny with a Chance*. Others, however, are more risqué, including music videos for Selena Gomez's 'Slow Down' (2013) and Miley Cyrus's 'Can't Be Tamed' (2010), both of which were released under Disney's more adult-oriented Hollywood Records label. The 'Slow Down' music video cuts between shots of cleavage-and-midriff-baring Gomez as she writhes seductively in a club, struts down a darkened street and slithers against a wall. The song's refrain is as follows: 'I just wanna feel your body right next to mine, all night long, baby slow down the song'. 'Can't Be Tamed', which provoked controversy in the US for countering Cyrus's wholesome persona on the TV show *Hannah Montana*, is similarly steeped in erotic imagery. The video depicts the singer, who plays a scantily clad, exotic winged creature, in a variety of steamy scenes – from seductively doing the splits in her caged nest to participating in a racy romp with other dancers in scant attire. While themes of girlhood strength and independence can be detected in Cyrus's assertive performance style and insistence that she 'can't be tamed', the shot compositions highlight her 'to-be-looked-at-ness' while the song lyrics centralize her heterosexual encounters with men. 'I go through guys like money, flyin' out the hands … if you're gonna be my man, understand, I can't be tamed'. Here, Cyrus's freedom seems less about forgoing male companionship than finding a guy who will put up with her wild ways. The message feels particularly out of place in a programme pitched at pre-teens.

In considering *Mini Studio*'s in-house video representations of Arab female youth alongside its commercial music video representations of American female youth, it would seem that the show's producers strive to have it both ways: to appeal to young viewers with images of attractive and mildly provocative local and Western performers, while also distancing themselves from racy imagery of Arab female stars that could potentially offend more conservative viewers. Perhaps because viewers in the Middle East are used to seeing sexualized media images of Western stars on satellite television, provocative images of Americans, such as Miley Cyrus, fly under the radar of social critique. In contrast, sultry images of Arab women, such as Haifa Wehbe, might arouse unwanted cultural criticism and backlash, especially given the show's dissemination throughout the region. Ultimately then, the mildly suggestive performances and baby-doll styling of *Mini Studio*'s princesses encapsulate gendered tensions surrounding the show's culturally hybrid, commercial form. On the one hand it sells a kind of grown-up sexiness while, on the other, it tries to keep it safely contained in the crib. As Marwan Kraidy argues:

> Hybrid media texts have the intertextual traces of an increasingly standardized global media industry where successful formats are adapted ad infinitum, hybridized to cater to the proclivities of one audience after another, but always remaining firmly grounded in the same commercial logic where hybrid texts are instruments finely tuned in pursuit of profit.[44]

This 'pursuit of profit' certainly includes what Kraidy and Khalil call the 'sexualized semiotics of global youth culture'.[45]

Perhaps it is worth noting that Elie, as host, has tried to distance the show from Miley Cyrus's more recent 'bad girl' images, such as her raunchy performance with a giant foam finger at the 2013 MTV Video Music Awards and her nude portrayal in the 2013 music video 'Wrecking Ball'. On 25 March 2014, before playing a clip of Cyrus's 2007 music video 'Nobody's Perfect', which featured Cyrus as the wholesome character Hannah Montana in pants and a long sleeved shirt, Elie told viewers:

> Miley has started her Bangerz tour. We can't say that it has been a big success but it is a success; there are some people who like it … We are going to tell Miley Cyrus good luck in everything she does, but we would still prefer if she would go back to how we knew her and how we will see her now in this *Hannah Montana* music video.[46]

Evidently, then, there are limits as to how far the show is willing to go in terms of supporting images of Western female artists that push at cultural and sexual boundaries of decency and taste. But, considering that Elie went on to endorse Cyrus's sexy performance of 'Can't Be Tamed' just two days later,[47] *Mini Studio* also clearly trades in gendered contradictions. It seeks to stamp out sexiness by turning back the clock one day, then enthusiastically celebrating it the next.

The Target Audience and Negotiation of Gendered Identities

Given that *Mini Studio* is part of the gendered institutions that conceive and distribute cultural expectations about gender, it plays a critical role in how young viewers learn about masculine and feminine identities.[48] Like a traditional family, the show's characters often replicate conventional gender norms. For instance, the princesses are kind, sensitive and fashion-conscious, while Prince Philippe is strong, sensible and good at solving problems. Yet it is noteworthy that traditional male roles, such as father and grandfather, are replaced on the show with male characters who tend to display feminine qualities. Elie, for example, usually opens the show in a turquoise and lavender suit adorned with a patchwork of pastel colours on his trousers and floppy bow tie, which is similar to a girlish hair bow worn by the princesses. His departure from more conventional codes of masculine dress pleasurably pushes at gender binaries and might be read as a small but important step towards depicting diverse masculine personas (even though, as we have seen, he also polices patriarchal gender norms for youthful female stars).

As noted, the show is also a site for 'doing gender', where interactions between individuals and groups often reproduce cultural/ideological expectations of gender.[49] The hosts exhibit customary power dynamics in their interactions with children; for example, Kikki is a motherly voice of order and discipline whereas Elie functions like the cool and clever older brother who benevolently shares his knowledge of youth cultures and trends. Interactions between the show's guest audience members also provide insights into the construction of gendered identities.[50] The practices and comments of contestants on the game sequence provide further evidence as to which of the show's gender norms are reinforced and incorporated and which are negotiated and/or resisted. During the game segment that aired on 19 October 2013, for instance, the female contestants, Pamela and Assil, shared with the audience their impressive career aspirations: lawyer and pediatrician, respectively.[51] Thus, although the show often advocates traditional roles for girls, Arab female youth demonstrate that they have exciting and sometimes unconventional plans of their own.

While advertisers have recognized the spending potential of young audiences, the absence of empirical research on gendered media selection has left media unable to produce content that appeals primarily to one gender or the other. With *Mini Studio*, the gendered media selection is assumed to skew towards a female audience. Producers suggest that young boys may be following less television and more online videos and games on portable devices. As a result, the show's material is perhaps geared to a predominantly female audience, which interestingly includes both mothers and daughters. This process of exclusion and inclusion of specific gendered identities, and the role advertising plays in this process, is worthy of further study.

Conclusion and Policy Implications

This chapter makes a preliminary foray into understanding the representation of males and females across a specific children's show. There is a need to examine not only media's gendered identity construction processes but also how girls and boys are portrayed, including their physical and socio-emotional characteristics and socio-cultural roles. Based on close analysis of *Mini Studio*, three themes seem to emerge as possible areas that affect a young person's development of a sense of self and other. The first of these themes relates to gender role beliefs, which often work in tandem with other gendered institutions and interactions. For example, a belief in the 'princess' role as an attractive one for girls is consistently reflected in a range of entertainment products and supported by parental and peer interactions.[52] The second belief is about 'suitable' gendered activities and occupations. For example, *Mini Studio* has always featured sponsored sequences that re-inscribe traditional occupational roles for future adults. The recent campaign for Banque Libano-Française (BLF), sponsor of the show's game segment, features a young boy and girl describing their aspirations for future jobs. In a stereotypical manner, the boy envisions becoming a doctor while the girl dreams of being a teacher (and dancing at *Mini Studio* in the afternoon.) These occupations carry clear gender, status and class attributes. Whereas the girl desires a conventionally 'feminine' career, the boy opts for a line of work that will presumably fund his consumer desires and bolster his social status, while also enabling him to assist others. As he explains, 'I want an airplane so I can go around the world, build my own house, and have a huge backyard. And I want to save money so I can help everybody'. While theoretically, a girl might have similar yearnings, the BLF promo does not consider them; the omission highlights how the advertisement's creators ascribe social and economic value to children along gendered lines. Indeed, the boy's voiceover segment, which airs first, runs for 35 seconds while the girl's segment lasts for less than half that time, at only 15 seconds.[53] The third belief relates to certain ascribed characteristics of physical beauty, which are almost exclusively restricted to young girls. For example, the princesses are put forward as a beauty benchmark that emphasizes thinness, make-up, hair and wardrobe, thereby limiting the scope of what matters in girls' lives.

Given the absence of clear and consistent regulatory policies, public engagement with children's media or state support for quality children's programming, in a context of increased media commercialization, we might ask whether anything can be done to decrease the potentially negative effects of stereotypical gender constructions on children's television. Parents and children stand to benefit from a new media environment characterized by increased 'on demand' content, but continuing on the current path does little to reduce the risks and misses the potential opportunities. A promising possibility is to introduce and encourage media literacy education of a kind that includes a gender awareness component and engages future parents and current children with practical tools and applications, such as those offered by Rebecca C. Hains in her book *The Princess Problem: Guiding Our Girls through the Princess-Obsessed Years*.[54] If media are a critical part of gender socialization, then it is ever more pressing to develop ways to improve children's media diet. Greater diversity in the hiring and promotional practices of the television and advertising industries, additional collaboration between television professionals and media scholars, and training young people to be socially responsible creators of media (as well as savvy critics and consumers), would also aid the effort to produce more diverse, inclusive and equitable programming for children – girls and boys alike.

The patterns observed in this chapter point to an increasingly differentiated media world. We might think that the dramatic increase of satellite channels and access to online digital content in the 21st-century would open up gender possibilities. Instead, it seems that media companies and advertisers often emphasize and reinforce traditional gendered pursuits as they attempt to realize, shape and capitalize upon the potentials of a younger audience.

Notes

1 The authors would like to thank Aisha Abduljawad, Dana Abu Nahl, Rawda Al-Thani, Hazar Eskandar, Kendra Johnston and Amin Zaky for their generous and helpful research assistance.

2 Joe F. Khalil's interview with Jawad Abbassi, CEO of Arab Advisors Group, Amman, 3 June 2014.

3 *Arab Media Outlook 2011–2015: Arab Media Vulnerability and Transformation*, 4th ed. (Dubai, UAE: Dubai Press Club, 2011).

4 Khalil's interview with a female presenter on *Mini Studio*, Beirut, 5 March 2014.

5 Marwan Kraidy and Joe F. Khalil, 'Youth, media and culture in the Arab world', in S. Livingstone and K. Drotner (eds), *The International Handbook of Children, Media and Culture* (Los Angeles: Sage, 2008), p. 343.

6 MTV and LBC are both Christian-owned channels out of eight leading Lebanese channels whose ownership reflects the confessional/sectarian mode of political organization in Lebanon.

7 Khalil's interview with a female creative team member at *Mini Studio*, Beirut, 5 March, 2014.

8 Khalil's interview with a female staff member at *Mini Studio*, Beirut, 6 March 2014.

9 Khalil's interview with a male host team member on *Mini Studio*, Beirut, 29 July 2014.

10 Dima Dabbous, *Regulating Lebanese Broadcasting: A Policy Analysis* (Saarbrücken: Lambert Academic Publishing, 2013), pp. 411–420.

11 L. Monique Ward, 'Understanding the role of entertainment media in the sexual socialization of American youth: A review of empirical research', *Developmental Review* 23/3 (1 September 2003), pp. 347–488.

12 Khalil's interview, Beirut, 6 March 2014.

13 Beckie Strum, '*Mini Studio Club* makes kids dance', *Daily Star*, 29 June 2012.
14 Khalil's interview, Beirut, 5 March 2014.
15 Shereen Abdel-Nabi, Jehan Agha, Julia Choucair and Maya Mikdashi, 'Pop goes the Arab world: Popular music, gender, politics, and transnationalism in the Arab world', *HAWWA: Journal of Women of the Middle East and the Islamic World*, 2/2 (2004), pp. 231–254; Kraidy and Khalil, 'Youth, media and culture in the Arab world', p. 341.
16 Khalil's interview, Beirut, 29 July 2014.
17 See, for instance, Rita Sommers-Flanagan, John Sommers-Flanagan and Britta Davis, 'What's happening on music television? A gender role content analysis', *Sex Roles*, 28, 11/12 (1993), pp. 745–753; *Dreamworlds 3: Desire, Sex and Power in Music Video*, DVD, written, narrated and edited by Sut Jhally (Northhampton, MA: Media Education Foundation, 2007); and Cara Wallis, 'Performing gender: A content analysis of gender display in music videos', *Sex Roles*, 64 (2011), pp. 160–172.
18 Ilana Nash, *American Sweethearts: Teenage Girls in Twentieth-Century Popular Culture* (Bloomington: Indiana University Press, 2006), p. 5.
19 Maya Götz and Dafna Lemish (eds), *Sexy Girls, Heroes and Funny Losers: Gender Representations in Children's TV around the World* (Frankfurt: Peter Lang, 2012). See also Kirsten Pike, 'Princess culture in Qatar: Exploring princess media narratives in the lives of Arab female youth', in M. Forman-Brunell and R. Hains (eds), *Princess Cultures: Mediating Girls' Imaginations and Identities* (New York: Peter Lang, 2015), pp. 139–160.
20 United Nations Development Programme, Regional Bureau for Arab States, *Arab Human Development Report 2002: Creating Opportunities for Future Generations*, p. 1. Available at http://www.arab-hdr.org/publications/other/ahdr/ahdr2002e.pdf (accessed 8 August 2014).
21 Maya Götz and Dafna Lemish, 'Gender representations in children's television worldwide: A comparative study of 24 countries', in M. Götz and D. Lemish (eds), *Sexy Girls, Heroes and Funny Losers: Gender Representations in Children's TV around the World* (Frankfurt: Peter Lang, 2012), p. 20.
22 *Mini Studio*, 15 September 2013. Available at http://mtv.com.lb/Programs/Mini_Studio/2013/videos/15_Sep_2013 (accessed 12 July 2014).
23 *Dreamworlds II: Desire, Sex and Power in Music Video*, VHS, written, narrated and edited by Sut Jhally (Northhampton, MA: Media Education Foundation, 1995); and Kirsten Pike, 'Music videos: Representations of men', in M. Kosut (ed), *Encyclopedia of Gender in Media* (Thousand Oaks, CA: Sage, 2012), pp. 242–245.
24 Karley Adney, 'Music videos: Representations of women', in M. Kosut (ed), *Encyclopedia of Gender in Media* (Thousand Oaks, CA: Sage, 2012) pp. 245–248.

25 *Mini Studio*, 1 March 2014. Available at http://mtv.com.lb/Programs/Mini_
Studio/2014/videos/01_Mar_2014 (accessed 14 July 2014).

26 *Mini Studio*, 15 November 2012. Available at http://mtv.com.lb/Programs/
Mini_Studio/2012/videos/15_Nov_2012 (accessed 19 April 2014).

27 While the majority of Barbies featured in the advertisement are white, a couple
appear to have light brown skin. All of the Barbies featured in the studio demonstration are white.

28 Dafna Lemish, 'The future of childhood in the global television market', in
G. Dines and J. M. Humez (eds), *Gender, Race and Class in Media: A Critical
Reader,* 3rd ed. (Thousand Oaks, CA: Sage, 2011), p. 359.

29 For an astute analysis of gender and consumer citizenship in children's television programming on Nickelodeon, see Sarah Banet-Weiser, *Kids Rule!
Nickelodeon and Consumer Citizenship* (Durham, NC: Duke University Press,
2007), pp. 104–141.

30 'Birthday celebration at *Mini Studio* CLUB house' (2014), [Digital photo
album]. Available at https://www.facebook.com/media/set/?set=a.746263632
059660.1073741926.138787699473926&type=3 (accessed 8 August 2014).

31 While the princesses use sexiness and flirtatiousness to appeal to viewers, the
male characters do not appear to do so. For example, Princess Jessica blows
a kiss to a six-year-old boy in the 1 August 2013 episode after he professes
his love in a letter. See http://mtv.com.lb/Programs/Mini_Studio/2013/videos/
01_Aug_2013 (accessed 20 April 2014).

32 Cara Wallis, 'Performing gender', p. 168.

33 Jeanne Prinsloo, 'Seductive little girls on children's TV: Sexualization and gen-
der relations', in M. Götz and D. Lemish (eds), *Sexy Girls, Heroes and Funny
Losers: Gender Representations in Children's TV around the World* (Frankfurt:
Peter Lang, 2012), p. 88.

34 See, for instance, *Dreamworlds 3*, DVD; Cara Wallis, 'Performing gender',
pp. 160–172; and Diane Railton and Paul Watson, *Music Video and the Politics
of Representation* (Edinburgh: Edinburgh University Press, 2011).

35 Naomi Sakr, *Arab Television Today* (London: I.B.Tauris, 2007), p. 85; and
Michael Frishkopf, 'Music and media in the Arab world and *Music and Media
in the Arab World* as music and media in the Arab world: A metadiscourse',
in M. Frishkopf (ed), *Music and Media in the Arab World* (Cairo: American
University in Cairo Press, 2010), p. 27.

36 For examples, see Abdel-Nabi et al, 'Pop goes the Arab world', pp. 248–253;
Patricia Kubala, 'The controversy over satellite music television in contempo-
rary Egypt', in M. Frishkopf (ed), *Music and Media in the Arab World* (Cairo:
American University in Cairo Press, 2010), pp. 173–212; and Walter Armbrust,
'What would Sayyid Qutb say? Some reflections on video clips', *Transnational
Broadcasting Studies*, Vol. 1: *Culture Wars: The Arabic Music Video Controversy*
(Cairo: American University in Cairo Press, 2005), pp. 18–25.

37 Elisabeth Cestor, 'Music and television in Lebanon', in M. Frishkopf (ed), *Music and Media in the Arab World* (Cairo: American University in Cairo Press, 2010), p. 103.

38 Cestor, 'Music and television', p. 103.

39 Salam Al-Mahadin, 'From religious fundamentalism to pornography? The female body as text in Arabic song videos', in K. Sarikakis and L. R. Shade (eds), *Feminist Interventions in International Communication: Minding the Gap* (Lanham, MD: Rowman & Littlefield, 2007), p. 149.

40 For an analysis of *Bratz* and *Winx*, see Prinsloo, 'Seductive little girls', pp. 76–88. For analyses of *Bratz* and other girl-oriented shows, see Dafna Lemish, *Screening Gender on Children's Television: The Views of Producers around the World* (New York: Routledge, 2010).

41 Diane Negra, *What a Girl Wants? Fantasizing the Reclamation of Self in Postfeminism* (London: Routledge, 2009), p. 12.

42 No videos were posted for 18 or 21 March 2014. See http://mtv.com.lb/Programs/Mini_Studio/2014 (accessed 9 July 2014).

43 Of course, an array of contemporary scholarship challenges this perception. See, for instance, Henry A. Giroux and Grace Pollock, *The Mouse That Roared: Disney and the End of Innocence*, 2nd ed. (Lanham, MD: Rowman & Littlefield, 2010); Janet Wasko, Mark Phillips and Eileen R. Meehan (eds), *Dazzled by Disney: The Global Disney Audiences Project* (London: Leicester University Press, 2001).

44 Marwan M. Kraidy, *Hybridity, or the Cultural Logic of Globalization* (Philadelphia: Temple University Press, 2005), p. 130.

45 Kraidy and Khalil, 'Youth, media and culture in the Arab world', p. 341.

46 *Mini Studio*, 25 March 2014. Available at http://mtv.com.lb/Programs/Mini_Studio/2014/videos/25_Mar_2014 (accessed 9 July 2014).

47 *Mini Studio*, 27 March, 2014. Available at http://mtv.com.lb/Programs/Mini_Studio/2014/videos/27_Mar_2014 (accessed 9 July 2014).

48 See, for instance, Joan Acker, 'From sex roles to gendered institutions', *Contemporary Society*, 21/5 (September 1992), pp. 565–569; and Kirsten Pike, 'Lessons in liberation: Schooling girls in feminism and femininity in 1970s ABC Afterschool Specials', *Girlhood Studies: An Interdisciplinary Journal* 4/1 (Summer 2011), pp. 95–113.

49 Candace West and Don H. Zimmerman, 'Doing gender', *Gender and Society*, 1/2 (June 1987), pp. 125–151.

50 Jeanne R. Steele and Jane D. Brown, 'Adolescent room culture: Studying media in the context of everyday life', *Journal of Youth and Adolescence*, 24/5 (1995), pp. 551–576.

51 *Mini Studio*, 19 October 2013. Available at http://mtv.com.lb/Programs/Mini_Studio/2013/videos/19_Oct_2013 (accessed 5 March 2014).

52 For thoughtful analyses of princess culture, see Miriam Forman-Brunell and Rebecca C. Hains (eds), *Princess Cultures: Mediating Girls' Imaginations and Identities* (New York: Peter Lang, 2015); and Rebecca C. Hains, *The Princess Problem: Guiding Our Girls through the Princess-Obsessed Years* (Naperville, IL: Sourcebooks, 2014).

53 See, for example, *Mini Studio*, 15 September 2013. Available at http://mtv.com.lb/Programs/Mini_Studio/2013/videos/15_Sep_2013 (accessed 5 March 2014). In this episode, the BLF ad featuring the boy airs at the beginning of the 'Let's Play' game segment, while the BLF ad featuring the girl airs at the end of the game segment.

54 Hains, *The Princess Problem*.

8

Domestication and Commodification of 'the Other' on Egyptian Children's TV

Ehab Galal

Painted on the wall of a building in Cairo is the easily recognizable cartoon figure of Bakkar. Beside the picture of the boy are the words '*min albu we ruhu masriy*' ('he is Egyptian, heart and soul'), a line from the cartoon's opening song. This piece of street art was displayed on the wall after the Egyptian revolution in 2011 and illustrates how a children's cartoon character is presented as a popular symbol of Egyptian national identity. More remarkable is that Bakkar clearly belongs to Egypt's Nubian minority. The cartoon in question, aired on Egyptian TV and the Egyptian Satellite Channel for a decade from 1998, was created by Mona Abul-Nasr, an Egyptian animator and director of national and international renown. One of very few people to have produced high-quality cartoons for Arabic-speaking children, Abul-Nasr seemed to have captured the mood of the times with Bakkar. The programme was popular not only in Egypt but was also shown, despite its obviously Egyptian setting and national sentiments, in the United Arab Emirates, Kuwait and Tunisia.[1]

In the context of children's television, the cartoon, entitled simply *Bakkar*, invites study for several reasons. It exists among the 'host of powerful images' in magazines, television and other media that, according to Mark A. Peterson,[2] 'serve as symbolic reservoirs for children growing up in global Cairo'. It was locally produced, in strong competition with financially much stronger and technologically more advanced competitors, such as Disney.[3] It was made for children, but was also watched by, and gained popularity with, adults. Its strong message about Egyptian national values did not detract from its transnational popularity. And, paradoxically although Bakkar belongs to a minority group, he is presented as Egyptian through and through – the very quintessence of 'Egyptianness'.

How can we explain these phenomena? To explore possible answers involves trying to understand Bakkar in the context of how children's TV is culturally produced and productive: how it constructs national diversity and unity in a global setting. This chapter therefore starts by setting the *Bakkar* cartoon within an Arab media landscape that has shown little interest in children's TV. It goes on to analyse the values and moral messages promoted by the cartoon; these include notions of national identity, which are also analysed. Bakkar is presented as both Egyptian and Nubian. The analysis therefore extends to his minority position and different modes of representation. Based on theories of representation, authenticity, national identity and minority, I argue that Bakkar is presented as the quintessential, but domesticated nation-centric Egyptian.

Bakkar's Place in Egyptian TV

Egypt is famous for its film industry, which for decades supplied popular films that were watched across the Arab world, until they came up against competition from other Arab countries in recent years. Yet neither animations nor other forms of children's content played any significant role in Egyptian film production.[4] The same was true of Egyptian television. A study in the mid-1990s, shortly before Bakkar was launched, showed that only 9 per cent of television air time was reportedly given over to children's television and only 3 per cent of cartoons shown on Egyptian television were locally made.[5] This is despite the large proportion of under-15s in the Egyptian population, reported by most demographic studies to account for around one third of the country's total population. According to Egypt's official Central Agency for Public Mobilization and Statistics (CAPMAS), the latter stood at 85 million in 2013, not counting another 9 million Egyptians living abroad.[6] Although Egyptian animation has been created for advertising purposes, experimentation has been limited. The mid-1990s study revealed that, unlike foreign animation, which features imaginary figures, Egyptian cartoons pictured only human characters. With little finance and technology and unable to compete with US animation studios[7], the Egyptian animation business faced many challenges, including the rise of privately-owned pan-Arab media outlets. Media liberalization across Arab countries since the 1990s created a more competitive environment that helped to stimulate new kinds of production for children,[8] while the emergence of cartoons aimed at adults added another dimension to the technological and artistic environment for children's animation.[9] As for typical values promoted by children's programmes, Noha al-Abd mentions a study of 35 hours of content transmitted on four satellite channels during the first three months of 2001, which found that independence, tolerance and generosity ranked very low, compared with values like competition, collaboration and respect for adults.[10] Bakkar differs somewhat from these findings, as the analysis will reveal.

Bakkar was broadcast on Egyptian Television Channel One for the first time in 1998 with short five-minute stories. In the following nine years, 252 episodes were produced and broadcast.[11] The creator, Mona Abul-Nasr, argued that the figure of Bakkar was inspired by the Egyptian authorities' labelling of 1997 as 'the year of Nubian child' with the intention of developing southern Egypt, particularly Nubia. The series was produced by the Egyptian Radio and Television Union (ERTU) and was taken off air in 2007 due to production problems.[12] In 2015 the series was resumed in Ramadan with episodes extended to 12 minutes. The script writer was still Amr Samir Atef, while Sharif Gamal took over as director after the death of his mother, Abul-Nasr.[13]

Bakkar is a boy around 10–12 years old. He lives alone together with his mother in a typical small Nubian village in South Egypt. All the episodes give a positive presentation of Bakkar as a very kind, but also sometimes naïve, boy. In each episode Bakkar faces new experiences and challenges related to his daily interaction with his friends, family and surroundings. He is at school; he is travelling, fishing, playing and so on. The dominance of male figures reflects a long-standing feature of children's cartoons in general. According to a study by Siham Abdel-Khaliq in 1996, 86 per cent of figures appearing on all cartoons (foreign and Egyptian) shown on Egypt national television (Channels 1, 2 and 3) in the three months from

July to September 1994 were male.[14] However, Bakkar is not presented as a superhero, but as a sensible and honest boy who learns from his mistakes, listens to grown-ups and loves people, animals and his country. He is presented as an 'authentic' Egyptian, characterized by being clean, loving, clever and brave. Bakkar's best friends are his pet goat, Rashida; his class mates Hasona, Hamaam and Faris; and a slightly younger girl, Hanya.

The series' success was evident not only in its popularity among Egyptian viewers, children as well as adults, but in praise it received at cultural festivals in the United Arab Emirates and Tunisia[15] and its distribution on cassette tapes, video tapes, DVDs and as printed books.[16] The creator, Mona Abul-Nasr, attributed this outcome to the programme's treatment of contemporary everyday life in an Egyptian context: 'A child from South Egypt, Bakar has been well-received by many people because he lives in our age. . . . Bakar is not like a hero'.[17] There may have been other reasons at work, however. One has to do with the series' position in the TV schedules. Another, linked with its prime time slot, is the way it constructs a proto-typical Egyptian 'character' and national identity in terms of the concept of authenticity.

The series was broadcast during the fasting month of Ramadan, just after the time for breaking the fast, when the whole family is together, sharing a meal. Many popular drama serials are aired in Ramadan every year, and are thereby established within a national and cultural frame of reference.[18] The period between the two prayer times of *maghreb* (sunset), which marks the end of the fast, and *isha*, a short while later, is a customary time for watching television, before welcoming evening visitors into the home or making visits to friends and family. Walter Armbrust has observed that the meshing of calls for prayer with television commercials and dramas marks 'religious time on a daily basis in the television flow'.[19] Although framed by the calls for prayer, neither the popular television dramas nor the cartoon *Bakkar* address a community of Muslims, but rather a national or imagined community.[20] For Armbrust, the television phenomenon is a secular Ramadan ritual.[21] Since each episode of *Bakkar* traditionally lasted no more than five minutes, it was easy for the family to stay together in front of the screen until it was over.

The character of the mass ritual is confirmed by the nation-centric moral messages contained in the programme, which can be distinguished from the religion-centric approach of Islamic children's programming. Islamic satellite channels, introduced with the launch of Iqra in 1998 and followed by several others, introduced forms of children's programming, including animations, that endorsed explicit religious values in an educational and moralizing manner, teaching children how to live in what was presented as a truly 'Islamic' way.[22] Although these channels' Gulf context and Saudi ownership would be poorly hidden, their aim seemed to be to propagate a context-free and universalized Islam.[23] Whereas such programmes emphasize Islam as the key to communal loyalty, the narratives of nation-centric programmes, in contrast, have their clear moral and educational message framed by a national context.

Egyptian state television, including its popular *musalsalat* (televised drama serials), has for long taken on the role of national educator.[24] According to Lila Abu-Lughod, Egypt TV first and foremost promotes a common national discourse nurtured by the government's interest in creating and mediating a shared imagined national identity. In this respect, the media under the regime of former president Hosni Mubarak were used as instruments in creating citizens of a modern nation state.[25] Whenever religion is part of the story, it is presented as a natural part of people's everyday lives.[26] The nation-centric approach underlying *Bakkar* was confirmed by Abul-Nasr in an interview in 2000, in which she pronounced herself 'pleased that the cartoon is consistent with government policies on Upper Egypt' and 'in line with the national goal of paying more attention to Upper Egypt'.[27] In order to promote certain educational and political messages, these are inscribed in a narrative of quintessential 'Egyptianness'. The nation is constructed as a natural given and its 'true' citizens as representing the 'essence' and 'authenticity' of the nation. Abul-Nasr conveyed this when she said in the interview that the show 'reflects the depth and authenticity of that region. Bakkar represents one aspect of a common Egyptian identity'.[28]

Bakkar's proclaimed 'authenticity' has to be analysed in light of literature that deconstructs representations of the quintessential Egyptian in Egyptian popular culture. Ramy Aly argues that the quintessential Egyptian character, *al-shakhsiyya al-masriyya*, represents a 'kind of biologically deterministic approach to Egyptian society, whereby certain types of women and men are produced through fixed notions of citizenship, belonging, gender, class, religion and social stratification'.[29] Within these fixed notions, rural people are routinely represented as 'honor-driven, violent, patriarchal simpletons' or as 'happy and colorful people'.[30] In the latter version, a character from the Egyptian countryside, whether Sa'idi (southern, or Upper Egyptian) or fellah (peasant farmer), is presented as ibn al-balad (son of the country), a figure Armbrust describes with the English-language equivalent stereotype as 'salt of the earth' or 'rough diamond'.[31] Ibn al-balad is typically contrasted with the aristocracy, or Westernized or nouveau riche Egyptians, who are defined by their greed and lack of modesty and manners.[32] The rural ibn al-balad is, in Aly's words, 'predictably parochial and authentically backward'.[33] The 'authenticity' of the peasant is inscribed in the national narrative by metaphors connected to the land and the landscape of Egypt. Lisa Malkki notes that metaphors embedded in nature and the biological are typical for the national narrative, having the function of emphasizing the community as territorially defined and 'naturally' given.[34] At the same time this construction of authenticity, as demonstrated by 'idealized represen-tations of Egyptian peasantry' in some Egyptian art, conceals the real-ity of Egypt's working classes and their situation.[35] Figures representing processes of urbanization and its new classes, such as the street vendor, are often portrayed as suspect and without morals – characteristics that ignore the societal context.

The position of Egypt's Nubians is likewise concealed by the idealiza-tion of 'authenticity'. Like the fellah, the figure of the Nubian in Egyptian popular culture is stretched between a negative and positive stereotype. A racialized version depicts certain African facial features that purport to dis-tinguish Nubians from other Egyptians and connote slavery in a way that conflates skin colour, class, ethnicity and geographic origin.[36] The implica-tions of such images map onto structural inequalities, including uneven distribution of national resources since independence in 1952 and neglect of Nubian towns and villages by central government, which concentrated development efforts around the capital and other major cities. Nubians were strongly marginalized, being considered racially and ethnically 'Other', since they have their own mother tongue and have a regional accent when speaking Arabic. The obvious political and social discrimination they have experienced is no less obvious in the media.[37] The more positive stereotype meanwhile conceals the structural inequalities. This is the image that inscribes Nubians into a united Egypt, as 'authentic' Egyptians who are close to nature and represent original and non-corrupted Egyptian values. Abul-Nasr, talking to the press about *Bakkar* in 2000, described the Nubian accent as 'beloved', saying that with his 'beloved Nubian accent, Bakkar fills the gap between city people and those from the south'.[38]

One risk of the domesticated and positive stereotype of the *ibn al-balad*, or 'authentic' Nubian, is that it slides easily into its negative counterpart of a minority people, seen as primitive, simple, lazy, unaccustomed to modern-day demands on labour, irrational and naïve. Even the *ibn al-balad* may end up being presented as crude, ill-mannered and ignorant.[39] The same kind of primitivism is routinely ascribed to Nubians, as discussed by Smith in relation to debates about the term *barabra* (singular *barbari*). *Al-barabra* is a historical term used in urban contexts to refer to Nubian and Sudanese male migrant workers, but currently turned into a derogatory reference to skin colour.[40] Another risk, as argued by Teun van Dijk, is that a positive stereotype is often used to stress the alleged 'bad behaviour' of other minority groups. The traditional 'authentic' minority group becomes a role model minority against which other minority groups are judged.[41]

Indeed, constructing Nubians as authentically Egyptian inscribes them into the country's dominant national discourse, which rejects the existence of minorities in Egypt. According to this discourse, Egypt 'does not "have" racism, ethnicities, or minorities', in the sense that the US or South Africa have institutionalized racism or countries like Turkey, Syria and Iraq have Kurdish ethno-nationalist separatist movements.[42] Formulating terms like 'racism' and 'ethnicity' by reference to global discourses obscures the specific application of racialist discourses to Nubians in Egypt.[43] While national unity is often presented through what Ismail Fayed calls vulgar propaganda[44] or Michael Billig calls 'banal nationalism',[45] such as the display of the flag and other national symbols, Nubians, and Copts too for that matter, are presented as part of the Egyptian web through a hegemonic narrative that acknowledges difference only in limited contexts, all the while privileging 'sameness' and national unity.[46] The question for the remainder of this chapter is where Bakkar is placed in this landscape of Egyptian-ness and what characteristics and values are ascribed to him as an 'authentic' Egyptian.

The Moral Message

On one hand the moral messages and values of *Bakkar* relate to universal values like honesty, hard work, responsibility and keeping promises. On the other, they relate to the particularistic value of love for one's country. By integrating these two aspects of the moral order, Egyptian citizens are constructed as loving their country but also responsible towards their country, as must be shown through their behaviour. The conflation of moral and national values is evident in several episodes where national symbols are to the fore.

One episode is about preparing for, and handling, an exam. Bakkar is reading and, when his mother asks him to go to sleep, he replies that he wants to read for the exam next day. His mother questions the need, since he has always done his homework on a regular basis. But Bakkar insists to keep on revising and asks his mother to wake him up in time for the dawn prayer. The next scene shows Bakkar's friend Hasona asking to come and play, but being rebuffed by Bakkar, who is working for his exam. Like the mother, Hasona asks why Bakkar needs to study more than he has already. Bakkar then asks Hasona if he has studied. Hasona says he has but that, if he is stuck on anything, he will cheat by getting help from Bakkar. The scene changes to the school building with the Egyptian flag waving on the roof. The national anthem is heard for a few seconds with the words that children sing in the playground when they salute the flag: *biladi biladi laki hubi wa fuadi* (my country, my country, you have my love and my heart). In the classroom Hasona is struggling to get the seat beside Bakkar, and when the exam begins, he is pestering Bakkar and disturbing him until the latter gives him the answers.

Their cheating is discovered and they are both expelled. Hasona blames Bakkar for not having given him the answers right away to avoid the teacher finding out, and he leaves Bakkar in anger. Bakkar is crying when the teacher gives him another chance, saying that he is a clever and kind pupil but that cheating is *haram* (forbidden). The teacher tells Bakkar that if he can convince Hasona that cheating is *haram*, he too will be given another chance. The moral message of the episode is simple: don't cheat and don't help anyone else to cheat. The easy way out not only spoils things for you, it also ruins things for others. And don't get misled by others out of consideration for them. The national framing of the message tells the viewer that moral responsibility is not only towards your family and friends, or even only towards God (as referenced in the labelling of cheating as *haram*), but also towards the nation.

Another episode holds some of the same elements, with slightly different messages. The opening scene shows a street vendor buying bad liver to sell in sandwiches. The scene shifts to the pupils singing the national anthem after which vaccinations are on offer at school. Hasona, scared of getting vaccinated, runs away from the class. The next scene shows Bakkar, Hasona and Faris on the square, with Faris wanting to borrow money to buy sandwiches, saying the vaccination has made him hungry again already. Bakkar is reluctant to lend money to Faris because the money he has with him is intended for books; he promised his mother he would use it for books and is not ready to break his promise. Hasona, on the other hand, is ready to use his book money to buy sandwiches for Faris, claiming that this is what friends do. Hasona and Faris buy three sandwiches but after having tasted a little, Hasona eats them all, leaving Faris with nothing to eat. Suddenly Hasona, who has been dismissive of Faris's complaints, gets a violent stomachache and falls ill. Bakkar says the illness must have come from the food bought from the street vendor. Again the message is that nothing good comes from breaking promises and neglecting responsibilities. People should keep their promises, not be greedy, accept to be vaccinated and avoid eating food from street vendors. Individual and collective interests are intertwined, placing participation in the state's vaccination programme and keeping one's promises as important elements of the national moral order.

In both of these examples Hasona is given the role of trouble maker, tease and bad sport. This is not the case in all episodes, but in the examples presented here this role is important to send a message. The generally unambiguous lesson of each episode is one that promotes national solidarity, personal responsibility and universal values of ethical behavior. Compared to the findings cited by Al-Abd, listed above, the values conveyed by Bakkar are somewhat different. He is socially responsible, loyal and helpful towards the collective (the nation and people in need, such as people with disabilities, rather than only friends); meanwhile competitiveness is often discredited as far as it reflects egoism, dishonesty and shortsightedness.[47]

Honesty is strongly emphasized, as are education and equality. Over and over again education and the ability to read are presented as the way out of trouble. Thus, in one episode, a poor and illiterate shopkeeper does not know he has inherited a fortune because he cannot read.

Equality is stressed across class and gender. In another episode, Bakkar is transported by magic back to Pharonic times in order to teach the young Pharaoh to be less arrogant and respect other people. When Bakkar's friends refuse to let Hanya play football with them because she is a girl, the plot of the episode ends up concluding that gender makes no difference. Altogether, the moral values of the series support the idea of a unified nation whose people are equal, educated and socially responsible. Bakkar, being the embodiment of these values, is thus constructed as a national role model, regardless of the particularities of his Nubian background. How is that done?

National Unity

Each episode starts with the same song, sung by the famous Nubian singer Mohamed Munir and starting with the following lines:

> Since he was young, he knew that he in his heart and soul is Egyptian; that the Nile runs in him; that his country's history is running in his blood.

The last three phrases are repeated by a choir of children. The song continues while Munir says the name 'Bakkar' between each line, making it clear that the sense of community comes with having Egypt's famous river and its history 'in the blood'. The song is thus a classic example of Malkki's point about the use of metaphors for the nation and national belonging that are embedded in nature and the biological.[48] While the song is being played, clips are passing by from other episodes showing the school, the Nile, Egyptian soldiers, the Egyptian flag, the Metro, Pharaohs, the Pyramids, military aircraft, the National Museum, musicians, and Bakkar with his goat and his friends, singing and dancing in the village. These images, accompanying the song, highlight national symbols and signal that visiting the sights of Egypt is a crucial aspect of the cartoon's narrative. Thus, one episode is about a visit to Al-Azhar, the oldest Muslim university and an important national symbol of Egypt. Another is about a trip to the Red Sea, another important spot for the national geography. A third talks of the High Dam at Aswan, a fourth of Pharonic sites and so on.

Several episodes are framed by key events in Egyptian history. One that deals with the October War of 1973 is followed by another in which a soldier who fought in 1973 has many years later become a successful businessman, working on a number of development projects in Sinai, which was regained for Egypt through the 1973 war. The businessman is seen surviving several assassination attempts, the perpetrators of which are indirectly identified as Israelis. In this way the series shows the national struggle for independence still continuing, tracing a line from the 1973 victory to events in the 1990s, and the state is seen caring for the population through defence as well as education and health.

Religion is seldom an explicit topic. Insofar as religion is included, as in the visit to Al-Azhar or the celebration of a saint's birthday in another episode, Islam is presented as an integrated and implicit part of the national community. When referring to what is considered *haram* (forbidden), the moral message has a universal character common to many religions. It is not so much a reference to Islam as to the national moral order. Hence, the religious language of Bakkar is very similar to the language of many Egyptian *musalsalat* (drama serials) and films, in which religious values tend to be linked to struggles against injustice. This struggle is embodied by the hero or heroine who represents the ideal human behaviour, but has to combat injustice to live in accordance with tradition, justice and human values, and defend them.[49] This is also the role of Bakkar.

In *Bakkar*, the Nubians as a numeric minority are turned into an integrated part of the national ecumene by being chosen to represent the moral right and normalized values of the nation. Whereas the minority is typically depicted as the strange 'Other', the stereotypical bad guys of the cartoon are not of one kind. From episode to episode the role of villain moves from urban dweller to fisherman from the north coast, southern Egyptian and so on. This diversity is further stressed by the presence of all skin colours, as seen, for instance, among the children taking a trip to Sinai. The key message seems to be that diversity is the basis for national unity and that the glue holding the nation together consists of shared values, history and symbols. Thus Bakkar seems to exemplify a traditional nationalism. In his book on media use in a cosmopolitan Cairo, Mark Allen Peterson writes about the most popular Arab children's magazines (*Samir, Al-Arabi Al-Saghir, Bolbol, Alaa-Eldin* and *Majid*), which he believes address an imagined transnational and interactive consumer community while promoting an 'ideology of regional identity that is simultaneously Arab, Islamic, and part of a larger global community of consumption'.[50] In *Bakkar*, however, although there is convergence of Islamic and national values and ideologies, what is constructed is an idea of authentic Egyptian-ness, rather than cosmopolitanism. Even though Bakkar travels in the programme to Yemen and the Red Sea, the ideological struggle remains within a symbolic battle of differentiations within Egyptian society rather than in an articulated opposition to, or conflation with, transnational or global values. Aspects of Islam are nurtured as Egyptian rather than looking out to a transnational or global Islamic community. It is notable that Islamic greetings, which became more prevalent as part of a general Islamization of Egyptian public practices in the 1990s, were prominent in the very first episode of *Bakkar* but seemed to become rarer and rarer as the series went on, while secular aspects of the promoted values arguably strengthened over time. Although the cartoon figures are Muslims, Islam as such is not seen as their driving force.

Images of a Minority

Being Nubian, or belonging to a minority group, does not emerge explicitly as an issue in the series. The viewer knows that Bakkar is Nubian from his appearance, language and setting; his skin is dark and his clothes have characteristics of traditional Nubian clothing. He speaks Egyptian Arabic with a Nubian accent and so do his friends. The village he lives in has Nubian features and some of the adults have Nubian names. These symbols reflect Mona Abul-Nasr's wish to present the audience with a Nubian setting. But, since neither Nubian languages nor the specific history of Nubian civilization are represented, it is clear that only selected Nubian signifiers are chosen at the expense of others. How does that compare with the general treatment of Nubians in Egyptian media?

It has to be said that, contrary to public discourse rejecting the idea that Egypt has minorities, Nubians are often not considered 'real' Egyptians.

They have historically been popular figures in Egyptian films, but in very limited roles. In films from before 1952 Nubians were given the role of servants to rich Egyptian families. After the 1952 revolution they were portrayed as caretakers: servants, doormen and cooks, reflecting the very jobs that were primarily on offer to those arriving as rural migrants to Cairo during Nasser's regime.[51] A Nubian character in film was typically portrayed as submissive, or even servile towards their employer, a 'white' Egyptian, who may be shown treating them badly. In this representation Nubians readily forgive and forget. They are presented as honest, naïve and funny, bordering on idiotic.[52] Similarly Bakkar, and especially his family, come across as naïve and funny to the point of being, if not stupid, then at least simpleminded. Their dialect and attire is reminiscent of the Nubian servants from 1930s films.[53] But their position within the narrative has changed. Instead of servants or subordinates they have the leading roles and their position in the society is normalized, as demonstrated by school scenes or the singer of the series' signature song. According to the social structure perspective on stereotypes, the ideas and conceptions of groups are based on their position in society.[54] The theory of social roles posits that the characteristics ascribed to a group depend on the roles that members of the group hold in a society.[55] Hence, the shift in Nubians' position in *Bakkar* invites a new ascription of characteristics to the group, notably positive elements of the stereotype: authenticity, honesty, truth and incorruptibility.

It is not uncommon for minority groups to be ascribed such positive characteristics as a nostalgic counter-image to what 'the majority' has supposedly lost due to modernization. The positive stereotype presents minority groups as those who still care for their families and each other, still live by traditional values and still believe in the good of other people. Thus, Bakkar is constructed as the positive representative of a true Egyptian, a Nubian version of the *ibn al-balad*. Instead of being contrasted with Egyptians who are Westernized or *nouveau riche*, Bakkar offers a contrast with a generalized set of faults that Egyptians attribute to their countrymen, such as laziness, corruption, shortsightedness and lack of education. This kind of stereotyping is what Eugenia Siapera denotes as a 'domesticated regime of representation', defined by its attempt to 'tame' and 'contain' difference within confines deemed safe and acceptable'.[56] Differences that are presented as having been assimilated or subsumed become irrelevant or banal, or they are tempered through 'mixing or hybridization'.[57] In the case of *Bakkar*, the trivialization is obvious. Difference is highlighted through clothes and speech, whereas contested differences, such as acknowledgement of the Nubian language, are ignored. Mixing and hybridization within this regime are not celebratory.[58] They are subject to the dominant culture and do not challenge the discourse on a national unity in which minorities do not exist.

In *Bakkar*, the central figure is certainly a role model. But he is not portrayed as a contrast to any easily identifiable other (minority) group. Instead, one could argue, the negative contrast is the *ibn al-balad* in different degenerated versions. There is Hasona, who tries to cheat on his exam because he was too lazy to study. There is the street vendor who sells contaminated meat, and there is the wholesaler who profited from selling the meat to the street vendor. Thus the immoral 'Others' are both small-time swindlers and big-money fraudsters. The class struggle inscribed in the term *ibn al-balad* is played down in favour of a broader call for patriotism that overlooks class, ethnicity or geographical origin. For this purpose Bakkar's Nubian identity is presented as Egyptian, rather than in terms of its Nubian particularities. Precisely because he is Nubian rather than a traditional *ibn al-balad*, it becomes possible to discredit all kinds of immoral behaviour as non-Egyptian, regardless of the perpetrator's identity.

At the same time, one should also not ignore the elements of what Siapera defines as a racist regime of representation.[59] Racist representation is the depicting of persons as members of a particular race, ethnicity or culture where their 'defining characteristics become those attributed to this race', ethnicity or culture.[60] Such representations may reflect, confirm or challenge dominant racial or cultural hierarchies. *Bakkar* may, as argued, pose some degree of challenge to a more traditional racist hierarchy in which Nubians are viewed as uneducated primitives, but it does contain a disturbing use of racial signifiers. While Bakkar and his friends and mother are all dressed in traditional Nubian clothing and have dark skin, his school teachers are all 'white' and dressed in the typical Western clothing of urban, educated and secular Egyptians. In a glaring departure from normal dress codes in countryside primary schools, the female teacher in Bakkar's school does not even cover her head. Thus, despite Bakkar's educational and national socialization, he is still depicted as 'Other'. His mother's facial features are those associated with black Africans. Hence remnants of Africanization and thus racialization of the Nubians, as examined by Smith,[61] are still present.

Consequently, Bakkar's main purpose is not to represent a Nubian minority, which is why Nubian identity is never mentioned. Instead he represents the Egyptian nation, and is able to do so strongly precisely because his Nubian identity allows him to take on all the positive characteristics of 'authenticity'. Although naïve he is given all positive attributes of an honest and hardworking modern youth. Although Bakkar is ingenuously forgiving, the offender or wrongdoer is always hit by his own offence or wrongdoing. In the background lurks the racialized Nubian; naïvety may turn into idiocy, Egyptian-ness into African-ness, and unity into differentiation.

Converging Commodification and Politicization

Bakkar succeeded not only as a television animation. The character was sold on cassette tapes, video tapes, DVDs and as printed books, making the domesticated Nubian marketable. Siapera suggests the term 'regime of commodification', whereby cultural differences are accepted but subsumed 'to another logic: that of the market'.[62] Within this regime the profitable identity is present and the less profitable is marginalized,[63] meaning that those identity markers susceptible to branding and marketing will be represented while others are ignored. Thus the Nubian accent of the Egyptian colloquial is marketable, but Nubian languages are not. The domesticated and commodified Bakkar converge, making the tamed and Egyptianized – but still 'authentic' – Bakkar marketable, unlike the Bakkar who belongs to a minority. His distinctive dress, food and music provide folkloristic markers that make him interesting, unique and a strong symbol. He is a cartoon figure, but also a boy from the south, who has lost his father and lives alone with his mother, a harmless 'Other' with none of the characteristics ascribed to the dangerous 'Other'. When the exotic 'Others' becomes a commodity, their differences are rendered harmless because any threat to the dominant Egyptian identity or challenge to the dominant discourse of the nation has been removed. The dominant narrative of the cartoon accords with the national discourse as it has been produced, promoted and mediated in popular culture since Egyptian independence.[64]

Moreover, the timing of the cartoon may also have influenced its success. The cartoon was introduced in 1998, after numerous violent attacks on tourists and other targets by extremist Islamist groups and clashes between Christians and Muslims.[65] There was an urgent need for national harmony, tolerance and unity, which was encouraged by the Mubarak regime in the years to follow. The media were particularly encouraged to include minorities, resulting in a growing production of television serials and films presenting Copts as key figures. Although these productions often sparked controversy, they did challenge the previous domestication of the Copts, which had placed them in marginal and minor roles to illustrate the diversities of daily life through comedy.[66] *Bakkar* was introduced at a time when the national unity narrative was being strongly promoted and supported in public by political forces as well as popular culture.

Conclusion

Bakkar belongs to a marginalized and stigmatized group in Egypt, which has rarely been visible in the media. Yet the voice he is given is not the voice of a minoritized Nubian but one characterized by ascribed 'authentic' qualities of the quintessential Egyptian, holding all Egyptians to account for the state of their society, regardless of their ethnicity, class or location. The series sends a message that behaviour matters, not ethnic or class particularities. This inclusive narrative is endorsed at the expense of acknowledging particularities like Nubian languages. The Nubians are acknowledged as Egyptians, not as Nubians. Bakkar is a funny and credible figure with whom a child audience can identify. His morality depends more on his patriotism than his religion.

Judging from the image of Bakkar that appeared during the 2011 revolution, the public at large considers him a symbol of Egypt. But despite being alluded to in a political context, Bakkar does not represent a politically mobilized citizen. Instead he is a loyal patriot who protects and embodies the values of the collective and who, as a Nubian, can be embraced by the audience in a spirit of nostalgia for an imagined past. In sum, Bakkar represents the fiction of Egyptian unity.

Notes

1 Rania Khallaf, 'One boy and his goat', *Al-Ahram Weekly Online* (29 November–5 December 2001), 562, http://weekly.ahram.org.eg/2001/562/fe3.htm (accessed 4 May 2013).

2 Mark Allen Peterson, *Connected in Cairo: Growing up Cosmopolitan in the Modern Middle East* (Bloomington, IN: Indiana University Press, 2011), p. 31.

3 Khallaf, Rania, 'Funny business', in *Al Ahram Weekly Online* (21–27 August 2003), 652, http://weekly.ahram.org.eg/2003/652/feat2.htm (accessed 4 May 2013).

4 Khallaf, 'Funny business'.

5 Noha Al-Abd, *Atfaluna we el-kawanat el-fadaiya* [Our Children and Satellite Channels] (Cairo: Dar al-Fikr al-Arabi, 2005), p. 155.

6 http://www.sis.gov.eg/En/Templates/Articles/tmpArticles.aspx?CatID=19#.U8lRK79OW1s (accessed 18 July 2014).

7 Khallaf, 'One boy and his goat'; Khallaf, 'Funny business'.

8 Samy Tayie, 'Children and mass media in the Arab world: A second level analysis', in U. Carlsson, S. Tayie, G. Jacquinot-Delaunay and J-M. Perez Tornero (eds), *Empowerment through Media Education: An Intercultural Dialogue* (Göteborg: Nordicom, 2008), pp. 67–87.

9 Mohammad Abdul Rahman, 'Cartoons for grown-ups, a new Ramadan trend', *Al-Akhbar*, 5 September 2008, http://www.menassat.com/?q=ar/news-articles/4560-cartoons-grown-ups-new-ramadan-trend (accessed 5 May 2013).

10 Al-Abd, *Atfaluna*, pp. 136–137. Al-Abd does not elaborate on the method or coding schedule for the content analysis.

11 Nada Nader, 'Iconic Egyptian cartoon *Bakkar* returns after eight years', *Daily News Egypt*, 16 March 2015.

12 Nader, 'Iconic Egyptian cartoon'.

13 Nader, 'Iconic Egyptian cartoon'. I will not go deeper into the new episodes of the 2015 production. According to Atef, there are no changes in the educational and moral messages. However, technological development is reflected in the topics as well as in the production of the new episodes.

14 Al-Abd, *Atfaluna*, p. 156. The method of the study is not presented.

15 Rania Khallaf, 'A token of respect', *Al-Ahram Weekly Online* (6–12 January, 2000), 463, http://weekly.ahram.org.eg/2000/463/li1.htm (accessed 14 August 2015).

16 Khallaf, 'A token of respect'.

17 Khallaf, 'One boy and his goat'.

18 Lila Abu-Lughod, *Dramas of Nationhood. The Politics of Television in Egypt* (Cairo: The American University in Cairo Press, 2005).

19 Walter Armbrust, 'Synchronizing watches: The state, the consumer, and sacred time in Ramadan television', in B. Meyer and A. Moors (eds), *Religion, Media, and the Public Sphere* (Bloomington, IN: Indiana University Press, 2006), p. 214.

20 Benedict Anderson, *Imagined Communities: Reflections on the Origin and Spread of Nationalism* (London: Verso, 1991).

21 Armbrust, 'Synchronizing Watches', p. 217.

22 Ehab Galal, 'Reimagining religious identities in children's programs on Arabic satellite-TV: Intentions and values', in J. Feldt and P. Seeberg (eds), *New Media in the Middle East* (Odense: Syddansk Universitetsforlag, 2006), pp. 104–118.

23 Galal, 'Reimagining religious identities'; Ehab Galal, 'Identity and Lifestyle on Islamic Satellite-television: A Content Analysis of Selected Programmes' Positioning of Muslims' [in Danish], PhD thesis (University of Copenhagen, 2009).

24 Lila Abu-Lughod, 'Finding a place for Islam: Egyptian television serials and the national interest', *Public Culture* 5/3 (Spring 1993), pp. 493–513; Abu-Lughod, *Dramas of Nationhood*.

25 Abu-Lughod, *Dramas of Nationhood*.

26 Abu-Lughod, 'Finding a Place for Islam'; Abu-Lughod, *Dramas of Nationhood*; Viola Shafik, *Arab Cinema: History and Cultural Identity* (Cairo: The American University in Cairo Press, 1998).

27 Khallaf, 'A token of respect'.

28 Khallaf, 'A token of respect'.

29 Ramy Aly, 'Rebuilding Egyptian media for a democratic future', *Arab Media and Society*, 114 (Summer 2011).

30 Aly, 'Rebuilding Egyptian media'.

31 Walter Armbrust, *Mass Culture and Modernism in Egypt* (Cambridge: Cambridge University Press, 1996), p. 25.

32 Armbrust, *Mass Culture and Modernism in Egypt*, p. 27.

33 Aly, 'Rebuilding Egyptian media'.

34 Liisa Malkki, 'National Geographic: The rooting of peoples and the territorialization of national identity among scholars and refugees', *Cultural Anthropology* 7/1 (1992), pp. 24–44.

35 Ismail Fayed, 'Dismal state: The 37th General Exhibition', *Mada Masr*, June 22 2015, http://www.madamasr.com/sections/culture/dismal-state-37th-general-exhibition (accessed 15 August 2015).

36 Elizabeth A. Smith, 'Place, class, and race in the Barabra Café: Nubians in Egyptian media', in D. Singerman and P. Amar (eds), *Cairo Cosmopolitan: Politics, Culture, and Urban Space in the New Globalized Middle East* (Cairo: The American University in Cairo Press, 2006), pp. 399–413; Viola Shafik, *Popular Egyptian Cinema: Gender, Class, and Nation* (Cairo: The American University in Cairo Press, 2007), p. 67.

37 Shafik, *Popular Egyptian Cinema*, pp. 68–71; Smith, 'Place, class, and race'.

38 Quoted in Khallaf, 'One boy and his goat'.

39 Armbrust, *Mass Culture and Modernism in Egypt*, p. 26.

40 Smith, 'Place, class, and race', p. 400. See also Armbrust, *Mass Culture and Modernism in Egypt*, p. 236, n. 27, on the historical use of the term *barbari* for a Nubian figure.

41 Van Dijk, Teun, *Elite Discourse and Racism* (Newbury Park, CA: Sage, 1993); Stacey J. Lee, *Unraveling the "Model Minority" Stereotype* (New York: Teachers College Press, 2009), p. 6.

42 Smith, 'Place, class, and race', p. 401.

43 Smith, 'Place, class, and race', p. 401.

44 Fayed, 'Dismal state: The 37th General Exhibition'.

45 Michael Billig, *Banal Nationalism* (London: Sage, 1995).

46 Cf. Lise Paulsen Galal, 'Coptic Christian practices: formations of sameness and difference', *Islam and Christian-Muslim Relations* 23/1 (2012), pp. 45–58.

47 See also Khallaf, 'One boy and his goat'.

48 Malkki, 'National Geographic'.

49 Cf. Abu-Lughod, *Dramas of Nationhood*.

50 Peterson, *Connected in Cairo*, p. 47–48.

51 Cf. Smith, 'Place, Class, and Race in the Barabra Café'.

52 Shafik, *Arab Cinema*; Shafik: *Popular Egyptian Cinema*.

53 Shafik, *Arab Cinema*; Shafik: *Popular Egyptian Cinema*.

54 Amanda Diekman, Alice Eagly, Antonio Mlandinic and Maria Cristina Ferreira, 'Dynamic stereotypes about women and men in Latin America and the United States', *Journal of Cross-Cultural Psychology*, 36 (2005), pp. 209–226.

55 Alice Eagly, Wendy Wood and Amanda Diekman, 'Social role theory of sex differences and similarities: A current appraisal', in T. Eckes and H. M. Trautner (eds), *The Developmental Social Psychology of Gender* (Mahwah, NJ: Lawrence Erlbaum Associates, 2000), pp. 123–174.

56 Eugenia Siapera, *Cultural Diversity and Global Media: The Mediation of Difference* (Malden and Oxford: Wiley-Blackwell, 2010), p. 139.

57 Siapera, *Cultural Diversity and Global Media*, p. 139.

58 Siapera, *Cultural Diversity and Global Media*, p. 140.

59 Siapera, *Cultural Diversity and Global Media*, p. 132ff.

60 Siapera, *Cultural Diversity and Global Media*, p. 132.

61 Smith, 'Place, class, and race in the Barabra Café'.

62 Siapera, *Cultural Diversity and Global Media*, p. 143.

63 Siapera, *Cultural Diversity and Global Media*, p. 143.

64 Abu-Lughod, *Dramas of Nationhood*; Armbrust, *Mass Culture and Modernism in Egypt*.

65 Saad Eddin Ibrahim, *The Copts of Egypt* (London: Minority Rights Group Report, 1996).

66 Samia Mehrez, *Egypt's Culture Wars: Politics and Practice* (Cairo: The American University in Cairo Press, 2010); Shafik, *Popular Egyptian Cinema*.

9

Representation of Language in Arab Media for Children[1]

Atef Alshaer

The Arabic language has far-reaching socio-political significance with existential implications for its Arab speakers. The nuanced reality of Arabic, namely, that it includes different levels[2] used in various contexts and occasions – affects its cultural projection in the public sphere, most manifestly in contemporary Arab media. What adds to the complexity of Arabic is its impressive longevity and its geographical scope. Its textual, cultural and political legacies have resonated in the everyday lives of Arabs up to the present day. The result is a complex linguistic palimpsest that cannot be explained in terms of prescriptive linguistic rules alone, as linguists often try to do. Instead, interpretive efforts are needed to unearth the embedded, culturally loaded structure of the Arabic language with all its uses and changes. Arab children grow up absorbing these varied linguistic realities alongside ideological understandings of the language projected through the media. Thus children's programmes in Arabic, or programmes involving children, offer fertile ground for the study of both the ideological and natural aspects of the language.

This chapter sets out to show that our understanding of the linguistic situation in the Arab world reflects a certain understanding of language itself and is subject to ideological forces. It highlights the various historical and contemporary levels and dimensions of Arabic and how these simultaneously differ from, and complement, each other. It then draws on examples from various media outlets to shed light on the ways in which media outlets present Arabic to children and how this presentation or representation is often governed by ideological factors. The conclusion reflects on the culture of Arabic, not only as a language, but as an epistemological system encompassed by what I refer to as a culture of communication.

Linguistic Realities, Language Acquisition and Intelligibility

Arabic is clearly divided into three well-known levels.[3] These include Classical Arabic (CLA), which constitutes pre-Islamic, Islamic and Medieval Arabic extending all the way back from the fourth century to the 14th century. Then there is Modern Standard Arabic (MSA), which is embedded in the writings and discourses of the 19th-century reform movements in the Arab world and carries the legacies of the earlier periods of Arabic. Last but not least, there is Colloquial Arabic (CA) with its several varieties, which are spoken on a daily basis in the Arab world and are connected with ordinary social interactions, mundane functions and intimacies. The varieties of Arabic differ among the 22 Arab countries in accordance with regional variation, class difference and geographic locations. All of them, alongside MSA, are encompassed within what Mustafa Shah describes as 'a continuum of affinity' that 'defines their Arabic status'.[4]

However, because these linguistic levels are separate enough from each other, particularly as between MSA and CA, there is a tendency among some scholars to treat them as if they are different languages, or as if one level is more significant and standardized than another. Historically speaking, Arabic has been known to project such various levels, the most clear of which are those that distinguish spoken Arabic in its colloquial sense and Modern Standard Arabic in its official, written and formal sense. As a result there has been a wide consensus among linguists on the validity and relevance to Arabic of the notion of diglossia as defined by Charles Ferguson, where he highlighted the two familiar sides of the same language, its classical and standard side and its colloquial one, as follows:

> A relatively stable language situation in which, in addition to the primary dialects of the language (which may include a standard or regional standards), there is a very divergent, highly codified (often grammatically more complex) superposed variety, the vehicle of a large and respected body of written literature, either of an earlier period or in another speech community, which is learned largely by formal education and is used for most written and formal spoken purposes but is not used by any sector of the community for ordinary conversation.[5]

Because of the noticeable gap in Arabic between its formal standard side and its informal colloquial one, various Arab media forums have tended to try to bridge it by incorporating elements from the various levels in their discourses. Clive Holes refers to this phenomenon as hybridization. He notes that, in addition to mixing the vernacular and 'Standard Arabic (SA)', 'more educated speakers' styles' often display 'a great deal of hybridization, whereby elements from the dialect are combined with elements from SA'.[6]

Meanwhile, there are media that accentuate the linguistic gap in favour of CLA and MSA or CA, depending on their ideological and class orientations. But the relatively new tendency is for the merging of levels in media in ways that emphasize the content and purpose of communication rather than its form. Therefore, even among the Arabs themselves, there are common outcries voiced by conservative or language purists over the blurring of lines between MSA and CA. Some view such mixing as cultural corruption and treason of the highest order.[7] Many Arabs see Arabic in its high form as the undeclared ambassador of the Arab-Islamic civilization. Islam affected Arabic and helped its spread among many communities that spoke different Semitic languages before the spread of Arabic from the seventh century onwards. As Edward Said put it in his erudite essay, 'Living in Arabic', 'Arabic is Islam and Islam Arabic at some very profound level'.[8]

As the political conditions of the Arab world worsen, and its cultural standing suffers, people increasingly view mixing between the various Arabic levels as a sign of inauthenticity, if not outright corruption. Such views are born of a certain, often dogmatic, understanding of the past that rejects the adaptability and dynamism that the very notion of language should embody. The cultural output of the past is presumed to have been expressed in CLA; when the medium of the past is no longer perceived as pervasive in the present, then Arabic is seen as deficient and even unfit for civilizational articulation and pride. Some Islamist dogmatists champion views to this effect and practice formalism in the use of language, even in songs and poetic renditions intended to be popular enough to seduce people to Islamist ideologies. They encapsulate their understanding of Arabic in past glories that can only be repeated through the use of that classical medium, which is viewed in reductive and manipulative terms that do not represent the complexity of the linguistic situation of either the past or the present. Linguistically, the situation has always been diverse and varied, with different levels of Arabic used for different purposes and contexts. Edward Said aptly characterizes the levels in terms of a relationship between CLA and CA: 'The two languages are porous and the user flows in and out of one into another as an essential aspect of what living in Arabic means'.[9]

However, the fact that many Arabs perceive CLA as the epitome of existential authenticity tends to make them see any deviation or promotion of colloquial forms as a sign of corruption and weakness rather than fluidity, naturalness and adaptability. In this respect, the linguistic landscape of Arabic is rife with ideological constructs that are related to people's understanding of the language in its historical and present states. Confusion regarding the difference between MSA and CA has been so marked that some even regard these two levels as two languages.[10] Arabic-speaking children acquire them at different stages of their lives; accordingly, Arab children are natives of CA and not MSA, to which they are exposed later. Some scholars, however, misinterpret the process of exposure. For example, Judith Rosenhouse concludes her study of the language of Arab children in Palestine-Israel, 'From a Child's Colloquial and Literary Arabic', with the following observation:

> Children who are native speakers of Arabic encounter a serious problem when they start formal school education. The acquisition of reading and writing skills involves the study of a different language from the one they have been using for daily communication.[11]

Several points in that statement reflect serious flaws in understanding the linguistic situation of Arabic at the structural, sociolinguistic and epistemological levels. The main problem lies in seeing Arabic through rigid lenses, bypassing the fluidity of Arabic with which Arabs, including Arab children, are familiar from the early stages of their linguistic acquisition. In fact, this misunderstanding is not uncommon, even among Arabs. Arabs tend to ascribe high values to CLA and MSA in ways that overlook the historical construction of the various levels of Arabic as well as the fluidity in language consumption and use. In addition, language acquisition normally takes place at an early age, during a child's first few years of life, these being relatively divided into stages from years 1 to 5 and 5 to 10, each stage marking further acquisition, learning and expansion of the linguistic and cognitive capacities.[12] During this period, Arab children would have inevitably been exposed to the various levels of Arabic at home, school and sites of formal articulation, such as mosques or churches, classical songs, media reports and other formal forums. Clearly, therefore, Arab children are not deprived of CLA or MSA, nor do they acquire it as a second language. Edward Said's observation about the Arab children he grew up with is more accurate and representative in terms of their language practices than that of Rosenhouse:

> I remember very clearly that young people my age in Lebanon or Palestine could sing the ditties and mimic the patter of Egyptian comedians with considerable panache, even though of course they never sounded quite as fast and as funny as the originals.[13]

The fact that children are mimicking the language of adults means that they are gearing themselves up to be like them: active language users with influences and agency of their own. Many Arab children, sometimes as young as 5 years old, appear on Arab television stations, speaking with elevated styles that echo their immersion in a diverse linguistic environment. Thus their language is not static, neither in its acquisition nor its learning; these processes, acquisition and learning, while different at some level, are substantively interlinked to a very important degree.

Children's acquisition of a language and the learning of writing, reading and other skills related to that language are two different things.

Reading and writing are always acquired skills that maturate or deteriorate in accordance with exposure and practice. The difficulty in acquiring them does not suggest that children are dealing with another language, simply that they are learning another level of the same language. If researchers assume that Arab children should not make obvious grammatical mistakes at an early age, and that their knowledge of the formal language should be higher than it is, this assumption shows they are confusing culture and pedagogy with language acquisition. The latter is subject to natural processes of exposure that vary in depth and degree from one environment to another. The notion that Arab children should be fluent or literate in all the forms of Arabic ignores the point that acquisition is gradual and that children become versed in their language and its culture as they grow up and become accustomed to their cultural surroundings and its linguistic habits. How could we explain the fluency of so many Arabs, who attach precious importance to eloquence in their culture and who switch seamlessly between the various forms of Arabic, had it not been for an acquaintance with all levels of the language in their early years? It cannot all be due to learning; it is also to do with an environment populated with a continuum of linguistic practices that children acquire and learn as they grow up.

Thus knowledge of language in the pedagogical sense is different from language acquisition. The latter is natural and gradual, the former constructed and often laborious. Overall, however, the point remains that there is no pure acquisition or pure learning for any language; there is a mix of both, and this applies to Arabic as much as it applies to any other language. While it is true that Arab children are exposed to different levels of their language, these levels are not mutually exclusive or produced in environments that are different enough for the levels to be classified as different languages. There are syntactic and semantic similarities among all the levels of the language that defy such a narrow logic of categorization. This renders problematic Restö's characterization of Arabic, which states:

> From a purely linguistic viewpoint the Arabic complex is dissolved into a large variety of languages that in varying degrees have elements in common with each other as well as with other Semitic languages.[14]

187

The idea that there is 'a purely linguistic viewpoint' divorced from the reality of language use and practice seems fictional or unhelpful at best. In addition, whereas Arabs can resort to other levels to communicate with each other, they cannot communicate with speakers of other Semitic languages. Between an Arabic speaker and a speaker of Hebrew or Tigrinya there is no mutual intelligibility, which is the essential test of a single language. Algerian and Palestinian speakers of Arabic may encounter difficulties in understanding each other, largely because of pronunciation. Yet there are ways in which they can modulate their speech in order to communicate. In addition, the wide spread of pan-Arab media and the popular culture of songs, television serials and talk shows associated with these media have made people aware of each other's dialects in very important ways that have helped and are helping what is known as 'educated Arabic' to provide a way of communicating through gaps between the diverse levels of Arabic. Again, Said has a more representative description of the Arabic language as lived:

> Thus, if I were to try to understand an Algerian I would get more or less nowhere, so different and widely varied are the colloquials from each other once one gets away from the shores of the Eastern Mediterranean. The same would be true for me with an Iraqi, Moroccan, or even a deep Gulf dialect. And yet paradoxically, all Arabic news broadcasts, discussion programs, as well as documentaries, to say nothing of meetings, seminars, and oratorical occasions from mosque sermons to nationalist rallies, as well as daily encounters between citizens with hugely varying spoken languages, are conducted in the modified and modernised version of the classical language, or an approximation of it which can be understood all across the Arab world, from the Gulf to Morocco.[15]

The currency in Said's description lies in not considering the two forms, classical and colloquial, as two different languages. Said's view of the sociolinguistic landscape of the Arab world is informative, based more on personal experience and powerful insight than sustained encounter with all these local dialects. The common view among Arabs, including this writer, seems to be that, with open attitudes to linguistic mutuality, they can largely understand the various colloquials, thanks in no small part to regional media for facilitating linguistic familiarity across the Arab world. As a Palestinian Arabic speaker, when travelling in Morocco and Tunisia, I have held many conversations in approximated Arabic with relative ease because the sociolinguistic base of Arabic, including its structure and the bulk of vocabulary, remains accessible.[16] Yet the view held by Restö, quoted above, does not seem uncommon among scholars. Nor is it uncommon among Arabs who subject the uses of Arabic to categorical demarcations rather than seeing the fluidity in the uses of Arabic as evident in media programmes and media in general or seeing how they can make use of this fluidity in productive ways rather than leaving it unacknowledged.

These demarcations help to explain why curriculum materials are often designed with a particular understanding of the language and its manifestations in mind, resulting in narrow judgments and contradictory outcomes, as will be further explained. Even Abdullah Mustafa al-Danan, author of a 'Guide on Arabic for Children', compiled for Al-Jazeera's two children's channels in 2012, opines in the Guide that

> there is not one single Arab society whose members use Classical Arabic (*Fuṣḥa*) in the common oral conversations. In other words, we say, the Arabs have two languages, a language for scholarship and knowledge and a language for daily conversations and interaction. Those two languages differ to a great extent in vocabularies, structures and styles.[17]

Al-Danan lists notable differences between classical Arabic and various colloquials and includes aims for introducing programmes in classical Arabic for children. Yet, suffice to say here that Al-Jazeera programmes often include an amalgam of linguistic practices and that such a prescriptive and normative view of language offers just one way, among many, of exposing Arab children to language. They could be familiarized more with the variety of linguistic levels that demonstrate the diversity of language practices and avoid potential ideological homogeneity and rigidity of the type such a linguistic education produces.

What amounts to fetishization of CLA has even driven some misinformed Arab parents to expose their children to CLA only, resulting in children being unable to communicate in the local dialect. This is rather than allowing children to acquire their mother tongue alongside their native language gradually within a process of acquisition and formal and informal learning. Erem News, a local channel, reported the story of a Palestinian child, named Abdul-Rahman, from Jenin, whose mother imposed *fus-ha/* CLA and exposed him only to television programmes in the formal language. This stunted his ability to interact with his classmates and others in CA at school. Whereas education is offered largely in the standard language, it is not offered in colloquial Arabic. Hence, Abdul-Rahman and others like him have been made deficient in their mother tongue at the hands of adults who deliberately limited their linguistic range.[18] The ideological narrowness is clear in this case.

The fact that there is a populist – even, in some respects, fastidiously romantic – understanding of Arabic and its cultural associations of the past makes educators and others agitate about its present state, as if the current moment can never catch up. Hence they are tempted to impose forms of learning that do not substantiate communication and interaction in the present as much as they serve ideological constructs within which language operates as a proxy. In what follows, I highlight the representation of Arabic in Arab culture for children and consider the broader consequences of this representation.

Classical Arabic and Perceptions of 'Existential Authenticity'

More than anything else, language reminds Arabs of their identity. Hourani explained the link succinctly:

> More conscious of their language than any people in the world, seeing it not only as the greatest of their arts but also as their common good, most Arabs, if asked to define what they meant by "the Arab nation", would begin by saying that it included all those who spoke the Arabic language.[19]

The various levels and diverse functions of Arabic are heard in the Arab world every day. Conversations take place in streets, homes and public places in the colloquial language, and specifically in the local variety. But these conversations are paralleled, interrupted or complemented by the call for prayer, Qur'anic recitations, formal speeches, occasions, gatherings and media coverage and by formal sayings and constructions. All the latter are handled in Arabic that differs from the intimate CA. There is thus no single Arab sphere for either CA or MSA; one level might dominate at one point but the public sphere at large is populated with several levels of Arabic. That is to say, Arabs use their language to fulfil communication needs of various kinds; it is these needs and their nature and contexts that determine the form of the communication. Here, the naturalness of language is not only innate, as formalist linguists contend, but also historical. It is born of practices and intersubjective interactions and familiarities that reinforce themselves to the point that they often become unconscious linguistic forms. These forms serve diverse functions and uses that fluctuate in accordance with socio-political changes and variations. To this end, language serves as the first point of reference if one wants conceptually to unearth intellectual and social changes in the society, alongside it being a distinguishing factor for the human species from other species.

Arab children, as indeed all children, are born into a multidimensional linguistic reality, which they grasp in doses and gradations until their language maturates and they become conscious of the wide scope of their linguistic – implicitly cultural – surroundings. They adapt and evolve from being largely consumers of language into producers and reproducers of it in accordance with their individual as well as collective experiences. To this end, one cannot study the language of Arab children in isolation from the language of Arab adults, who pass their own language acquisition and experiences onto children. Adults working in media often have a particular understanding of Arabic, in light of which they devise ways to expose children to the language through stories and shows. Such media-driven attempts often emanate from within an ideological understanding of the language and its variations as outlined above, resulting in inflexible linguistic forms being presented to the children as the 'only' or the 'perfect' norms of communication that they should adopt. In this respect, media 'educators' do not take into account the full range and levels of Arabic that could be used for the benefit of the intended message and could thus lessen the focus on the linguistic form and its alleged perfection in favour of forms and messages that convey plurality within Arabic itself. Those who attempt to force one form of Arabic to the exclusion of others often fail to understand that the dynamism of language depends on its users, as does its potential to be an engine of improving people's lives.

However, if one strand of Arab media reflects linguistic purism of some sort, where CLA and MSA are rigidly maintained, others show linguistic variation. Arab media are a space within the public sphere in the Habermasian sense, where different social, political and psychological rationalities are projected. Thus the form of the language tends to adapt to the intended message, creating a linguistic fusion that serves the purpose of rational and interactional communication. In this light it can be seen that even the most ardent Islamist channels and forums, which indulge in purist linguistic practices, thinking that they are the bearers of the message of Islam as originally delivered in classical Arabic, end up using a medley of linguistic forms as dictated by the nature of the message in question and its context. Children are therefore exposed to multiple linguistic public spheres where Arabic is interwoven within ideologies and social space.

For example, the widely watched Jordan-based satellite channel for children, Ṭuyur al-Jannah, founded in 2008, seems on the face of it to adhere to formal classical or standard Arabic in its programmes, especially since it appears to uphold and instil Islamic values in children through educational and entertainment programmes that derive their content and inspiration from an Islamic culture.[20] The channel's choice of name is interesting, as it derives its very nature and identity from an Islamic reference, where children are regarded as *tuyūr al-jannah* (birds of paradise), being beyond the rules and frameworks of reward and punishment applied to adults within the Islamic faith. Here, 'birds' are a metaphor for innocence and exoneration from wrongdoing, which can be corrected through subtle teachings and good examples and practices on the part of the adults responsible for children. Therefore, the name is chosen with an Islamic culture in mind – one which entertains, teaches and facilitates a childhood unburdened with the heavy and conscious responsibilities of adulthood. Just as children are seen to be free like 'birds in paradise', children's language and the language that is used to appeal to and educate them is one that denotes freedom, ease and informality, albeit one that foregrounds its understanding and pedagogy in a modernized and adaptable Islamic culture. To this end, the channel uses what is practically a medley of linguistic forms to convey its values in a way that emphasizes the content of the message rather than its form. In this way, it modernizes Islamism or Islamic values more broadly in a novel and intimate way, as it uses everyday language and mannerisms.

Tuyur al-Jannah promotes Islamic norms, which are often associated with CLA. Yet it communicates these in a fluid and free style in songs and programmes that mix not only forms of Arabic but also use English concepts and expressions derived from Western cultures. The song for Eid al-Fiṭr (festival marking the end of Ramadan) in 2015 was delivered in colloquial Arabic and even interspersed with English. It started with the words, 'Happy, Happy, Happy Eid', and continued in a mixed style, '*Kull 'ām wintū bikhayr, 'asākū min 'uwāduh*' (and many happy Eid returns). This Eid is happiness, for every Muslim in the world/happy, happy Eid, *'eidkum mabrūk*' (may your Eid be blessed). Whereas some high-profile personalities, such as Muslim Brotherhood icon Yousef al-Qaradawi writing in an article entitled 'Our beautiful language and the media',[21] believe the media should safeguard Arabic from colloquial uses and Western influences as they are considered corrupting practices, the spontaneous and intimate style of the Eid song cited here suggests that media are pragmatic, commercial and indeed entertaining to a degree that diversifies Islamic-oriented channels and makes them wide-ranging in terms of the ways in which they speak and interact with the Arab society.

In the same vein, other famous programmes on Tuyur al-Jannah use the same style of mixing concepts from Arab and Western cultures, but still retain the spirit of popularized sayings and resonant discourses from the Islamic tradition, such as *Mughamarāt Camping*' ('Camping Adventures').[22] This programme is specifically devoted to sports such as horse riding, jumping and climbing in order to instil in children the value of activity and movement, as opposed to moods of inactivity and laziness. Here the children, girls and boys, are involved in activities that strengthen them physically and encourage them to cooperate, as the activities require team effort. The channel's discourse seems driven by socio-cultural values and interests, yet its conservatism is apparent through the absence of women guiding and training the children alongside the men. Even so the example shows that some channels with Islamic backgrounds and agendas are able to adapt and use mixed linguistic forms, thus undermining the potentially more purist tendencies that are prevalent in other extreme and often austere channels, whose programmes and messages are delivered in CLA and MSA in a way that reflects the rigidity of the pedagogical ideology in question.

The Saudi channel Iqra is a case in point. Founded by Saudi investors in 1998 and purportedly aiming to reinforce the Islamic creed and values, Iqra's use of the Arabic language appears as the outward tool through which these orientations are maintained. The name Iqra means 'read', in the imperative form of the verb, which was the first word in the Islamic revelation dictated to the Prophet Muhammad as attested in the Islamic tradition. As the first word of the Qur'an, 'iqra' is a word charged with seriousness and formality. Thus, all the programmes, including the traditional songs (*anāshīd*), which in Tuyur al-Jannah are delivered in free styles including colloquial Arabic and sometimes English expressions, are here delivered in the classical and standard Arabic language. Songs on Iqra are heavily inflected with the past and its aura, recalling the glories of what is known in Islamic culture as the golden age of Islam, which represents the early years of Islam and its spread.[23] For example, one song eulogizing Prophet Muhammad runs as follows:

> *Lā taqul māta al-ḥabīb al-muṣṭafā*
> *Lā taqul anna al-ṭiyā' qadd inṭafā*
>
> (Do not say that the beloved chosen Prophet had passed away
> Do not say that the light had been extinguished)

The song is a eulogy for the Prophet, which reinforces his message and affirms his eternal presence in the life of the Muslims. It focuses on theological aspects of the Islamic faith and represents them in the classical language. Certainly, the tradition and its presence today is the driving force behind the channel; it plays on the resonant effects of the past and its associated glories rather than the present with its modernist imperatives, which are facilitated through a discourse of practicality and ease of communication. Modernity uses language to address its concerns and attitudes, and does not allow the prior rules of language to restrict or frame its articulation, as has been most readily demonstrated by poets such as Syria's Adonis,[24] Palestinian Mahmoud Darwish and others. In other words, modernity has no past except that which serves its present; in that sense, it is bound not so much by rules as by attitudes.

Iqra, on the other hand, is set in its subscription to rules and norms: rules of thought as well as rules of language. Its programme intended to teach Arabic language to children outside the Arab world is rigidly observant of the rules and constructions of classical and standard Arabic[25] and thus devoid of any colloquial or entertaining aspects that would accord with the potentialities and flexibility of children's general social environments. Children are introduced to language in a rule-based manner that restricts their appreciation of the wide spectrum pertaining to the flexible sociolinguistic conditions of Arabic.

To this end, language serves as a mirror, through which facets of social life like ideologies can be explored and explained. Looking at the way children's language is represented in Arab media, one cannot sidestep the fact that practices of representation extend far beyond the media themselves, forming part of the cultural and political, not to say linguistic, fabric of the world, including the ideological and existential spheres where language is situated. Thus, while media play a role in reflecting linguistic practices and orientations as well as in shaping them, the media are also subject to preceding ideologies that shape their form and content. In this sense, media represent different aspects of the Arab world, one that is entrenched in particular perceptions of the past and its rules and modes, and another that subjects the past to present sensibilities and attitudes. Linguistically, this means that the Arabic language appears as dichotomous between its 'high' and 'low' levels as well as fluid, interactive and adaptable when all levels at hand are used to articulate the intended message. These diverse aspects are liable to cause confusion as to how to describe the sociolinguistic conditions of Arabic and its representation in Arab media. The eminent sociolinguist Yasir Suleiman describes disagreement among linguists over the nature and number of levels in use between MSA and CA in terms that define the dynamic composition of Arabic and the various uses to which it could lend itself. He writes:

> The fact that Arabic sociolinguists have not been able to agree on the number of Arabic levels or categories on the diglossic continuum, or on their ontology (whether they are levels/ registers/ styles or categories of self-contained classification)

reflects the semi-liquidity or viscosity of the Arabic language situation at its outer ends and its liquidity in the middle. This further reminds us of the difficulties Ferguson had in drawing up his definition of diglossia.[26]

What Suleiman refers to as the 'semi-liquidity' or 'viscosity of the Arabic language situation' exposes the reductive selectivity of those Arab media programmes that target children through one chosen form of language to the exclusion of others, thereby elevating the chosen form to the detriment of other forms and the potential dynamism embedded in Arabic itself. Producers' choice of certain forms for children reflects their ideology about language acquisition. Those who resort to *fus-ha*/CLA do so because they feel that is how children will acquire the 'accurate', if not 'pure', language. Producers who use CA are often condemned for doing so, as if they are corrupting the language. But they are also not immune from particular ideological motivations, often related to class issues. The champions of CA tend to come from secular and high-class backgrounds. They reason that the structure of CLA is archaic, that it somehow prevents the present reality from evolving and that it manipulates reality rather than expressing it. The Egyptian thinker Salama Musa espoused such a view in the 1940s, as did Palestinian scholar Hisham Sharabi in the latter part of the 20th century, advocating use of local colloquial Arabic as an immediate form of communication. Sharabi, as quoted by Suleiman, expressed his position as follows:

> Classical Arabic produces a sort of discourse that mediates reality through a double ideology: the ideology inherent in the 'trance of language' – produced and reproduced by the magic of catchwords, incantations, verbal stereotypes and internal referents – and the ideology supplied by the 'encractic' language –produced and disseminated under the protection of political or religious orthodoxy.[27]

Many enlightened Arab thinkers came to condemn conditions in the Arab world through language, conflating and indeed mistaking ideology for linguistic realities, given that language can bend to almost any chosen use. Ultimately, discourse about the use of Arabic seems inevitably to revert to the relationship between language and the past, including the rise of Arab nationalism. It seems it would take a revolution, or at least a mammoth effort, involving the sensibilities of individuals and society as a whole, to let go of the past, even at the risk of loss, to end the situation where attitudes to Arabic language are so closely aligned with ideologies built on historical examples and aspirations.

Cultures of Communication and Intimations of Political Legitimacy

The fact that Islamist and traditionalist Arabs rely heavily on the past in their ideologies, viewing the past as a site of perfection of some sort, reinforces Arabic in its past tense rather than its present contexts. There is what I called a culture of communication, which exists in every culture, whereby diverse verbal, written and visual forms of communication relate to each other in intricate ways and require orderly discursive interpretation.[28] The culture of communication has peculiar aspects in the Arab world, being heavily associated with a distant past, particularly the early days of Islam. Such invocations of the past are often unrelated to current events and their needs and responses, serving ideological consolidation and cohesion, not fulfilment of tangible and practical purposes. To this end, some strands of this culture, mainly Islamist or dictatorial, have been materially effective in manipulating realities and concealing them through communication which lacks practical and immediate values of societal currency, but is rather engrossed in metaphysical references and justifications that often stultify the present rather than enliven and reveal it. Indeed, it is worthwhile highlighting cultures of communication as a way to emphasize the materiality of language within human life as well as to explain some of the ways in which Arabic language is taught and represented for Arab children in media. As I have written elsewhere:

> What defines a culture of communication is the process of enactment that stems from the historical-anthropological root-edness of action in language and culture. In other words, a culture of communication is a communicated compendium of religious, historical, literary and mythological references used by a community as valid tropes for all time which, as such, are

acted upon and treated as having authenticity. 'Authenticity' in a culture of communication serves to manipulate language as a locus of resonant power embodied in culture as an anthropological, historical and literary space, in which the powerful, the spiritual and the pertinent (to the moment) are drawn upon, selectively reproduced, idolized, talked of and visualized. Essentially, the resonant power of language, which a culture of communication acts upon, serves to highlight the historical and spiritual dimensions that culture embodies.[29]

As far as Arabic is concerned, the glories of the past are perceived to have been constructed and articulated through CLA. It is that form of the language that is emphasized as the legitimate one for the public sphere and all aspects that have collective bearings on the Arab world. In this context, CLA is associated with authenticity, virtue and eloquence and is a source of cultural and political legitimacy. When children appear on Arab media speaking in the high register of MSA, this garners attention and, most often, admiration. For example, a Palestinian child who spoke on Al-Jazeera about the Israeli assault on Gaza in 2008–2009 drew wide Arab media attention because he did so in a language similar to that of educated adults. His language largely characterized what has come to be known as educated Arabic, which amalgamates features from MSA and CA in a way that mitigates the severity of the perceived diglossic situation of Arabic, as described above. It was specifically played by Arab media because of the linguistic maturity the child expressed, as well as the emotional effects his message had on the Arab world. At one point, the Al-Jazeera anchor was moved to exclaim to the child: 'You speak classical Arabic better than me!' Indeed, the 8-year-old child in question, Ahmad 'Awad Zayed, used a highly charged formal (classical/standard) language with expressions such as the following: 'We (the Palestinians) tasted the depth of bitterness' [*dhuqnā al-amrayn*]; 'I will not forget the children of Palestine' [*Lan ansa atfāl filisṭīn*]; 'I found everything being turned upside down' [*wajadtu kull shay maqlūban ra'san 'alā 'aqib*] (referring to the Israeli destruction of Palestinian houses); and 'That which does not kill us makes us stronger' [*aḍ-ḍarbah al-latī lā tumītanā tazīdunā quwah*] – referring pointedly to a famous saying repeatedly uttered by the former Palestinian president Yasir Arafat, who made Nietzsche's statement part of his rather random and limited rhetorical repertoire.[30]

While the linguistic abilities of this particular child are notable, they are not so uncommon among Arab children. Several Syrian, Palestinian and Iraqi children have been brought to the public eye through the media because of their eloquent, albeit innocent, linguistic renderings of their miserable conditions. In this context, the children echo their environment and its dense verbal associations without being necessarily conscious of the meanings and implications of what they say. It is this verbal imitation, sometimes masquerading as bravery and eloquence, which strikes roots in their character in a way that makes them subject to others' ideology-driven life, which they in return inherit and perpetuate. The learning of language, and its most important function – namely, communication – becomes descriptive, imitative and rhetorical rather than analytical, deductive and innovative.

The above characterization can be explained by reference to the fact that, while several regional networks such as Al-Jazeera have programmes for children in CLA, they also have others in CA that amalgamate expressions from the various dialects, often depending on the national origins of the speakers in these programmes. Children's programmes conducted in CLA, such as the rendition of the *Arabian Nights* on Jeem TV, the Al-Jazeera channel for children aged 7–12, are highly accomplished in the classical language with visual effects.[31] Yet, by reproducing the language in set forms, they take away from the vitality embedded in the story itself, which in its origin is peppered with vernacular elements and expressions. In contrast, when children are interviewed on screen they are addressed in CA. This situation results in contradictions, which, albeit confusing, are productive in reflecting the reality of the language ideologies at hand.

Similarly national channels and partisan media, such as Al-Aqsa channel of Hamas in Gaza, produce local shows for children in CLA while also featuring children in shows where CA is employed. The same applies to Hizbullah's channel, Al-Manar. Thus the projection of these Islamist movements as ideological and rigid in their use and consumption of the language is true to some extent. Yet they have also been accommodated within nation-state structures and consequently use phrases and expressions from CA where this suits their political interests. This use shows openness to CA, particularly in producing songs and writing effective slogans.[32] At the same time, each country produces programmes for children in a variety of levels, equipping them as they grow with Arabic as a multidimensional language, along the lines described above. In light of this, it can be seen that Al-Danan, who wrote the Al-Jazeera Guide on language for children mentioned earlier, conflated between language and ideology when he enumerated a list of aims that the channel wished to realize. He reflected a particular linguistic understanding that does not address the reforms required and the pedagogical needs of Arab children, which are more than linguistic reforms. Of six aims that Al-Danan highlighted as important and to be achieved through the Al-Jazeera channels Baraem and Jeem TV, Aims 1, 5 and 6 were as follows:

- To provide the children with knowledge and skills which they require in their forthcoming school life in order to help them in their practical life in the future.
- To teach children how to think in a sound manner and solve problems.
- To realize the objectives of the programmes in an atmosphere of happiness and entertainment.[33]

These aims are not all related. They require different processes and techniques and do not all contribute to linguistic novelty as much as to useful media programmes that can attract children and enhance their conceptual and linguistic capacities. Learning about language and its intricacies can enrich the culture and eloquence, traits that are rooted in Arabic culture. However, as for linguistic reforms, which are usually invoked from various standpoints, secular or Islamist, these cannot be separated from cultural reforms and a better understanding of the role of language in culture. The pervasive problem seems to lie in the rigid manipulation of the past within a culture that stultifies language in its attempt to restore the past without consideration to the present and its imperatives. Modern Arab poets and writers, particularly the secular ones among them, have been able to demonstrate the vitality of Arabic by injecting it with modern dimensions of narrative and uses that confirm both its dynamism and the view that language is subject to people's uses. Likewise some media for children have shown the impressive range of Arabic through programmes that demonstrate the language's multidimensional reality and its potential vitality once freed from narrow ideological considerations.

Conclusion

Nobody can claim that Arabic has not changed since its beginnings. The various levels of Arabic are a testament to an environment that adapted to socio-political and technological advances. Yet, more often than not, language change is slow. Since Islam and Arabic are interlinked and the former has always affected Arabs' life, its idioms and meanings remained relevant as Arabic carries its spirits and the heritage associated with it. Many television shows for children aim to instil in them a particular linguistic ethos. Embedded in that ethos is a constant discourse of crisis and fear that Arab children will not be able to use classical Arabic in the future and that this will rob the Arabs of the future of a significant heritage that once made them a great nation. This discourse of crisis goes back centuries, having had particular traction in the 19th century, and is laden with ideological undertones and short-sighted assumptions. Had Arabic really been threatened to such an extent, CLA and MSA would not have been in use today.

These days, Islamist movements and other ideologies, which idolize the Arabic language and its association with Islam, have through their access to media attempted to indoctrinate Arab children in the virtues of Arabic and its past associations through inflexible forms of the language. It is this image of the past and its various meanings that need to be properly understood and situated within their contexts so that the present can be freed from irrelevant indoctrinations. When that happens, language can be made to echo the present and its imperatives and needs rather than the past and uses of it that are limited and unproductively ideological.

Insight 3

Educational Priorities and Language Use in *Shara'a Simsim*

Choosing the level of Arabic most suited to screen content for preschool children is subject to many influences and considerations. Here **Daoud Kuttab** *reviews the rationale behind the use of local dialect in a Palestinian co-production with Sesame Workshop (formerly Children's Television Workshop) in the US.*

Shara'a Simsim began in 1995 as a Palestinian co-production of the US programme *Sesame Street*. It aired first on Al-Quds Educational television and then on Palestine TV. Initially Palestine TV was reluctant to be part of the actual production for political reasons, because Season 1 had a few elements of coordination with Israelis. But from Season 2 they started broadcasting it and replaying it over and over because it was so successful. The show used colloquial Arabic from the outset. Language only becomes a big issue for *Sesame Street* projects that are done in cooperation with Arab ministries of education or state-run media, where they are the dominant power. In our case we were television producers, with a different perspective from academics or ministry of education officials, and from day one we said the show would be in colloquial Arabic because we knew as communicators that is how you reach people.

Our perspective was that of producers and parents, whose goal was to reach young children. For that we knew we had to talk to them in the colloquial language. Unlike the Egyptian and Gulf co-productions, we did not do any formal formative research. It was not a big fight for us and we had no internal argument. Our research was anecdotal; we just talked to people. The issue of language was never raised with us in viewers' feedback on the show. We were also free from the financial pressures that often dictate why television stations use classical language; namely, that it makes sense financially to broadcast across all Arab countries and hence to use a form of language that works for all. Without those financial pressures, and without pressure from an education ministry, it was a slam dunk for us to use colloquial Palestinian Arabic.

People often misunderstand the role of language in educational programming. Language is both a means of communication and a goal. You want children to learn classical Arabic but you also want to communicate. There is a thick curriculum document that is produced for every *Sesame Street* series; it takes around a year to produce jointly with academicians and educators to decide on the goals. Our team, headed by Dr Cairo Arafat, created our curriculum through meetings with non-governmental organizations that are interested in education, like Save the Children, with the council of Palestinian private schools, and with the United Nations Relief and Works Agency for Palestinian Refugees (UNRWA) which has hundreds of schools in Gaza. We also met with people from the Palestinian Ministry of Education.

Every script in the series has to have a goal, even if it's a 30-second animation. So we had language as a goal in *Shara'a Simsim*, but it was not our number one goal: it was there as a goal but not a very high priority. But if you talk about language not as a goal in itself but as a means of communication – as the medium and not the result – there was no disagreement at all that the best way to reach the children of Palestine was to speak to them in their local language. Our number one goal with *Shara'a Simsim* was pride in your country and culture; another one was mutual respect, respecting handicapped people, respecting women and men. Those were higher priorities in terms of the goals of different segments.

For example, the goal of teaching children the difference between sizes might be goal number 1.3.5. If you wanted to write a script about big things and small things you would identify that by the goal number. If, on the other hand, you wanted to do something addressing language it would have been something like goal number 5.4.3. If we had opted to use classical Arabic, then the goal of language would have been the number one goal and would have weakened all the other goals. Look at the team who co-produced the Egyptian *Sesame Street* series, *Alam Simsim*, in colloquial Egyptian Arabic. They thought girls' literacy was important. So when they wrote the curriculum document they prioritized the goal of girls' literacy and then subdivided it into goals such as encouraging girls not to drop out of school, to have careers and so on; you break down the goals into line items. Then as a producer you give the curriculum book to the writers and you say, 'Make me a 30-second animation that addresses goal number one' and they look it up. But sometimes they may just come up with an idea first and then start searching the curriculum to find which goal it fits because you cannot submit a *Sesame Street* script idea for approval without identifying a goal.

Sometimes you have two goals, maybe language and age group or size, or language and understanding the other, or respecting, tolerating people of different cultures. But every single segment in *Sesame Street* has to be fun and funny and entertaining at the same time as addressing at least one of the goals, and that's what makes it so difficult. Sometimes addressing the goal is done with a very light touch. We did a lot of work on the alphabet. Most kids in the Arab world today can sing the 'ABC' song in English, but we have nothing like it in Arabic, no unifying song in Arabic that helps children to know the alphabet. So we created different animations in which the muppets do the alphabet. Sometimes also we would have a pop-up with a word and talk about that word. So we introduced vocabulary and letters, but with preschoolers you don't want to go too much into the pedagogical part because they don't get it, and anyway different people have different ideas about what you want to do for children in preschool. Everyone will tell you that children should enjoy education, love it, be interested in it, identify with it. What you want is for children, when they're with their parents in a car, to tell them, 'Oh, look, it says "souq"' or whatever, so that the parents are proud and say, 'Bravo'. In other words, vocabulary and literacy are very important, but you don't want to get into grammar or poetry and literature.

It is true that producing *Shara'a Simsim* was very, very expensive, which might be seen as a reason to make the language accessible to children beyond Palestine. It cost literally millions of dollars to produce. So the need for value for money is extremely high, which is why it needs to be subsidized by government or rich foundations. But if you are doing a version for Palestine, your live action and documentaries are all about Palestine, about children in Palestine, addressing the needs of children in Palestine. A pan-Arab version would dilute the Palestine part, making it just one of many. With the new series of *Iftah ya Simsim*, made in Abu Dhabi and first aired in 2015, the material is intended for all countries of the Gulf Cooperation Council. That means the live action, which is the most culturally sensitive kind of content, has to come from each Gulf country. So, even though the series is produced from Abu Dhabi, there are stories from Oman and so on, which dilutes the focus. We were fortunate to have five seasons funded and produced for children of Palestine, which is a small community compared to the whole Arab community.

Notes

1 All translations in the text of this chapter are the author's, unless indicated otherwise.

2 The term 'level' is chosen here in recognition of disagreement among sociolinguists as to the number and nature of different forms of Arabic, as discussed later in the chapter.

3 The notion of linguistic levels in Arabic is mostly associated with El-Said Badawi, who, considering its use in Egyptian media, divided Arabic into five levels. Starting from the most to the least formal, he called these: 'heritage classical', 'contemporary classical', 'colloquial of the cultured', 'colloquial of the basically educated' and 'colloquial of the illiterates'. See Reem Bassiouney, *Arabic Sociolinguistics* (Edinburgh: Edinburgh University Press, 2009), pp. 14–15.

4 Mustafa Shah, 'The Arabic language', in A. Rippin (ed), *The Islamic World* (Abingdon: Routledge, 2008), pp. 261–277.

5 Charles Ferguson, 'Diglossia', *Word*, 15 (1959), pp. 34–35.

6 Clive Holes, 'Orality, culture and language', in J. Owens (ed), *The Oxford Handbook of Arabic Linguistics* (Oxford: Oxford University Press, 2013), pp. 281–300.

7 See Yasir Suleiman, *Arabic in the Fray: Language, Ideology and Cultural Politics* (Edinburgh: Edinburgh University Press, 2013); Yasir Suleiman, *The Arabic Language and National Identity* (Edinburgh: University of Edinburgh Press, 2003).

8 Edward Said, 'Living in Arabic', *Al-Ahram Weekly*, 677, (12 February 2004), http://weekly.ahram.org.eg/2004/677/cu15.htm (accessed 25 February 2015).

9 Said, 'Living in Arabic'.

10 See Jan Restö, 'What is Arabic?' in J. Owens (ed), *The Oxford Handbook of Arabic Linguistics* (Oxford: Oxford University Press, 2013), pp. 433–541.

11 Judith Rosenhouse, 'Colloquial and literary Arabic in Israel: An analysis of a child's texts in colloquial Arabic', in M. Piamenta, J. Rosenhouse and A. Elad (eds), *Linguistic and Cultural Studies on Arabic and Hebrew* (Wiesbaden: Otto Harrassowitz Verlag, 2001), p. 109.

12 Karin Christina Ryding, 'Second-language acquisition', in J. Owens (ed), *The Oxford Handbook of Arabic Linguistics* (Oxford: Oxford University Press, 2013), p. 393.

13 Said, 'Living in Arabic'.

14 Restö, 'What is Arabic?', p. 446.

15 Said, 'Living in Arabic'.

16 For reference to colloquial Arabic and its relationship to standard and classical Arabic, see Muhin Haji Zadeh and Farida Shahrstani, 'Silat al-lahjāt

al-mu'asirah bil-fusha wa-atharaha fiha', *Fasliyat Dirasat al-Adab al-Mu'asir*, 11 (2003).

17 Abdullah Mustafa al-Danān, *Ad-Dalil fī al-Lugha al-'Arabiyyah al-Muyassara lil-'Amilin fī Baramij al-Atfal at-Tilfaziyyah* (Internal JCC document, Damascus, 2012), p. 7.

18 https://www.youtube.com/watch?v=2BLfGgxr5L0, (accessed 28 February 2015).

19 Albert Hourani, *Arabic Thought in the Liberal Age: 1798–1939* (Cambridge: Cambridge University Press, 1963), p. 1.

20 For example, several programmes are devoted to sports mentioned as note-worthy in the tradition of the Prophet Muhammad, such as swimming and horse-riding. It also broadcasts songs by children in the style of *anashid* (rhymed poems/songs with resonant effects). These are often entertaining and value-laden, aiming to inspire children to be virtuous, interactive and modest in accordance with mannerisms having Islamic appeal.

21 See Atef Alshaer, 'Language as culture: The question of Arabic', in T. Sabry (ed), *Arab Cultural Studies: Mapping the Field* (London: I.B.Tauris, 2011), pp. 275–297.

22 See for example, https://www.youtube.com/watch?v=VnL5IJi7mq0 (accessed 26 July 2015).

23 For example, see http://iqraa.com/ar/videos.aspx?VideoID=50A103A103B11 7C53&SubSectionID=5 (accessed 26 July 2015).

24 Adonis, *An Introduction to Arab Poetics* (London: Saqi Books, 2003).

25 See http://lettergarden.com/fullflash/LetterGarden.htm (accessed 26 July 2015).

26 Yasir Suleiman, 'Arabic folk linguistics', in J. Owens (ed), *The Oxford Handbook of Arabic Linguistics* (Oxford: Oxford University Press, 2013), p. 265.

27 Quoted in Suleiman, *Arabic in the Fray*, p. 235.

28 Atef Alshaer, 'Towards a theory of a culture of communication: The fixed and the dynamic in Hamas' communicated discourse', *Middle East Journal of Culture and Communication*, 1/2 (2008), pp. 101–121.

29 Alshaer, 'Towards a theory of a culture of communication, p. 104.

30 https://www.youtube.com/watch?v=BE8kpbm0c9s, and https://www.youtube.com/watch?v=JLNG4G7WOUM (accessed 25 February 2015).

31 http://www.jeemtv.net/en/shows/1001-nights/2 (accessed 25 July 2015).

32 http://aqsatv.ps/ar/index.php; see the link here for the expressions used in supposedly formal media.

33 Al-Danān, *Ad-dalil fi al-Lugha al-'Arabiyyah*, p. 6.

10

(Mis)trust, Access and the Poetics of Self-Reflexivity

Arab Diasporic Children in London and Media Consumption

Nisrine Mansour and Tarik Sabry

This chapter reflects on ethnographic research conducted in London over a period of 28 days in February, September and December of 2013, involving family observations and four workshops with young children of Arab origin between the ages of 7 and 12. The ethnographic research was part of a larger, interdependent three-year research project funded by the UK's Arts and Humanities Research Council (AHRC), which examined pan-Arab programming for children through a holistic and relational approach to three strands: audiences, texts and the political economy of screen production and distribution for children. The audience strand of the research project entailed ethnographic research in the UK, Morocco and Lebanon. In all these localities our prime objective was to steer away from the well-rehearsed media audiences models and experiment with new methods that would allow us to make sense of the ways in which children live and communicate their media and culture worlds. In the case of the London children, we were especially interested in the ways in which British children of Arab origin intentionally perform being in the world by navigating through multiple forms of subjectification and cultural tastes. This, we argue below, drawing on Bourdieu's concept of 'habitus'[1] together with studies of the

207

'mnemonic imagination' whereby remembering is understood as creative practice,[2] results in a mnemonic diasporic habitus.

In this chapter we reflect not so much on material emerging from the participant observations and children's creative workshops, but on the methodological issues that emerged from fieldwork in the UK. The range of issues and challenges we faced in the field as two Arab diasporic ethnographers, researching Arab diasporic children living in London, triggered so much reflexive debate and discussion among the two researchers and the rest of the research team that we consider the methodological issues we faced important enough to form this chapter's main object of enquiry. These concerns resonate with methodological and ethical questions arising from research with London children from other ethnic backgrounds.[3] The methodological process of framing, planning and conducting ethnography became a site for re-negotiating the subjectivities of researcher and research subject. In our case, the 'field' of research moved from anthropology's conventional positioning as 'being "out there" practiced by "other" people' and was discursively relocated within the researchers' and research subjects' 'home'.[4] Thus it contested the delineations of what is meant by Arab diaspora, how the diasporic researcher constructs herself or himself in relation to the diasporic subject, and the ways in which research subjects negotiate their participation in the research process.

The chapter is organized around five key themes, which we believe encapsulate our experience in and out of the field. In the first theme we reflect briefly on a pilot study we conducted in February 2013 in preparation for the longer fieldwork in London. In the second we discuss difficulties encountered by the ethnographers in recruiting participants for the research. We contextualize the politics of access and (mis)trust within larger debates around Otherness, racism and Islamophobia in the UK. This theme also engages, reflexively, with the politics of implicated-ness on the part of Arab diasporic ethnographers researching Arab diasporic children. In the third theme, which we call 'doing being self-reflexive as poetics', we further discuss the politics of (mis)trust by showing how performing a mnemonic diasporic habitus (negotiation of memory and self in a diasporic context) is different from the habitus that is being performed, and how it is through the affective performing of habitus that a *third* mnemonic language of identification is created. Similar research on transnational childhoods notes that, even when ethnography actually takes place in what is physically a single site, it still relates to what are effectively transnational constructions of childhood, constructed through everyday experiences of home and exile. Throughout the ethnographic conversation, research subjects express their transnational selves by 'evok[ing] multiple sites through an explicit reference to other sites which are "off-stage" [… resulting in] strategically situated (single site) ethnography'.[5] This performance, we argue, is negotiated through and across parent cultures, the cultures of researchers as mediators and the London cultures.

The fourth theme looks at the technologies and types of affective performances and narrativity that children use while navigating and seeking to know the parents' and mediators' cultures. We approached this theme while aware that '[i]deas about children directly impinge upon the experience of childhood which children themselves have'.[6] Hence, we sought to conduct reflexive research that involves deconstructing the dominant notions of childhood and explicating the power relations inherent in the relationship among researchers, parents and children. In the final theme we discuss what our methodological experiences in the field have taught us and what implications this might have for interpreting diasporic cultures. We also outline how our concept of the 'mnemonic diasporic habitus' may be a useful tool for unpacking the politics of diasporic identities.

Pilot Study: London Borough of Hackney, February 2013

The pilot study, conducted in February 2013, included visits to Arabic-speaking children of North African origins in their homes. In total we visited five families. It involved children keeping viewing diaries in sketchpad form, as well as a three-hour workshop. The study was conducted in preparation for the first phase of the main fieldwork, which took place in London in August–December 2013. The pilot examined how and whether Arabic and non-Arabic programming (consumed media texts) was open to different spaces of subjectification. It explored how the children's media uses informed their positioning vis-à-vis domesticity (diasporic space/local space/worldly space) and cultural temporality. The pilot was specifically concerned with investigating how Arabic-speaking children living in London respond to Arabic-language and other programming aimed at them, how they choose it, how they make sense of it and what they think about it.

The pilot deployed a three-stage methodology. In the first stage we conducted a three-hour workshop with seven school children between the ages of 7 and 10 years at the Childhood Museum in Bethnal Green, exploring their use of pan-Arab television, using drawings, group interviews (where children interviewed each other as journalists) and other interactive activities based around play. The three-hour workshop was a useful way to get to know the children, to establish trust and to recruit participants for the family viewing observations. In the second stage, we developed a 14-day media-viewing diary, which we used as a prompt for the selected participants taking part in the third stage of the research: family observations. Regardless of its small sample, the pilot's findings provided us with good insight into young children's everyday lives and media uses. It extended our enquiry beyond pan-Arab satellite channels to include new media, mobile phones and music. One of the pilot's key findings was that most of the participants preferred programming broadcast by British public service broadcasters and not Arabic programming broadcast from the countries of origin of the children's families. We also learnt that the children actively and selectively consumed different media, the internet being a preferred platform. This made us rethink and modify our methodological strategies to suit new and complex audience realities on the ground.

In the rest of this chapter, we reflect on methodological issues emerging from the main fieldwork we conducted in London, which included four workshops with children of Maghrebi and Mashreqi heritage and four family observations lasting a period of 25 days.

Framing Problems of Access and Trust within a Socio-Political Context

Having access to and establishing a relationship of trust with children and their families are, as ethnographic processes, rarely contextualized within the socio-cultural environments and the material realities by which they are determined. In preparation for our ethnographic research in London we had to locate four families of Arab origin, for the purpose of conducting home ethnography, and 24 children of Arab origin for the purpose of conducting four separate workshops.

As researchers residing in London for over a decade, we have been part of the changing public discourses on the UK's Arab diaspora. We each came to London individually without any links to the Arab diaspora. The compound and fluid selving process gradually blended the migrant narrative with increasing daily involvement with the UK as a final destination country. Over time, we both have joined the many Londoners who juggle with a native cultural repertoire and a British lived experience. Thus, questions like 'Where are you from?' have become harder to answer. Our social networks did not rely on our respective diasporic groups, and we both were at the margins of the intra-diasporic subjectification dynamics within the Arab diaspora in London. Engaging in this research necessitated an active performative process to connect with the Arab diaspora and to reposition ourselves as insiders to the Arab community. This process required engaging with the stratifying techniques of belonging and otherness vis-à-vis our native communities that are culturally familiar to us but which we effectively knew little about.

With no prior connection to the Arab diaspora in London, it was not possible to rely on personal contacts to recruit children between 7 and 12 years old – the target age of the research project. The prominent physicality of diasporic communities within the geography of London made London an obvious choice to initiate access. Our aim was to find entry points linking us to the varied loci of Arab communities rather than going through elitist and structured channels of Arab cultural production or education in London. While these channels are conventionally used in children's research because of their potential for easy access, they remain laden with power dynamics that could hinder children's ability to opt out and their willingness to express themselves freely.[7] We planned instead to gain entry by hitting the streets of the local Arab neighbourhoods, contacting commercial outlets and religious community centres.

Our strategy was to head for enclaves in London, including schools, known to have a predominant or at least a significant Arab diasporic population. We targeted places like Ladbroke Grove and Shepherds Bush with a sizeable Moroccan population, and Marble Arch, Kilburn and Edgware

Road, known to attract a largely Middle Eastern population (including Iraqi, Lebanese and Egyptian). We had designed a leaflet written both in Arabic and in English explaining the purpose of the research and the source of funding. We then approached a number of schools, mainly heads of Year 7, asking for help in recruiting children of Arab origin to take part in the research. In total we contacted eight schools, all of which, after a fair exchange of emails, said that lack of staff and time rendered them unable to help. To focus our energies, we then opted to target our native Arab diasporic communities, with whom we as researchers share a common culture and structure of feeling. We each concentrated on localities in London that had a significant Lebanese or Moroccan population and leafleted in the street, cafés, supermarkets and grocery shops. After six weeks of trying, it was the religious communities of these two groups – a mosque in Ladbroke Grove and a church in Swiss Cottage – that allowed us access to workshop participants. However, the agreement to give us access was followed by another eight-week period during which we, as researchers, were coaxingly and politely interrogated again and again about the nature and objectives of the research. We were only let in after literally dozens of email exchanges and a number of one-to-one meetings with community leaders in these religious establishments.

Negotiating access threw us into the contextual dynamics of our respective communities because it involved tapping into networks linked to local retailers, such as grocers and butchers. Nisrine's interaction with Lebanese shopkeepers in Kilburn is an example of the complex politics of diasporic relations, the insider–outsider positionality of researcher and migrant, and the continuous crossing over, rearticulating and blurring lines between 'us' and 'them'.[8] With every visit, shopkeepers tested the insider–outsider positionality in relation to the many facets of the intra-Lebanese habitus that revolve around the religion of birth. Through Lebanon's recent history of civil war (1975–1990) and until today, religion of birth remains a marker of difference, since it is a compulsory legal political category enshrined in the civic records of every Lebanese citizen regardless of their personal beliefs. Queries around this matter occurred smoothly, reflecting, in indirect ways, the importance of context in negotiating access. A seemingly basic question like 'Where are you from?' unfolds a powerful categorizing subtext that locates one's religious affiliation within a geographic location, since the Lebanese civil war resulted in a geographic segregation of population on the basis of religion of birth. When birthplace, and hence religion of birth, matched those of the shopkeeper in question, it was a first step into establishing an initial insider rapport tracing connections back in Lebanon and in the Lebanese diaspora in London. However, religion of birth is only a partial marker of the intra-Lebanese diasporic habitus. Further queries aimed to discern the researcher's links with social and religious institutions and practices within the Shi`a community in London. When the researcher could not show prior involvement with members of the community, the shopkeeper restricted access to it.

In contrast, the researcher's lack of identification with a specific Shi`a diasporic habitus guaranteed access to the Christian community through the Lebanese Maronite church in London. The priest, who was the main person in the church, went through the same geographic categorizing exercise to probe the researcher's birthplace, noting the researcher's religious 'Otherness'. However, more probing revealed the researcher's individual migration trajectory, lack of religious involvement with the Shi`a community in London and professional occupation. For the priest, these attributes were markers of a 'civilised Other', reflected in his comments such as, 'Wow you are well educated. Nowadays the Shi`a community in Lebanon has evolved'. Hence, an invitation to become an insider was extended to visit the church and engage with the religious rituals, as 'the church is open for all Lebanese regardless of their religious affiliation'. Effectively, performing the friendly Other through attending the Sunday Mass turned out to be the main channel for recruiting Lebanese respondents.

We have no doubt the difficulties we experienced in recruiting participants were largely due to the ethical sensitivities implicit in researching children and concern for the protection and well-being of minors as research participants. However, we also attribute them to socio-cultural and political variables. These include interpretations of domesticity as a private space, Arabophobia/Islamophobia and gender roles. Since the terrorist attacks of 9/11 in New York and 7/7 in London, there has been a conspicuous and ceaseless coverage of Islam and Muslims in British mainstream media. Such coverage tends, on the whole, to discursively link Islam, Muslims, Islamism and terrorism together as though these were inseparable categories. Over time, this has created a great sense of suspicion (and hatred in the case of fascist groups and many of their members who come largely from disgruntled poor working classes) towards Muslim and Arab communities in the UK.[9] Islamophobia is the result of an intersection between the encoding and the decoding of racist representations of Muslims and Arabs as Others, two aspects of which are seldom studied. The first is how a systematic consumption of negative coverage about Islam and Muslims affects British Muslim identities and their conceptions of Otherness. The second is what implications it has for access to ethnographic research with Muslim and Arab communities in the UK.[10] We believe the challenge we faced as researchers in getting access to Arab families' homes is largely due to suspicion, which Arab communities have themselves developed towards British media and the establishment they represent. We were denied access (mistrusted) because we were seen, regardless of our apparent traces of Arabness, as part of a racist system. Our research focus on London children of Arab origin and their media worlds may well have been misread by the parents as a sneaky attempt on our part (since we represent the system) to spy on Muslim/Arab children (to catch them early on). One of the parents with whom we conducted periodic home observations over eight weeks and who trusted us enough to sing for us and his children, jokingly remarked in the last family visit that we 'could be spies after all'.

Our constant insider–outsider repositioning was tested in our role as researchers conducting intra-diasporic research on Arab children and media. The nature of the inquiry called for home visits over a three-week time span. Through our contacts, a sense of anxiety and suspicion emerged as to the purpose of the research project. Questions such as 'Why are you looking at Arab kids?', 'What do you want to know?', 'Who is funding this research?' reflected a deep-seated anxiety about a growing Islamophobic climate in the UK. Muslim contacts were the most reluctant to participate in the research, in contrast to Christian contacts who were little concerned with any underlying motives. In this instance, our positioning as intra-diasporic researchers was embedded with a sense of paranoia from some contacts, who suspected that we were potentially acting as double agents, delving into the intimate lives of our 'own' communities and reporting back to the British system, since the funding was granted by the AHRC.

The problem of access and mistrust is the product of a relational structure and has to be understood more widely, in conjunction with factors such as gender and discourses of domesticity. We felt that our genders as researchers were unquestionably implicated not only in problems of access, but also in power relations between the researcher and the researched or the observer and the observed. Being a male ethnographer with an intention to observe children and families in their homes brought two challenges. First, there is a general bias against males working with children due to the recent explosion of highly mediatized legal cases of paedophilia involving famous children's programme presenters, educators and other males engaging in direct professional contact with children. Second, some families found it culturally inappropriate to allow a male researcher into their home when the male head of the household was absent. Whether due to a traditional, patriarchal form of domesticity (perhaps with roots in religious discourse) or to the general gender bias discussed above, some mothers of participants felt more at ease conversing with and being observed by a female rather than a male researcher. Being a male researcher meant that Tarik could not attend all the family observations on his own; indeed a mixed gender team proved quite effective in diffusing these gender-related obstacles. Researching children of any origin is usually fraught with ethical implications and the problems of access and trust discussed here are certainly not limited to our targeted group. However, we believe it is reasonable to argue that, in the case of Arab and Muslim children living in London, problems of access and trust are further complicated by an increasingly privatized media sphere where representations of Arab ethnicity and Islam are still deeply rooted in an orientalist discourse. Similarly, entry into private spaces is problematic regardless of the participants' origin. Researchers remain relative strangers and entry into private spaces, regardless of geography or culture, will always be challenging.

Being a woman facilitated access to children because of the conventional caring roles associated with women. But it also involved a process of negotiating gender performativity in relation to the dominant sociocultural discourses on gender within the Arab diasporic communities. Various Lebanese contacts within the Lebanese diaspora in London found that being a single Lebanese woman with no family ties in London represents a set of non-conforming social practices. These gendered moralities hold the potential to position the female researcher at the margins of the diaspora's dominant gender norms. For instance, one contact person interpreted it as a sign of sexual availability and licence for sexual harassment. However, the overwhelming majority of contact persons went beyond these moralities. They accepted the researcher's different ways of life as a marker for a 'friendly outsider' and sought to maintain friendship ties after the end of the fieldwork.

Mnemonic Diasporic Habitus between Performance and Affect

Once in the field and in family homes we were extremely conscious of the important task of building a rapport of trust with the children and their parents. While power relations between adult researchers and young respondents are part and parcel of research methodologies,[11] we wanted our encounters with the families to mimic structures of ordinary everyday talk in an attempt to destabilize binaries between researcher and researched and produce textured types of knowledge beyond ageist, ethnic and sociocultural biases. We cannot say with certainty to what extent what was said and how the families behaved was totally free or untainted by relations of power or by the simple fact that we were 'strangers', but we certainly shared intimate moments with the families we observed, which involved dancing, singing and telling jokes.

A three-way relationship among the diasporic researcher, parents and children developed within the performative site of the home. Initially, parents displayed tacit mistrust as they intently sat around the first few meetings with the children. Gradually, they loosened their involvement, yet they remained omnipresent as a silent and seemingly distracted audience. In most instances, parents were first generation immigrants, attached to the cultural practices of their country of birth. They also avidly engaged with Arabic-speaking global satellite TV channels on daily basis, a finding resonating with existing research on Arab diasporas in Europe.[12] They spoke limited English and mingled primarily and almost exclusively with fellow diaspora members. We related to parents through tracing commonalities in our diasporic trajectories, an issue that children did not closely relate to. We exchanged narratives about our migration history, our legal status and our perceptions of life in Lebanon/Morocco and the UK. The researchers' diasporic performativity with parents revolved around narratives of nostalgic belonging, manifested in an affinity over food, pop culture, childhood experiences and current anxiety in relation to the political insecurity engulfing the Arab region.

The mnemonic diasporic habitus was further expanded by our presence. Our performativity relied on making sense of, and navigating through, these overlapping cultural layers when relating to children and parents. Thus we brought our own diasporic cultural repertoire into the dynamics, opening doors to exploration of the selving process. In many instances, we were positioned at the edge of the insider–outsider mnemonic diasporic boundaries. For example, Moroccan children were curious about Nisrine's age and marital status and noted her short haircut as a novelty for an Arab woman. Lebanese children expressed a pronounced notion of sectarian and ethnic differences and considered Tarik different because of his darker complexion. We were able to relate to the children through London-focused cultural practices, an area with which the parents struggled. For instance, our conversations covered popular audio-visual culture, articulations of London's urban youth culture and contemplations on beliefs, hopes and worries.

However, in listening to the children talk about their friends, family members, schools and media worlds, often in the presence of their parents, we sensed early on that the telling of life stories/life worlds/the unfolding narratives of self were mnemonically performed for us in a way that produced a discursive language we had to unpack semiotically. This language we later attributed to the workings of a mnemonic diasporic habitus, manifested in a dialectical relationship between different narratives of self and contextual environment (in our case, parents' culture and researchers' culture). We found it useful in our grappling with the children's performed narrativity to distinguish between 'habitus' as the sum of accumulated socio-cultural attributes and as, as will be shown, an affectively performed habitus using mnemonic imagination, allowing navigation and negotiation of self between past and present and among parent cultures, the culture of the researchers as Arabs and London cultures. It is through the mnemonic imagination and the affective performance of diasporic habitus that a third discursive language about self is created.

What we are describing here as 'a mnemonic diasporic habitus' emerges from our implicated-ness in the research and in the lives of the children whom we were observing. As such, making sense of this type of habitus is for us not merely a matter of cultural interpretation, but also an object of methodological reflection, for the two things are inextricably linked. Our theoretical pursuit in unpacking the structures of a 'mnemonic diasporic habitus' is inspired by Emily Keightley and Michael Pickering's work on the 'mnemonic imagination', in which they steer away from sociologically and psychologically deterministic interpretations of memory and advocate a focus on the relations between personal and popular memory and interplay between situated and mediated experience.[13] The authors argue that the mnemonic imagination is key to these relations and this interplay because it facilitates 'the transactional movement necessary for their co-existence'.[14] Here, the redrafting of memories of our past experience is not a fixed process. Experience in this case is ceaselessly traversing a temporalized space between the remembering subject and the changing intervening social forces with which it enters a dialectical relationship. In the case of our research with children from the Arab diaspora in London, the 'traversing of temporalized space' is a perpetual performance of selfhood, oscillating between an 'unlived' spatio-temporality, mnemonically performed by the parents for the children, which enters into dialogue with the children's 'lived' experience, their implicated-ness in being in, and part of, spatio-symbolic London and their 'futuralness', to use Heidegger's term,[15] where children mnemonically imagine different ways of being in the world. Our role as ethnographers in this dialectical type of diasporic traversing was to facilitate the children's mnemonic imagination, to nurture it and encourage the parents to overcome their gatekeeping instincts and become aware of the imaginative work their children were doing.

Staying clear of modernist and deterministic interpretations of 'experience', Keightley and Pickering define experience as 'never exclusively personal or public, interiorised or outwardly facing, self-directed or the blind product of social forces', but always in flux and crossing between 'these mutually informing categories'.[16] The traversal movement of experience is predicated on a dual temporal structure, 'characterised by its continual unfolding in time while also acting back on the continuing development across time'.[17] This dual structure allows the modern subject to creatively reflect 'narratively' about self across time. It is because of our access to

Erfahrung[18] (the point where accumulated experience is evaluated) that our knowledge about self is crystallized. For the London children, accumulated experience is crystallized in a mnemonic, third discursive and performative space. In other words, while accumulated experience may shape their identities, it is through their intentional and performative narrative of self, which they negotiate between memory and imagination, that their subject-hood comes to light.

Taking their cue from Dilthey's work on *Poetry and Experience*, Kant's distinction between reproductive (*re-collective*) and productive (*inventive*) imagination, and Marleau Ponty's situating of the 'real' and the 'unreal' within a dialectical relationship, Keightley and Pickering build a strong case against 'the deleterious consequences of analytical separation of memory and imagination'. Their concept, 'mnemonic imagination', moves beyond this tendency, insisting instead on a 'continuous interpenetration' of memory and imagination.[19]

As we began to understand how habitus was performed for us through different affective strategies, we became conscious that we as ethnographers needed to modify our line of questioning, moving from being mere interviewers to performing being audiences. By 'poetics', we mean the mnemonic performativity that the children used to dialectically navigate through and between individual agents (habitus) and environment (field) to create a third meaning of self that lies at an intersection between the past, the present and the future, but which strategically embodies and champions the present and the future over the past. A 12-year-old female participant, who was talking to us about her favourite music, showed us parts of a music video where a young female US pop singer is almost naked. The participant mimed the lyrics she knew by heart as she gazed at the pop star with admiration, then shyly glanced at her mother and us and complained about the pop star's decadent and debauched behaviour. The child displayed a range of subtle expressions in relation to explicit pop culture that could be picked up by researchers through the process of 'interpretive poetics ... whereby layers of meaning in narrative texts are interrogated and interpreted in a way that mirrors a sophisticated reading of a poem' of which 'languages of the unsayables and woven and torn signifiers' are key interpretation registers.[20]

However, children evoked their Arab past when intentionally invited by parents. Experiences and practices across temporality and geography were manifested in the diasporic habitus through the parents' media capital. Lebanese children were exposed to Lebanese and Arabic-speaking TV, since it was the parents' default viewing choice. Lebanese parents also actively encouraged them to watch specific Lebanese TV shows ranging from comedy to talk shows and sometimes news. Children eagerly followed these shows on a daily basis, several times recounting the content to us. Similarly, they had regular contact with their relatives in Lebanon through online apps like Skype, Viber and WhatsApp. Sometimes these relatives featured as part of their closest daily contacts.

Children located the Arab past within mnemonic recollections of a nostalgic heritage rather than an articulation of the present physicality of Lebanon or Morocco in relation to London. For instance, children of Lebanese origin were not able to place Lebanon on the world map, and were not aware of the precarious security situation there. However, the physicality of London was pronounced in their articulation of their daily lives. Their native language was English, with only little understanding of Arabic. Their friends were primarily Lebanese, in contrast to Moroccan children who socialized regularly with various ethnicities. Their choice of music reflected London's urban and pop culture. Their Arabic music playlists were limited to patriotic songs and pop music, with an avid appetite for celebrity fandom. However, their English speaking playlists were much longer and, regardless of their religiosity, they were up to date with the most explicit music video clips of artists such as Miley Cyrus and Rihanna.

This mnemonic past was projected into the future in varying ways. Lebanese children who had never been to Lebanon referred to their parents' country of origin in romantic terms of a homeland and exile that are far removed from their existence in London. Their accounts focused on the beauty of their village, and their hope to go back to the big house, pets and garden they own there, contrasting it with their tiny one-bedroom flat in Shepherds Bush. Moroccan children meanwhile evoked images of exoticism reminiscent of an ideal holiday destination. They talked at length of the good times they have in Morocco, especially recounting the food, the music, the sun, the sea, as well as the friendly relatives.

Technologies of Self and Children's Media Worlds

When we initially designed the rationale for our overall research project, with three relational strands including audiences, texts and producers, we devised a clear set of objectives at the heart of which lay a key focus on Arab children's reading and engagement with media texts broadcast by pan-Arab satellite channels. No sooner had we entered the field than we were challenged to rethink not only our audience research questions (for UK children) but also our assumptions about the 'what' and 'how' of media consumption among children of Arab origin in the UK. The pilot study, which consisted of family observations and one workshop, had unveiled a key finding: British children of Arab origin spoke little if any Arabic and preferred watching children's programming on the BBC and ITV over the pan-Arab satellite channels that their parents watched. This finding helped us rethink our media focus, line of questioning and the design of media diaries in ways that allowed the children to creatively map out their social and media worlds for us.

As a consequence, our starting point for researching the children's media consumption habits had shifted from an idea in the ethnographer's head about what media were to how the children thought about them and used them. As we embarked on the family observations it became clear to us that the children's media consumption relied on multiple devices (mobiles, tablets) and media (video games, music, social media). In this sense, the practices of Londoner children of Arab origin coincided with findings from an EU-wide research that found children using media in individual and private spaces like their bedrooms and their mobile devices.[21] As we became more involved with family observations and having reworked our participant observation methods to allow for a freer and a more reflexive account of the children's narratives about self and media-cultures, we realized that the children use different media platforms (online and offline) not only strategically and for different purposes, but also as technologies of self through embodiment, where media become 'cultural frames'[22] and act as extensions of habitus. The children wove narratives of subject-hood through identification with and in relation to media characters, sounds and visuals. This type of narrativity was further helped by designing an experimental media diary, through which we attempted to explore not only the children's everyday media consumption habits but also how what they consume was used to operationalize their mnemonic diasporic habitus, giving us an insight into their media and social worlds. The diaries were a creative tool to get around the rigid communication dynamics that might ensue between researchers and children. Increasingly, diaries proved to be a particularly useful and versatile tool complementing ethnographic research.[23] The diaries had the merit of repositioning children as researchers engaged in recording and reflecting upon their own diasporic and media worlds. It also combined both qualitative and quantitative entries, allowing children to document their media consumption habits at the end of each day, in addition to reflecting on their diasporic and mnemonic habitus.

Using the diaries as a starting point for discussion, our line of questioning during family observations followed a fluid, semi-structured (sometimes unstructured) approach where the children felt comfortable enough to move from one subject to another. In most cases we only interfered or changed the line of questioning to stimulate further talk. In one instance a 7-year-old danced for us, performed a rap song and switched minutes later to telling us about a family member whom we were told was 'possessed'. As the discussion went on, this time including the father and a sister, the talk fluidly drifted to assertions about major pop stars like Madonna and Michael Jackson being Satan worshippers and part of a global conspiracy by the Illuminati secret society against Muslims around the world. Rather than seeing this as an incoherent form of narrativity, we picked on its theme/performance (pop culture, healing practices and religious persecution) as a stimulus for further insight into the workings of a mnemonic diasporic habitus. What might appear on the surface as a non-linear, fragmentary and therefore incoherent narrative of self can under scrutiny be extremely useful in unpacking the constituent elements of a performed mnemonic diasporic habitus.

We extended the flexible design of the media diary (which was intended to encourage talk about self) to the tasks we devised for the workshops, one of which was asking the children to work in groups as media producers to create a new Arab satellite channel targeting young Arabs living in the Arab region and in the diaspora. The task included designing a one-week running schedule for the new channel. Methodologically our objective from simulating this task was to further explore the children's media uses and preferences. Since consumption is deeply implicated in habitus, we also wanted to investigate the choices, modalities and socio-cultural attitudes/values informing their production choices, negotiative processes and decision-making in a gendered environment. We were keen to understand how and whether the children's choice of programming informed their mnemonic habitus. For example, even though workshop participants were recruited through religious cultural centres, none of the hypothetical new satellite channels had any programming remotely close to a religious theme. Was this because the parents were not present? Might the children have negotiated a different set of programmes had the parents been present at the workshops? Although our focus in this chapter is purely on method and not on our ethnographic findings as such, we want to emphasize how creative audience research approaches can delineate self-reflexive spaces that allow for a closer and a deeper insight, less into what we the researchers think about the world than into how the researched subjects think and experience the world. What we were keen to learn was how the children, as active audiences, understood, spoke about and mnemonically imagined their habitus in relation to their everyday media consumption.

Concluding Remarks

Audience research rarely reflects on the intricacies and challenges posed by the designed research methods. Findings are always privileged as an end, even if they are always inextricably linked to the rationalizing processes that come with method design. In our case it was clearly the methods and how we used them that shaped our conceptual framework, not vice versa. It was the conduct of the pilot and the reworking of the method that expanded the object of our enquiry and altered our interviewing techniques. Our method and conceptual framework entered a dialectical relationship. For example, as we began to grapple with the mnemonic diasporic habitus and its constituent elements (parent culture, London culture and a third performative language), we intentionally varied our line of questioning and approach to participant observation to further probe and test our grappling with a type of habitus where, like Bhabha's 'third space', identities are always in flux, navigating and negotiating meaning through an ambivalent space of enunciation.[24] Once we realized children's identities were intentionally and affectively performed for us through everyday talk,[25] dance and music, we strategically moved towards a more qualitative and a far less structured line of questioning. We became, as Bird would have put it, 'opportunist ethnographers'.[26]

This gave the third space a performative third language that disrupted cultural time and enunciated, through interactions among parent, researcher and London cultures, a carefully orchestrated form of subjecthood. The conceptualizing/theorizing of the mnemonic diasporic habitus was taking place simultaneously with our grappling with method and the fieldwork's materiality: we transformed the methods as we went along to better understand what the mnemonic diasporic habitus meant. It was our experience in the field that dictated methodological strategies and not an *a priori* objective or theoretical world outside it. As we progressed with the research we learned to relax more as ethnographers. We also learnt that singing along with a child or dancing to the sounds of their music can be more rewarding methodologically than following a rigid, possibly intimidating line of questioning, which often denies us access to what people are really like, what they really think and what their desires are really about. Deploying flexible, fluid and experimental methods that are ceaselessly open to change and reflection has, in our experience, been key towards grappling with the relational constituents of a mnemonic, performative habitus.

Our Arab-ness as ethnographers was deeply implicated in the research because we were by default part of the relational performative circuit through which children had to navigate discourses of selfhood. However, while the parents subtly acted as gatekeepers, we were asking the questions and encouraging the children's mnemonic diasporic performance. We facilitated the third language, which we then had to unpack. So, our relation to the parent culture, regardless of our age (equal to that of the parents) and our Arab-ness (appearance and language) does not occupy the same hierarchical position.

Notes

1 The concept of habitus expresses the way in which individuals develop attitudes and dispositions that make them who they are, and the ways in which they engage in culturally and historically constituted practices. See Jen Webb, Tony Schirato and Geoff Danaher, *Understanding Bourdieu* (London: Sage, 2002), p. xii.

2 Emily Keightley and Michael Pickering, *The Mnemonic Imagination: Remembering as Creative Practice* (Basingstoke: Palgrave Macmillan, 2012).

3 For example, see Samantha Punch, 'Research with children: The same or different from research with adults?', *Childhood*, 9/3 (2002), pp. 321–341; Allison James, 'Ethnography in the study of children and childhood', in P. Atkinson, A. Coffey, S. Delamont, J. Lofland and I. Lofland (eds), *Handbook of Ethnography* (London: Sage, 2001), pp. 246–257; Benjamin Zeitlyn and Kanwal Mand, 'Researching transnational childhoods', *Journal of Ethnic and Migration Studies*, 38/6 (2012), pp. 987–1006.

4 Zeitlyn and Mand, 'Researching transnational childhoods', p. 988.

5 George Marcus, 'Ethnography in/of the world system: the emergence of multi-sited ethnography', *Annual Review of Anthropology*, 24 (1995), pp. 95–117, quoted in Zeitlyn and Mand, 'Researching transnational childhoods', p. 989.

6 Allison James, *Childhood Identities: Self and Social Relationships in the Experience of the Child*, (Edinburgh: Edinburgh University Press, 1993), p. 72.

7 Karen Fog Olwig and Eva Gulløv, 'Towards an anthropology of children and place', in K. F. Olwig and E. Gulløv (eds), *Children's Places, Cross-Cultural Perspectives* (London: Routledge, 2003), pp. 1–22.

8 Marcus, 'Ethnography in/of the world system', pp. 95–117.

9 Dina Matar, 'Diverse diasporas, one meta-narrative: Palestinians in the UK talking about 11 September 2001', *Journal of Ethnic and Migration Studies*, 32/6 (2006), pp. 1027–1040; Zahera Harb and Ehab Bessaiso, 'British Arab Muslim audiences and television after September 11', *Journal of Ethnic and Migration Studies*, 32/6 (2006), pp. 1063–1076; Khalil Rinnawi, 'Instant nationalism' and the 'cyber mufti': The Arab diaspora in Europe and the transnational media, *Journal of Ethnic and Migration Studies*, 38/9 (2012), pp. 1451–1467.

10 See Marta Bolognani, 'Islam, ethnography and politics: Methodological issues in researching amongst West Yorkshire Pakistanis', *International Journal of Social Research Methodology*, 10/4 (2007), pp. 279–293; Ali Sundas, 'Second and third generation Muslims in Britain: A socially excluded group? Identities, integration and community cohesion' (Oxford, 2008), http://www.portmir.org.uk/assets/pdfs/second-and-third-generation-muslims-in-britain-a-socially-excluded-group.pdf; Jonathan Scourfield, Sophie Gilliat-Ray and Asma Khan Sameh Otri, *Muslim Childhood: Religious Nurture in a European Context* (Oxford: Oxford University Press, 2013).

11 See Pia Christensen and Allison James (eds), *Research with Children: Perspectives and Practices* (London: Falmer Press, 2000).

12 See Harb and Bessaiso, 'British Arab Muslim audiences and television after September 11'; Matar, 'Diverse diasporas, one meta-narrative'; Noureddine Miladi, 'Satellite television news and the Arab diaspora in Britain: comparing al-Jazeera, the BBC and CNN', *Journal of Ethnic and Migration Studies*, 32/6 (2006), pp. 947–960; Verena Stolcke, 'Talking culture: new boundaries, new rhetoric of exclusion in Europe', *Current Anthropology*, 36/3 (1995), pp. 1–13.

13 Keightley and Pickering, *The Mnemonic Imagination*.

14 Keightley and Pickering, *The Mnemonic Imagination*, p. 9.

15 Heidegger's *Zukünftigsein* (futuralness) is the state of readying oneself to 'receive the right impetus from the past in order to open it up'. See Martin Heidegger, *The Concept of Time: The First Draft of Being and Time* (trans. Ingo Farin) (London: Bloomsbury Academic 2011), p. 80.

16 Keightley and Pickering, *The Mnemonic Imagination*, p. 19.

17 Keightley and Pickering, *The Mnemonic Imagination*, p. 24.

18 Keightley and Pickering, *The Mnemonic Imagination*, p. 26.

19 Keightley and Pickering, *The Mnemonic Imagination*, p. 76.

20 Annie Rogers, Mary Casey, Jennifer Ekert, and Jim Holland, 'Interviewing children using an interpretive poetics', in S. Greene and D. Hogan (eds), *Researching Children's Experience: Approaches and Methods* (London: Sage, 2005), p. 160.

21 Sonia Livingstone, 'From family television to bedroom culture: Young people's media at home', in E. Devereux (ed), *Media Studies: Key Issues and Debates* (London: Sage, 2007), pp. 302–321; Sonia Livingstone, Leslie Haddon, Jane Vincent, Giovanna Mascheroni and Kjartan Ólafsson, *Net Children Go Mobile: The UK Report* (London: London School of Economics and Political Science, 2014).

22 Elizabeth Bird, *The Audience in Everyday Life: Living in a Media World* (Abingdon: Routledge, 2003), p. 3.

23 Lauri Hyers, Janet Swim and Robyn Mallet, 'The personal is political: Using daily diaries to examine everyday prejudice-related experiences', in S. Hesse-Biber and P. Leavy, *Emergent Methods in Social Research*, (London: Sage, 2006), pp. 313–336.

24 Bhabha's 'third space', in Homi Bhabha, *The Location of Culture*, (Abingdon: Routledge, 1994).

25 See Caroline Dover, 'Everyday talk: Investigating media consumption and identity amongst school children', *Particip@tions*, 4/1 (2007).

26 Bird, *The Audience in Everyday Life*.

Bibliography

Abdel-Nabi, Shereen, Jehan Agha, Julia Choucair, and Maya Mikdashi, 'Pop goes the Arab world: Popular music, gender, politics, and transnationalism in the Arab world', *HAWWA: Journal of Women of the Middle East and the Islamic World*, 2/2 (2004), pp. 231–254.

Abu-Lughod, Lila, 'Finding a Place for Islam: Egyptian Television Serials and the National Interest', *Public culture*, 5/3 (1993), pp. 493–513.

———, *Dramas of Nationhood: The Politics of Television in Egypt* (Chicago: University of Chicago Press, 2005).

Acker, Joan 'From sex roles to gendered institutions', *Contemporary Society*, 21/5 (September 1992), pp. 565–569.

Adney, Karley, 'Music videos: Representations of women' in M. Kosut (ed), *Encyclopedia of Gender in Media*, (Thousand Oaks, CA: Sage, 2012), pp. 245–248.

Adonis, *An Introduction to Arab Poetics* (London: Saqi Books, 2003).

Al-Abd, Noha, *Atfaluna we el-qawanat el-fadaiya* [Our children and satellite channels] (Cairo: Dar al-Fikr al-Arabi, 2005).

Alexander, Alison and James Owers, 'The economics of children's television' in J. Alison Bryant (ed), *The Children's Television Community* (Mahwah, NJ: Lawrence Erlbaum Associates, 2007), pp. 57–74.

Al-Khayr, Misbah and Hashim Al-Samira'i, Hashim (trans. Ahmad Sweity), 'Iftah Ya SimSim (Open Sesame) and Children in Baghdad' in E. Fernea (ed), *Children in the Muslim Middle East* (Austin, TX: University of Texas Press, 1995), pp. 464–469.

Al-Mahadin, Salam, 'From religious fundamentalism to pornography? The female body as text in Arabic song videos' in K. Sarikakis and L.R. Shade (eds), *Feminist Interventions in International Communication: Minding the Gap* (Lanham, MD: Rowman & Littlefield, 2007), pp. 146–160.

Al-Najjar, Abeer, 'Pure Salafi broadcasting: Al-Majd Channel (Saudi Arabia)' in Khaled Hroub (ed), *Religious Broadcasting in the Middle East* (London: C. Hurst & Co, 2012), pp. 35–55.

Alshaer, Atef, 'Towards a theory of a culture of communication: The fixed and the dynamic in Hamas' communicated discourse', *Middle East Journal of Culture and Communication*, 1/2 (2008), pp. 101–121.

Alshaer, Atef, 'Language as culture: The question of Arabic' in Tarik Sabry (ed), *Arab Cultural Studies: Mapping the Field* (London: I.B.Tauris, 2012), pp. 275–297.

Bibliography

Aly, Ramy, 'Rebuilding Egyptian Media for a Democratic Future', *Arab Media and Society*, 14 (Summer 2011).

Ammar, Hamed, *Growing Up in an Egyptian Village* (London: Routledge, 1954).

Anderson, Benedict, *Imagined Communities: Reflections on the Origin and Spread of Nationalism* (London: Verso, 1991).

Arab Media Outlook 2011–2015: Arab Media Vulnerability and Transformation, 4th ed. (Dubai: Dubai Press Club, 2011).

Ariès, Philippe, *Centuries of Childhood* (trans. Robert Baldick) (New York: Vintage Books, 1962).

Armbrust, Walter, *Mass Culture and Modernism in Egypt* (Cambridge: Cambridge University Press, 1996).

Armbrust, William, 'What would Sayyiid Qutb say? Some reflections on video clips', *Transnational Broadcasting Studies* Vol. 1, *Culture Wars: The Arab Music Video Controversy* (Cairo: American University in Cairo Press, 2005), pp. 18–29.

Armbrust, Walter, 'Synchronizing Watches: The State, the Consumer, and Sacred Time in Ramadan Television' in B. Meyer & A. Moors (eds), *Religion, Media, and the Public Sphere* (Bloomington, IN: Indiana University Press, 2006).

Aronczyk, Melissa, *Branding the Nation: The Global Business of National Identity* (New York: Oxford University Press, 2013).

Azer, Adel and Sohair Mehanna, Mulki al-Sharmani and Essam Ali, *Child Protection Policies in Egypt: A Rights Based Approach*, Monograph in the *Cairo Papers in Social Science* series, 30/1 (2010).

Banet-Weiser, Sarah, *Kids Rule! Nickelodeon and Consumer Citizenship* (Durham, NC: Duke University Press, 2007).

Barakat, Halim, 'The Arab family and the challenge of social transformation' in E. Fernea (ed), *Women and Family in the Middle East – New Voices of Change* (Austin, TX: University of Texas Press, 1985), pp. 27–48.

——, *The Arab World: Society, Culture and State* (Berkeley, CA: University of California Press, 1993).

Barker, Martin and Julian Petley (eds), *Ill Effects: The Media Violence Debate* (London and New York: Routledge, 1997).

Bassiouney, Reem, *Arabic Sociolinguistics* (Edinburgh: Edinburgh University Press, 2009).

BBC Trust, *Review of the BBC's Children's Services* (London, 2013). Available at: http://downloads.bbc.co.uk/bbctrust/assets/files/pdf/our_work/childrens_services/childrens_services.pdf (accessed 17 September 2015).

Belarbi, Aicha (trans. Moncef and Wafaa Lahlou) 'The child as economic investment: Preliminary reflections' in E. Fernea (ed), *Children in the Muslim Middle East* (Austin, TX: University of Texas Press, 1995), pp. 230–234.

Benson, David and Andrew Jordan, 'What have we learned from policy transfer research? Dolowitz and Marsh revisited', *Political Studies Review*, 9 (2011), pp. 366–378.

Bibliography

Berkey, Jonathan, 'Review of Avner Giladi "Children of Islam: Concepts of childhood in medieval Muslim society"', *Speculum*, 69/3 (1994), pp. 780–781.

Bettelheim, Bruno, 'Do Children need television?' in P. Löhr and M. Meyer (eds), *Children, Television and New Media: A Reader of Research and Documentation in Germany* (Luton: University of Luton Press, 1999), pp. 3–37.

Bhabha, Homi, *The Location of Culture* (London: Routledge, 1994).

Billig, Michael, *Banal Nationalism* (London: Sage, 1995).

Bird, Elizabeth, *The Audience in Everyday Life* (New York and Abingdon: Routledge, 2003).

Boerwinkel, Felia, *The First Lady Phenomenon in Jordan: Assessing the Effect of Queen Rania's NGOs on Jordanian Civil Society* (Amsterdam: University of Amsterdam and Hivos, March 2011).

Bolin, Göran and Per Ståhlberg, 'Mediating the nation state: Agency and the media in nation-branding campaigns', *International Journal of Communication*, 9 (2015), pp. 3065–3083.

Bolognani, Marta, 'Islam, ethnography and politics: Methodological issues in researching amongst West Yorkshire Pakistanis', *International Journal of Social Research Methodology*, 10/4 (2007), pp. 279–293.

Boyd-Barrett, Oliver, 'Pan-Arab satellite television: the Dialectics of identity' in H. Tumber (ed), *Media Power, Professionals and Policies* (London and New York: Routledge, 2000), pp. 314–331.

Boyden, Jo, 'What place the politics of compassion in education surrounding non-citizen children?', *Educational Review*, 61/3 (2009), pp. 265–276.

Brack, Hans, *The Evolution of the EBU through its Statutes from 1950 to 1976* (Geneva: European Broadcasting Union, 1976).

Brunsdon, Charlotte, 'Problems with Quality', *Screen*, 31/1 (1990), pp. 67–90.

Bryant, J. Alison, 'Understanding the children's television community from an organizational network perspective' in J. Alison Bryant (ed), *The Children's Television Community* (Mahwah, NJ: Lawrence Erlbaum Associates, 2006), pp. 35–55.

Buccianti, Alexandra, 'Dubbed Turkish soap operas conquering the Arab world: Social liberation or cultural alienation?', *Arab Media and Society* 10 (Spring 2010).

Buckingham, David, 'The commercialisation of childhood? The place of the market in children's media Culture', *Changing English*, 2/2 (1995), pp. 17–40.

———, 'New media, new childhoods? Children's changing cultural environment in the age of digital technology" in M. J. Kehily (ed), *An Introduction to Childhood Studies*, 2nd ed. (Maidenhead: Open University Press, 2009), pp. 124–139.

Buckingham, David, Hannah Davies, Ken Jones and Peter Kelley, *Children's Television in Britain* (London: BFI Publishing, 1999).

Buckingham, David et al., *The Impact of the Commercial World on Children's Wellbeing: Report of an Independent Assessment* (London: Department for

Children, Schools and Families and Department of Culture, Media and Sport, 2009).

Caves, Richard, *Creative Industries: Contracts between Art and Commerce* (Cambridge, MA: Harvard University Press, 2000).

Cestor, Elisabeth, 'Music and television in Lebanon' in M. Frishkopf (ed), *Music and Media in the Arab World* (Cairo: The American University in Cairo Press, 2010), pp. 97–110.

Christensen, Pia and Allison James (eds), *Conducting Research with Children* (London: Falmer Press, 2000).

Cole, Alexander, 'Distant neighbours: the new geography of animated film production in Europe,' *Regional Studies*, 42 (2008), pp. 891–904.

Collier, David, 'Understanding process tracing,' *Political Science and Politics: PS*, 44/4 (October 2011), pp. 823–830.

Communication and Media Research Institute, *Orientations in the Development of Screen Content for Arabic-speaking Children: Findings Report*, (London: University of Westminster, September 2015).

Cooke, Miriam, *Tribal Modern: Branding New Nations in the Arab Gulf* (Oakland, CA: University of California Press, 2014).

Cunningham, Hugh, *Children of the Poor: Representations of Childhood since the Seventeenth Century* (Oxford: Blackwell, 1991).

——, *Children and Childhood in Western Society since 1500* (Harlow: Pearson Education, 1995).

Dabbous, Dima, *Regulating Lebanese Broadcasting: A Policy Analysis* (Saarbrücken: Lambert Academic Publishing, 2013).

Dabbous-Sensenig, Dima, 'Ending the War? The Lebanese Broadcasting Act of 1994,' PhD thesis (Sheffield Hallam University, 2003).

D'Arma, Alessandro, Gunn Enli and Jeanette Steemers, 'Serving children in public service media' in G. Ferrell Lowe (ed), *The Public in Public Service Media* (Göteborg: Nordicom, 2010), pp. 227–242.

D'Arma, Alessandro and Jeanette Steemers, 'Children's television: the soft underbelly of public service broadcasting'. Paper presented to the RIPE@2008 conference on Public Service Media in the 21st Century (Mainz, October 2008).

——, 'Public service media and children: Serving the digital citizens of the future,' in P. Iosifidis (ed), *Reinventing Public Service Communication* (Basingstoke: Palgrave Macmillan, 2010), pp. 114–127.

——, 'Children's television: markets and regulation' in Karen Donders, Caroline Pauwels and Jan Loisen (eds), *Private Television in Western Europe: Content, Market, Policies* (Basingstoke: Palgrave Macmillan, 2013), pp. 123–135.

Davis, Susan and Douglas Davis, 'Love conquers all? Changing images of gender and relationship in Morocco' in E. Fernea (ed), *Children in the Muslim Middle East* (Austin, TX: University of Texas Press, 1995), pp. 93–108.

Deeb, Mary Jane, 'The 99: Superhero comic books from the Arab world' in P. Karimi and C. Gruber (eds), *Images of the Child and Childhood in Modern Muslim Contexts*, special volume of *Comparative Studies of South Asia, Africa and the Middle East*, 32/2 (2012), pp. 391–407.

Diana, Chiara, 'Children's citizenship: Revolution and the seeds of an alternative future in Egypt' in Linda Herrera (ed), *Wired Citizenship: Youth Learning and Activism in the Middle East* (Abingdon: Routledge, 2014), pp. 60–75.

Diekman, Amanda, Alice Eagly, Antonio Mlandinic and Maria Cristina Ferreira, 'Dynamic stereotypes about women and men in Latin America and the United States', *Journal of Cross-Cultural Psychology*, 36 (2005), pp. 209–226.

Dodge, Toby, 'Bringing the bourgeoisie back in: Globalization and the birth of liberal authoritarianism in the Middle East' in T. Dodge and R. Higgott (eds), *Globalization and the Middle East: Islam, Economy, Society and Politics* (London: Royal Institute of International Affairs, 2002), pp. 169–187.

Dorsky, Susan and Thomas Stevenson, 'Childhood and education in highland North Yemen' in E. Fernea (ed), *Children in the Muslim Middle East* (Austin, TX: University of Texas Press, 1995), pp. 309–324.

Dover, Caroline, 'Everyday talk: Investigating media consumption and identity amongst school children', *Particip@tions*, 4/1 (2007).

Eagly, Alice, Wendy Wood and Amanda Diekman, 'Social role theory of sex differences and similarities: A current appraisal' in T. Eckes and H. M. Trautner (eds), *The Developmental Social Psychology of Gender* (Mahwah, NJ: Lawrence Erlbaum Associates, 2000), pp. 123–174.

Elahi, Maryam, 'The rights of the child under Islamic law: Prohibition of the child soldier' in E. Fernea (ed), *Children in the Muslim Middle East* (Austin, TX: University of Texas Press, 1995), pp. 367–374.

Ferguson, Charles, 'Diglossia', *Word* 15 (1959), pp. 325–340.

Fernea, Elizabeth, '*Children in the Muslim Middle East*' in E. Fernea (ed), *Childhood in the Muslim Middle East* (Austin, TX: University of Texas Press, 1995), pp. 3–16.

Fernea, Robert, 'Gender, sexuality and patriarchy in modern Egypt', *Critique: Critical Middle East Studies*, 12/12 (2003), pp. 141–153.

Forman-Brunell, Miriam and Rebecca C. Hains (eds), *Princess Cultures: Mediating Girls' Imaginations and Identities* (New York: Peter Lang, 2015).

Frishkopf, Michael, 'Introduction: Music and media in the Arab world and *Music and Media in the Arab World* as music and media in the Arab world: A meta-discourse' in M. Frishkopf (ed), *Music and Media in the Arab World* (Cairo: The American University in Cairo Press, 2010), pp. 1–64

Galal, Ehab, 'Reimagining religious identities in children's programs on Arabic satellite-TV: intentions and values' in J. Feldt and P. Seeberg (eds), *New Media in the Middle East* (Odense: Syddansk Universitetsforlag, 2006), pp. 104–118.

Bibliography

Galal, Ehab, 'Identity and Lifestyle on Islamic Satellite-television: A content analysis of selected programmes' positioning of Muslims' [in Danish], PhD thesis (University of Copenhagen, 2009).

Galal, Lise Paulsen, 'Coptic Christian practices: formations of sameness and difference', *Islam and Christian-Muslim Relations*, 23/1 (2012), pp. 45–58.

George, Alexander and Andrew Bennett, *Case Studies and Theory Development in the Social Sciences* (Cambridge, MA: MIT Press, 2005).

Giladi, Avner, 'Some notes on the Qur'anic concepts of family and childhood' in F. Georgeon and K. Kreiser (eds), *Childhood and Youth in the Muslim World* (Paris, 2007), pp. 15–26.

——, 'Herlihy's thesis revisited: Some notes on investment in children in medieval Muslim society', *Journal of Family History*, 36/3 (2011), pp. 235–247.

——, 'Concepts of childhood and attitudes towards children in medieval Islam: A preliminary study with special reference to reaction to infant and child mortality', *Journal of the Economic and Social History of the Orient*, 32/2 (1989), pp. 121–152.

Giroux, Henry A. and Grace Pollock, *The Mouse That Roared: Disney and the End of Innocence*, 2nd ed. (Lanham, MD: Rowman & Littlefield, 2010).

Gittins, Diana, 'The historical construction of childhood' in M. J. Kehily (ed), *An Introduction to Childhood Studies*, 2nd ed. (Maidenhead: Open University Press, 2009), pp. 35–49.

Götz, Maya and Dafna Lemish, 'Gender representations in children's television worldwide: A comparative study of 24 countries' in M. Götz and D. Lemish (eds), *Sexy Girls, Heroes and Funny Losers: Gender Representations in Children's TV around the World* (Frankfurt: Peter Lang, 2012), pp. 9–48.

Haas, Peter M., 'Introduction: Epistemic communities and international policy coordination', *International Organisation*, 46/1 (Winter 1992), pp 1–35.

Hains, Rebecca C., *The Princess Problem: Guiding Our Girls through the Princess-Obsessed Years* (Naperville, IL: Sourcebooks, 2014).

Hanson, Karl, 'Schools of thought in children's rights' in M. Liebel (ed), *Children's Rights from Below: Cross-Cultural Perspectives* (Basingstoke: Palgrave Macmillan, 2012), pp. 63–79.

Harb, Zahera and Ehab Bessaiso, 'British Arab Muslim audiences and television after September 11', *Journal of Ethnic and Migration Studies*, 32/6 (2006), pp. 1063–1076.

Heidegger, Martin, *The Concept of Time: The First Draft of Being and Time* (trans. Ingo Farin) (London: Bloomsbury Academic, 2011).

Hendrick, Harry, 'Constructions and reconstructions of British childhood: An interpretive Survey, 1800 to the present' in A. James and A. Prout (eds), *Constructing and Reconstructing Childhood: Contemporary Issues in the Sociological Study of Childhood* (London: Falmer Press, 1997), pp. 34–62.

Bibliography

——, 'Origin and evolution of childhood in Western Europe, c.1400–1750' in J. Qvortrup, W. Corsaro and M-S. Honig (eds), *Palgrave Handbook of Childhood Studies* (Basingstoke: Palgrave Macmillan, 2009), pp. 99–113.

Heydemann, Stephen, 'Upgrading Authoritarianism in the Arab World', Brookings Institution Saban Center for Middle East Policy, Analysis Paper No 13 (October 2007).

Heywood, Colin, *A History of Childhood: Children and Childhood in the West from Medieval to Modern Times* (Cambridge: Polity Press, 2001).

Higson, Andrew, 'The Concept of National Cinema', *Screen*, 30/4 (1989), pp. 36–46.

Holes, Clive, 'Orality, culture and language', in Jonathan Owens (ed), *The Oxford Handbook of Arabic Linguistics* (Oxford: Oxford University Press, 2013), pp. 281–300.

Hourani, Albert (1963) *Arabic Thought in the Liberal Age: 1798–1939* (Cambridge; Cambridge University Press, 1963).

Human Rights Watch, *Charged with Being Children: Egyptian Police Abuse of Children in Need of Protection* (Washington: Human Rights Watch, February 2003).

Hunt, Peter, 'Children's literature and childhood' in M. J. Kehily (ed), *An Introduction to Childhood Studies*, 2nd ed. (Maidenhead: Open University Press, 2009), pp. 50–69.

Hyers, Lauri, Janet Swim and Robyn Mallet, 'The personal is political: Using daily diaries to examine everyday prejudice-related experiences' in S. Hesse-Biber and P. Leavy (eds), *Emergent methods in social research* (London: Sage, 2006), pp. 313–336.

Ibrahim, Barabara and Hind Wassef, 'Caught between two worlds: Youth in the Egyptian hinterland' in R. Meijer (ed), *Alienation or Integration of Arab Youth: Between Family, State and Street* (London: Routledge, 2000), pp. 161–188.

Ibrahim, Saad Eddin, *The Copts of Egypt* (London: Minority Rights Group, 1996).

James, Allison, *Childhood Identities: Self and Social Relationships in the Experience of the Child*, (Edinburgh: Edinburgh University Press, 1993).

——, 'Ethnography in the study of children and childhood' in P. Atkinson, A. Coffey, S. Delamont, J. Lofland and I. Lofland (eds), *Handbook of Ethnography* (London: Sage, 2001), pp. 246–257.

James, Allison, Chris Jenks and Alan Prout, *Theorizing Childhood* (Cambridge: Polity Press, 1998).

Jancovich, Mark and James Lyons, *Quality Popular Television* (London: BFI Publishing, 2003).

Jenks, Chris, *Childhood*, 2nd ed. (Abingdon: Routledge, 2005).

——, 'Constructing childhood sociologically' in M. J. Kehily (ed), *An Introduction to Childhood Studies* (Maidenhead: Open University Press, 2009), pp. 93–111.

Jhally, Sut, *Dreamworlds II: Desire, Sex and Power in Music Video* [VHS] (Northhampton, MA: Media Education Foundation, 1995).

——, *Dreamworlds 3: Desire, Sex and Power in Music Video* [DVD] (Northhampton, MA: Media Education Foundation, 2007).

Johnson, Catherine and Paul Grainge, 'From broadcast design to "On-Brand TV": Repositioning expertise in the promotional screen industries' in M. Banks, B. Conor and V. Mayer (eds), *Production Studies: The Sequel!* (Abingdon: Routledge, 2016), pp. 46–58.

Jordan, Amy B., 'Children's media policy', *The Future of Children*, 18/1 (Spring 2008), pp. 235–253.

Joseph, Suad, 'Connectivity and patriarchy among urban working-class Arab families in Lebanon' *Ethos*, 21/4 (1993), pp. 452–484.

———, *Intimate Selving in Arab Families: Gender, Self, and Identity in Arab Families* (New York: Syracuse University Press, 1999).

Kamrava, Mehran, *Qatar: Small State, Big Politics* (Ithaca, NY: Cornell University Press, 2013).

Kaneva, Nadia, 'Nation branding: Toward an agenda for critical research', *International Journal of Communication*, 5 (2011), pp. 117–141.

Karam, Imad, 'Satellite television: A breathing space for Arab youth?' in N. Sakr (ed), *Arab Media and Political Renewal: Community, Legitimacy and Public Life* (London: I.B.Tauris 2007), pp. 80–95.

Karimi, Pamela and Gruber, Christiane., 'Introduction: The Politics and Poetics of the Child Image in Muslim Contexts' in P. Karimi and C. Gruber (eds), *Images of the Child and Childhood in Modern Muslim Contexts*, special volume of *Comparative Studies of South Asia, Africa and the Middle East*, 32/2 (2012), pp. 273–293.

Kehily, Mary Jane, 'Understanding childhood: An introduction to some key themes and issues' in M. J. Kehily (ed), *An Introduction to Childhood Studies,* 2nd ed. (Maidenhead: Open University Press, 2009), pp. 1–16.

Keightley, Emily and Michael Pickering, *The Mnemonic Imagination: Remembering as Creative Practice* (Basingstoke: Palgrave Macmillan, 2012).

Khatib, Lina, *Qatar and the Recalibration of Power in the Gulf* (Beirut: Carnegie Middle East Center, 2014).

Kinder, Marsha, *Playing with Power in Movies, Television, and Video Games: From Muppet Babies to Teenage Mutant Ninja Turtles* (Berkeley/Los Angeles: University of California Press, 1991).

Kingdon, John W., *Agendas, Alternatives and Public Policies*, 2nd ed. (Glenview, IL: Longman, 2011).

Kleeman, David W., 'PRIX JEUNESSE as a Force for Cultural Diversity' in D. G. Singer and J. L. Singer (eds), *Handbook of Children and the Media* (Thousand Oaks, CA: Sage, 2001), pp. 521–531.

Kline, Steven, *Out of the Garden: Toys, TV and Children's Culture in the Age of Marketing* (London: Verso, 1993).

Kohstall, Florian, 'Free transfer, limited mobility: A decade of higher education reform in Egypt and Morocco', *Revue des mondes musulmans et de la Méditerranée*, 131 (June 2012), pp. 91–109.

Bibliography

Kraidy, Marwan, *Hybridity, or the Cultural Logic of Globalization* (Philadelphia: Temple University Press, 2005).

Kraidy, Marwan and Joe F. Khalil, 'Youth, media and culture in the Arab world' in K. Drotner and S. Livingstone (eds), *International Handbook of Children, Media and Culture* (London: Sage, 2008), pp. 336–350.

Krätke, Stefan, 'Network analysis of production clusters: the Potsdam/Babelsberg film industry as an example,' *European Planning Studies,* 10 (2002), pp. 27–54.

Kubala, Patricia, 'The controversy over satellite music television in contemporary Egypt' in M. Frishkopf (ed), *Music and Media in the Arab World* (Cairo: The American University in Cairo Press, 2010), pp. 173–224.

Lee, Stacey, *Unraveling the "Model Minority" Stereotype*, 2nd ed. (New York: Teachers College Press, 2009).

Lemish, Dafna, *Screening Gender on Children's Television: The Views of Producers around the World* (Abingdon: Routledge, 2010).

———, 'The future of childhood in the global television market' in G. Dines and J. M. Humez (eds), *Gender, Race and Class in Media: A Critical Reader* (Thousand Oaks, CA: Sage, 2011), pp. 355–364.

Lesser, Gerald, *Children and Television: Lessons from Sesame Street* (New York: Random House, 1974).

Livingstone, Sonia, 'From family television to bedroom culture: Young people's media at home' in E. Devereux (ed), *Media Studies: Key Issues and Debates* (London: Sage, 2007), pp. 302–321.

Livingstone, Sonia, Leslie Haddon, Jane Vincent, Giovanna Mascheroni and Kjartan Ólafsson, *Net Children Go Mobile: The UK Report* (London: London School of Economics and Political Science, 2014).

Locke, John, *Some Thoughts Concerning Education.* Internet Modern History Sourcebook (1692). Available at: http://www.fordham.edu/halsall/mod/modsbook.html (accessed 15 February 2013).

Lull, James, 'The social uses of television,' *Human Communication Research,* 6 (1980), pp. 197–209.

Malkki, Liisa, 'National Geographic: The rooting of peoples and the territorialization of national identity among scholars and refugees,' *Cultural Anthropology,* 7/1 (1992), pp. 24–44.

Malmelin, Nando and Johanna Moisander, 'Brands and branding in media management – Toward a research agenda,' *International Journal on Media Management,* 16/1 (2014), pp. 9–25.

Marcus, George E. 'Ethnography in/of the world system: the emergence of multi-sited ethnography,' *Annual Review of Anthropology,* 24 (1995), pp. 95–117.

Martinez, Luis, 'Youth, The Street and Violence in Algeria' in R. Meijer (ed), *Alienation or Integration of Arab Youth: Between Family, State and Street* (London: Routledge, 2000), pp. 83–113.

235

Bibliography

Matar, Dina, 'Diverse diasporas, one meta-narrative: Palestinians in the UK talking about 11 September 2001', *Journal of Ethnic and Migration Studies*, 32/6 (2006), pp. 1027–1040.

Mattern, Shannon, 'Font of a nation: Creating a national graphic identity for Qatar', *Public Culture* 20/3 (2008), pp. 479–496.

Mazawi, Andre Elias and Ronald G. Sultana, *World Yearbook of Education 2010: Education and the Arab World* (Abingdon: Routledge, 2013).

Mehrez, Samia, *Egypt's Culture Wars: Politics and Practice* (Abingdon: Routledge, 2010).

Meijer, Roel (ed), *Alienation or Integration of Arab Youth: Between Family, State and Street* (Abingdon: Routledge, 2000)

Messenger Davies, Máire, 'Academic literature review: The future of children's television programming' (2007). Available at: http://www.ofcom.org.uk/consult/condocs/kidstv/litreview.pdf (accessed 14 February 2014).

——, *Children, Media and Culture* (Maidenhead: Open University Press, 2010).

Michalis, Maria, *Governing European Communications* (Plymouth: Lexington Books, 2007).

Miladi, Noureddine, 'Satellite television news and the Arab diaspora in Britain: Comparing al-Jazeera, the BBC and CNN', *Journal of Ethnic and Migration Studies*, 32/6 (2006), pp. 947–960.

Mitchell, Timothy, *Colonising Egypt* (Cambridge: Cambridge University Press, 1988).

Morley, David, *Family Television: Cultural Power and Domestic Leisure* (London: Comedia, 1986).

Nash, Ilana, *American Sweethearts: Teenage Girls in Twentieth-Century Popular Culture* (Bloomington, IN: Indiana University Press, 2006).

Negra, Diane, *What a Girl Wants? Fantasizing the Reclamation of Self in Postfeminism* (London: Routledge, 2009).

Ofcom, *The Future of Children's Television Programming* (London, 2007). Available at: http://stakeholders.ofcom.org.uk/consultations/kidstv/statement/ (accessed 16 February 2015).

——, *Children and Parents: Media Use and Attitudes Report* (London, 2013). Available at: stakeholders.ofcom.org.uk/binaries/research/media-literacy/october-2013/research07Oct2013.pdf (accessed 16 February 2014).

Olwig, Karen Fog and Eva Gulløv, 'Towards an anthropology of children and place' in K. F. Olwig and E. Gulløv (eds), *Children's places, Cross-Cultural Perspectives* (Abingdon: Routledge, 2003), pp. 1–22.

Orme, Nicholas, *Medieval Children* (New Haven: Yale University Press, 2001).

Ozment, Steven, *Ancestors: The Loving Family in Old Europe* (Cambridge, MA: Harvard University Press, 2001).

Palmer, Sue, *Toxic Childhood* (London: Orion, 2006).

Parkes, Aisling, *Children and International Human Rights Law: The Right of the Child to be Heard* (Abingdon: Routledge, 2013).

Bibliography

Peterson, Mark Allen, 'The *jinn* and the computer: Consumption and identity in Arabic children's magazines', *Childhood*, 12/2 (2005), pp. 177–200.

———, '*Imsukuhum kulhum!* Modernity and morality in Egyptian children's consumption', *Journal of Consumer Culture* 10/2 (2010), pp. 233–253.

———, *Connected in Cairo: Growing up Cosmopolitan in the Modern Middle East* (Bloomington IN: Indiana University Press, 2011).

Piaget, Jean, *The Language and Thought of the Child* (London: Routledge, 1977).

Pieterse, Jan Nederveen, 'Globalization as hybridization' in M. Featherstone, S. Lash and R. Robertson (eds), *Global Modernities* (London: Sage, 1995), pp. 45–68.

Pike, Kirsten, 'Lessons in liberation: Schooling girls in feminism and femininity in 1970s *ABC Afterschool Specials*', *Girlhood Studies: An Interdisciplinary Journal*, 4/1 (Summer 2011), pp. 95–113.

———, 'Music videos: Representations of men' in M. Kosut (ed), *Encyclopedia of Gender in Media* (Thousand Oaks, CA: Sage, 2012), pp. 242–245.

———, 'Princess culture in Qatar: Exploring princess media narratives in the lives of Arab female youth' in M. Forman-Brunell and R. Hains (eds), *Princess Cultures: Mediating Girls' Imaginations and Identities* (New York: Peter Lang, 2015), pp. 139–160.

Postman, Neil, *The Disappearance of Childhood* (New York: Delacorte Press, 1982).

Prince, Russell, 'Policy transfer as policy assemblage: making policy for the creative industries in New Zealand', *Environment and Planning A*, 42 (2010), pp. 169–186.

Prinsloo, Jeanne, 'Seductive little girls on children's TV: Sexualization and gender relations' in M. Götz and D. Lemish (eds), *Sexy Girls, Heroes and Funny Losers: Gender Representations in Children's TV around the World* (Frankfurt: Peter Lang, 2012), pp. 69–90.

Prout, Alan and Allison James, 'A new paradigm for the sociology of childhood: Provenance, promise and problems' in A. James and A. Prout (eds), *Constructing and Reconstructing Childhood* (London: Falmer Press, 1997), pp. 7–32.

Punch, Samantha, 'Research with children: The same or different from research with adults?', *Childhood*, 9/3 (2002), pp. 321–341.

Railton, Diane and Paul Watson, *Music Video and the Politics of Representation* (Edinburgh: Edinburgh University Press, 2011).

Restö, Jan, 'What is Arabic?' in J. Owens (ed), *The Oxford Handbook of Arabic Linguistics* (Oxford, 2013), pp. 433–451.

Rinnawi, Khalil, (2012) '"Instant nationalism" and the "Cyber Mufti": The Arab diaspora in Europe and the transnational media', *Journal of Ethnic and Migration Studies* 38/9 (2012), pp. 1451–1467.

Rogers, Annie, Mary Casey, Jennifer Ekert and Jim Holland, 'Interviewing children using an interpretive poetics' in S. Greene and D. Hogan (eds), *Researching Children's Experience: Approaches and Methods* (London: Sage, 2005), pp. 158–174.

Rooke, Tetz, 'Escape from the family: A theme in Arab autobiography' in R. Meijer (ed), *Alienation or Integration of Arab Youth: Between Family, State and Street* (London: Routledge, 2000), pp. 207–222.

Rosenhouse, Judith, 'Colloquial and literary Arabic in Israel: An analysis of a child's texts in colloquial Arabic' in M. Piamenta, J. Rosenhouse and A. Elad (eds), *Linguistic and Cultural Studies on Arabic and Hebrew* (Wiesbaden: Otto Harrassowitz Verlag, 2001), pp. 107–134.

Ryding, Karin Christina, 'Second-language acquisition' in J. Owens (ed), *The Oxford Handbook of Arabic Linguistics* (Oxford: Oxford University Press, 2013), pp. 392–411.

Sabel, Charles F. and Jonathan Zeitlin, 'Neither modularity nor relational contracting: Inter-firm collaboration in the new economy: A critique of Langlois and Lamoreaux, Raff, and Temin', *Enterprise and Society*, 5/3 (2004), pp. 388–403.

Sabry, Tarik, *Cultural Encounters in the Arab World: On Media, the Modern and the Everyday* (London: I.B.Tauris, 2010).

Sainton Rogers, Wendy, 'Promoting better childhoods: Constructions of child concern' in M. J. Kehily (ed), *An Introduction to Childhood Studies*, 2nd ed. (Maidenhead: Open University Press, 2009), pp. 141–160.

Sakr, Naomi, *Satellite Realms: Transnational Television, Globalization and the Middle East* (London: I.B.Tauris, 2001).

——, *Arab Television Today* (London: I.B.Tauris, 2007).

Sakr, Naomi and Jeanette Steemers, 'Co-producing content for pan-Arab children's TV: State, business and the workplace' in M. Banks, B. Conor and V. Mayer (eds), *Production Studies: The Sequel!* (Abingdon: Routledge 2016), pp. 238–250.

Salais, Robert and Michael Storper, 'The four "worlds" of contemporary industry', *Cambridge Journal of Economics*, 16/2 (1992), pp. 169–193.

Sandler, Kevin S., ' "A kid's gotta do what a kid's gotta do": Branding the Nickelodeon experience' in H. Hendershot *Nickelodeon Nation* (New York: New York University Press, 2004), pp. 45–68.

Santo, Avi, ' "Is it a camel? Is it a turban? No, it's The 99": Branding Islamic superheroes as authentic global cultural commodities', *Television & New Media*, 15/7 (2014), pp. 679–695.

Schleicher, Klaus, *Sesame Street für Deutchland? Die Notwentigheit einer Vergleichender Mediendidaktik* (Düsseldorf: Schwann, 1972).

Schor, Juliet, *Born to Buy: The Commercialized Child and the New Consumer Culture* (New York: Scribner, 2004).

Scourfield, Jonathan, Sophie Gilliat-Ray, Asma Khan and Sameh Otri, *Muslim Childhood: Religious Nurture in a European Context* (Oxford: Oxford University Press, 2013).

Seiter, Elen, *Sold Separately: Parents and Children in Consumer Culture* (New Brunswick: Rutgers University Press, 1993).

Bibliography

Shafik, Viola, *Arab Cinema: History and Cultural Identity* (Cairo: The American University in Cairo Press, 1998).

———, *Popular Egyptian Cinema: Gender, Class, and Nation* (Cairo: The American University in Cairo Press, 2007).

Shah, Mustafa, 'The Arabic language' in Andrew Rippin (ed), *The Islamic World* (Abingdon: Routledge, 2008), pp. 261–277.

Siapera, Eugenia, *Cultural Diversity and Global Media: The Mediation of Difference* (Oxford: Wiley-Blackwell, 2010).

Singerman, Diane, 'The economic imperatives of marriage: Emerging practices and identities among youth in the Middle East', *Middle East Youth Initiative Working Paper* (Washington and Dubai: Wolfson Center for Development and Dubai School of Government, 2007).

Smith, Elizabeth A., 'Place, class, and race in the Barabra Café: Nubians in Egyptian media', in D. Singerman and P. Amar (eds), *Cairo Cosmopolitan: Politics, Culture, and Urban Space in the New Globalized Middle East* (Cairo, 2006), pp. 399–413.

Sommers-Flanagan, Rita, John Sommers-Flanagan and Britta Davis, 'What's happening on music television? A gender role content analysis', *Sex Roles*, 28, 11/12 (1993), pp. 745–753.

Stainton Rogers, Wendy (2009) 'Promoting better childhoods' in M. J. Kehily (ed), *An Introduction to Childhood Studies*, 2nd ed. (Maidenhead: Open University Press, 2009), pp. 141–160.

Steele, Jeanne R., and Jane D. Brown, 'Adolescent room culture: Studying media in the context of everyday life', *Journal of Youth and Adolescence*, 24/5 (1995), pp. 551–576.

Steemers, Jeanette, *Creating Preschool Television: A Story of Commerce, Creativity and Curriculum* (Basingstoke: Palgrave Macmillan, 2010).

———, 'Production studies, transformations in children's television and the global turn', *Journal of Children and Media*, 10/1 (2016), pp. 123–131.

Steemers, Jeanette and Alessandro D'Arma, 'Evaluating and regulating the role of public broadcasters in the children's media ecology: the case of home-grown television content', *International Journal of Media and Cultural Politics*, 8/1 (2012), pp. 67–85.

Stolcke, Verena, 'Talking culture: new boundaries, new rhetoric of exclusion in Europe', *Current Anthropology*, 36/1 (February 1995), pp. 1–24.

Stone, Diane, 'Learning lessons, policy transfer and the international diffusion of ideas', University of Warwick Centre for the Study of Globalisation and Regionalisation Working Paper No 69/01 (April 2001).

Storper, Michael and Robert Salais, *Worlds of Production* (Cambridge, MA: Harvard University Press, 1997).

Strandgaard Jensen, Helle, 'TV as children's spokesman: Conflicting notions of children and childhood in Danish children's television around 1968', *Journal for the History of Childhood and Youth*, 6/1 (2013), pp. 105–128.

239

Straubhaar, Joseph, 'Beyond media imperialism: Asymmetrical interdependence and cultural proximity', *Critical Studies in Mass Communication*, 8 (1991), pp. 39–59.

——, '(Re)Asserting national television and national identity against the global, regional, and local levels of world television' in J. Chan and B. McIntyre (eds) *In Search of Boundaries* (Westport, CT: Praeger, 2002), pp. 181–206.

——, *World Television: From Global to Local* (Thousand Oaks, CA: Sage, 2007).

Suleiman, Yasir, *The Arabic Language and National Identity* (Edinburgh: Edinburgh University Press, 2002).

——, *Arabic in the Fray: Language Ideology and Cultural Politics* (Edinburgh: Edinburgh University Press, 2013).

——, 'Arabic folk linguistics: Between mother tongue and native language' in J. Owens (ed), *The Oxford Handbook of Arabic Linguistics* (Oxford: Oxford University Press, 2013), pp. 264–280.

Tayie, Sami, 'Children and mass media in the Arab world: a second level analysis' in U. Carlsson et al (eds), *Empowerment Through Media Education: An Intercultural Dialogue* (Göteborg: Nordiskt Informationscenter, 2008), pp. 67–87.

Tschang, Ted, 'Production and political economy in the animation industry: Why insourcing and outsourcing occur', a paper presented at the DRUID Summer Conference 2004 on Industrial Dynamics, Innovation and Development, Elsinore, Denmark, 14–16 June 2004). Downloaded from: http://www.druid.dk/conferences/summer2004/papers/ds2004-92.pdf.

Ulrichsen, Kristian Coates, *Qatar and the Arab Spring* (London: C. Hurst & Co, 2014).

UNHCR, *World at War: UNHCR Global Trends – Forced Displacement in 2014* (Geneva: United Nations, 2015).

UNICEF, *The State of the World's Children 2015* (New York: United Nations, 2014).

——, *Education under Fire* (New York: United Nations, September 2015).

United Nations Development Programme, *Arab Human Development Report 2002* (New York: United Nations Development Programme, Regional Bureau for Arab States, 2002).

Van Dijk, Teun, *Elite Discourse and Racism* (Newbury Park, CA: Sage, 1993).

Waisbord, Silvio, 'McTV: Understanding the global popularity of television formats', *Television & New Media*, 5/4 (2004), pp. 359–383.

Walkerdine, Valerie, 'Developmental psychology and the study of childhood' in M. J. Kehily (ed), *An Introduction to Childhood Studies*, 2nd ed. (Maidenhead: Open University Press, 2009), pp. 112–123.

Wallis, Cara, 'Performing gender: A content analysis of gender display in music videos', *Sex Roles*, 64 (2011), pp. 160–172.

Ward, L. Monique, 'Understanding the role of entertainment media in the sexual socialization of American youth: A review of empirical research', *Developmental Review*, 23/3 (1 September 2003), pp. 347–388.

Bibliography

Wasko, Janet, Mark Phillips and Eileen R. Meehan (eds) *Dazzled by Disney: The Global Disney Audiences Project* (London: Leicester University Press, 2001).

Webb, Jen, Tony Schirato and Geoff Danaher, *Understanding Bourdieu* (London: Sage, 2002).

Wedeen, Lisa, *Ambiguities of Domination: Politics, Rhetoric, and Symbols in Contemporary Syria* (Chicago: University of Chicago Press, 1999).

Wells, Paul, *Animation Genre and Authorship* (London: Wallflower Press, 2002).

West, Candace and Don H. Zimmerman, 'Doing gender,' *Gender and Society*, 1/2 (June 1987), pp. 125–151.

Whitaker, Lynn, 'Producing UK Children's Public Service Broadcasting in the 21st Century: A Case Study of BBC Scotland', PhD Thesis (University of Glasgow, 2011).

White, Cindy L. and Elizabeth Hall Preston, 'The spaces of children's programming', *Critical Studies in Media Communication*, 22/3 (2005), pp. 239–255.

Winder, Catherine and Zahra Dowlatabadi, *Producing Animation* (Boston: Focal Press, 2001).

Winn, Marie, *The Plug-in Drug* (New York: Bantam, 1977).

Woodhead, Martin, 'Childhood studies: Past, present and future' in M. J. Kehily (ed), *An Introduction to Childhood Studies*, 2nd ed. (Maidenhead: Open University Press, 2009), pp. 17–34.

Yacoub, Rania Nafez Mahmoud, 'Ideological Aspects of Dubbing into Arabic for Children – With Special Reference to Language Variety', PhD thesis (University of Salford, 2009).

Yoon, Hyejin and Edward J. Malecki, 'Cartoon planet: Worlds of production and global production networks in the animation industry', *Industrial and Corporate Change*, 19/1 (2010), pp. 239–271.

Zahlan, Rosemarie Said, *The Making of the Modern Gulf States* (London: Unwin Hyman, 1989).

Zeitlyn, Benjamin and Kanwal Mand, 'Researching transnational childhoods', *Journal of Ethnic and Migration Studies*, 38/6 (2012), pp. 987–1006.

Zelizer, Viviana, *Pricing the Priceless Child: The Changing Social Value of Children* (New York: Basic Books, 1985).

Index

Index